GAIA'S QUANTUM LEAP

GAIA'S QUANTUM LEAP

A Guide to Living through the Coming Earth Changes

Marko Pogačnik

Translated by Tony Mitton

2011
Lindisfarne Books

Published by Lindisfarne Books
An imprint of SteinerBooks/Anthroposophic Press
610 Main Street, Great Barrington, Massachusetts 01230
www.steinerbooks.org

Text and illustrations © Marko Pogačnik 2011

Published in German as *Quantumsprung der Erde von der
gegenwaertigen Erwandlung,* Baden und München, AT Verlag 2010.

Library of Congress Cataloging-in-Publication Data

Pogacnik, Marko, 1944-
[Quantensprung der Erde. English]
Gaia's quantum leap : a guide to living through the coming earth changes /
Marko Pogacnik ; translated by Tony Mitton.
    p. cm.
ISBN 978-1-58420-089-5
1. Earth—Miscellanea. 2. Spiritual life—Miscellanea. I. Title.
BF1999.P58713 2011
001.94—dc22

                    2010050817

Printed in the United States

CONTENTS

Preface   7

Chapter 1: Surprise! The Earth Is Changing

Introduction   9
Dream 1. The Earth Soul's Invitation   13
Dream 2. Unforeseen Consequences of the Earth Changes   15
Dream 3. Unknown Forces   17
Dream 4. It Can Get Quite Dramatic   19
Dream 5. A New Principle of Time Is Born   21
Dream 6. It Can Get Quite Bewildering   23
Dream 7. Don't Be So Arrogant   25
Dream 8. New Birth   27
Exercises on the Theme "The Earth Is Changing"   28

Chapter 2: Birth of a New Earth Space

Introduction   31
Dream 9. A Shocking Message   35
Dream 10. The Usual Spatial Structure Is Vanishing   37
Dream 11. Space Turned Upside Down   39
Dream 12. A New Space Is Born   41
Dream 13. A New Creative Set of Tools   45
Dream 14. Reality Pulsates on Two Levels Simultaneously   47
Dream 15. Tasks of the Transition Time   49
Exercises on the Theme "The New Earth Space"   52

Chapter 3: The Dramatics of Earth Change

Introduction   55
Dream 16. Dynamite in the Baggage   59
Dream 17: An Obstacle to the Soul's Relationship to the Earth   61
Dream 18: The Exaggerated Yang   63
Dream 19: There Are Contrary Powers   65
Dream 20: The Voice of Intellect   67
Dream 21: The False Inborn Pattern   69

Dream 22: The Life Force Is About To Disappear *71*
Dream 23: The Code of Life Is Endangered *73*
Exercises on the Theme "Overcoming the Barriers" *74*

Chapter 4: New Creative Tools

Introduction *77*
Dream 24: The Phenomenon of Archetypal Forces *81*
Dream 25: The Archetypal Powers of Heaven and Earth *83*
Dream 26: Where Are the Roots of Our Creative Power? *85*
Dream 27: Discovery of a Channel of Archetypal Power *87*
Dream 28: The Other World Announces Itself *89*
Dream 29: The Role of Humanity *93*
Dream 30: A Change in the Realm of Emotional Forces *95*
Dream 31: An Interdimensional Portal *97*
Dream 32: Cooperation from the All *99*
Dream 33: The Angel-World's Offer *101*
Exercises on the Theme "The New Creative Tools" *102*

Chapter 5: The Powers that Work Against Earth Change

Introduction *105*
Dream 34: A Panorama of Contrary Powers *109*
Dream 35: Our Dependence on Alien Forces as a World Problem *111*
Dream 36: The Lucifer Syndrome *113*
Dream 37: Religious Bondage *115*
Dream 38: Do the Contrary Powers Self-Destruct? *117*
Dream 39: Travesty of the Dark Powers *119*
Exercises on the Theme "Dealing with the Contrary Powers" *122*

Chapter 6: Rebirth of Holiness

Introduction *125*
Dream 40: Reversal of the Divine *129*
Dream 41: Return of the Goddess *131*
Dream 42: The Dark Aspect of God *135*
Dream 43: Change Is Not To Be Avoided *138*
Dream 44: "The Green Christ" *141*
Exercises on the Theme "The Rediscovery of Holiness" *142*

Chapter 7: Change on the Personal Plane

Introduction *145*
Dream 45: Grounding the Heart *149*
Dream 46: The Cosmic Invitation *151*
Dream 47: Valuable Advice *153*
Dream 48: The Epoch of the Great Cleansing *155*
Dream 49: An Offer from the Nature Forces *157*
Dream 50: Identity Crisis *159*
Dream 51: The Inner Child *161*
Dream 52: The Human Being's Elemental Twin *163*
Dream 53: The Master's Offering *165*
Exercises on the Theme "Personal Evolution" *168*

Chapter 8: Views of the Near Future

Introduction *171*
Dream 54: The Great Hope *175*
Dream 55: Cooperation with the Fairy World *177*
Dream 56: Removal Problems *181*
Dream 57: Midwife Wanted *183*
Dream 58: An Animal Fable *185*
Dream 59: The Tall Guest *187*
Dream 60: The Lost Telephone *191*
Dream 61: The Valuable Find *193*
Exercises on the Theme "Processes that Point to the Future" *194*

Late-Breaking News

The First Dream *197*
The Second Dream *198*
A Closing Exercise *198*

PREFACE

OUTWARDLY, one scarcely notices what is happening, but as individuals and as a civilization we are now being drawn into a cosmic event whose breadth and depth we can hardly guess. What may be readily observed are the constantly worsening crises in the ecological, economic, health and social realms. Yet we still fail to ask about the deeper reasons for the repeated breakdowns in our environment, as well as in many people's personal lives.

The aim of this book is to testify that we are not facing "the End of the World," but rather a fundamental change in the environment that allows the further evolution of nature and humankind on the earth's surface. We are looking at a radical process of deep change that has repeatedly occurred in earth's history. This change shakes up and thoroughly sifts the earth's surface and its life forms—not to destroy them, but to create new circumstances which will open new horizons of being for nature and civilization.

In the language of modern physics, one could speak of a "quantum leap" by earth and its life forms—our human civilization included.

I developed the concept and coined the term "earth change" in 1998, and described it shortly afterward in the book *Earth Changes, Human Destiny.* I took this major step after discovering, in the course of my geomantic practice, that the earth's intelligence had set in motion certain energy-related measures to avert the threatening terrestrial destruction—I am referring to the destruction that threatens earth and its life forms because of our civilization's irresponsible conduct.

The energy-related measures that the earth has initiated can be seen as a unique self-healing process which will enable earth space to receive a completely new quality. But one thing is certain: this hope for a healing process can become part of our everyday reality only if at least some numbers of us human beings become aware of the quite fantastic possibilities for earth and its life forms contained in this quantum leap. We should then begin to incorporate them in our own lives.

If the cosmos' offer of the quantum leap is not accepted, it stays in the belly of the universe as an unrealized possibility. After that, do the life of earth and humanity still have a chance?

Because it is hard to conceive of the complex process of change in earth and humans in any logical form, I have decided to describe individual aspects of the process through dreams that I had in the years between 1998 and 2009. So their message can be directly comprehended, I have not only described the pictures of my dream visions but have also drawn them. To this end, I have called back to life an art form that I used in the 1960s, the time of Pop Art and the so-called "comics." I wanted to transmit the message of the dreams as vividly as possible through the drawings. The accompanying commentary should help put the reader on the track of the message hidden in the relevant dream. One can then also better compare one's own insights relating to earth change with my dream messages.

I sense dreams to be messages from a parallel world dimension where the causes of events are rooted, which later emerge on the level of everyday life.

I have developed meditative exercises on the differing themes of change in earth and humans and placed these at the ends of the relevant chapters. They should enable readers to advance further in the course of their own attunement to the cosmic processes of change. The exercises have been comprehensively developed from the dream messages described, similar to the way I shape my cosmograms: intuitively, at rest in my center, and with the clear objective of supporting life and the successful transformation of our earthly cosmos.

Marko Pogačnik, September 19, 2009

Chapter 1

SURPRISE! THE EARTH IS CHANGING

IN COMMON, I suspect, with many of earth's people, I eye the future with some uncertainty. Around me I see the regular occurrence of serious natural catastrophes and social upheavals. I have just read the latest newspaper report of the American scientific group that won the Nobel Prize in 2008 for their research in the area of climate change. Their further investigations in 2009 have shown that the situation will not essentially improve for at least one thousand years. The oceans have already reacted to the global warming trend, and it will take at least a millennium for nature to reverse such a long-term process. Nature takes its own time. It is not as fast as our cybernetic civilization!

So, what is to be done?

At a gloomy point ten years ago, I found a reason for hope that has since continually been confirmed in different ways.

The scientific prognostications are based solely on the traditional structures of time and space. At that level it would seem that earth's catastrophic destruction can no longer be averted. My geomantic work experience, however, has taught me that earth is a multidimensional being that can initiate specific change processes, not only at the physical level, but also at other more subtle levels of existence. In theory, if it is impossible to heal our planet's situation effectively by any means available on the physical level, the possibility may nonetheless exist on other levels of reality, which are known to us from our geomantic experiences. To be more precise, this possibility arises through the interaction between the physical and the so-called subtle levels of reality.

We have been speaking of geomantic experiences as key, which raises the question, what is geomancy really? Rather than give a general definition, I will tell of my personal experiences.

As an artist, I have been occupied all my life with the concept of space. In my profession as landscape artist I have tried for decades to penetrate more deeply into the invisible spaces of the landscape, those which our physical eyes cannot see. One could call them subtle, perhaps etheric, archetypal, or even fairy-tale dimensions. I have to thank my personal sensitivity for my success in gradually entering these above-mentioned dimensions of space.

I landed in a world that can scarcely be explained by my intellect. First I discovered that there are power centers and power streams that scoop up the life force[1] from the depths of the earth and distribute it to the natural world and its living beings (including humanity). I am always amazed at this world of light when I get the opportunity to attune to its structure and observe its constant movement. On this level, reality is not firm, but flowing![2]

Even more fascinating is the dimension of earth's intelligence! For a long time now, I have recognized that the earth is a conscious being with which one can communicate, provided that one is prepared to learn her language. This is no sort of mental language, but a picture-like way of communicating, combined with the transmission of different qualities of feeling. It is related to the language of our dreams and the expressive forms that appear in crop circles worldwide.[3]

Related to the danger of earth's destruction, there is the possibility of taking up once again the interrupted communication with earth's intelligence—with Gaia—and exchanging ideas with her. One might address her directly and persuade her to undertake specific steps toward self-healing. But who speaks with the Earth Soul today or with her units of consciousness—the elemental beings known to us in fairy tales as sylphs, gnomes and fairies?[4]

Earth has a quite extraordinary consciousness. It is not lodged anywhere in the depths of the planet but uses for its capacious memory, mountains, rivers, trees, all sorts of plants, animals, and lately, humans too—to say nothing of crystals. The intelligence of earth is distributed everywhere in us and around us, working, guiding and creating. Why do we never talk with the earth when her consciousness is distributed so closely among us? We should surely be talking with the Earth Consciousness about the possibilities for saving the wonderful life of Nature and Humanity from catastrophic earth changes.

And look at my experience! Earth Consciousness has of itself begun to contact us, and of her own accord to initiate a process, unnoticed by humanity, which is known as the process of earth transformation.

To inform me and humanity in general about this amazing development that will safeguard the future, the Earth Soul must seek a form of language that people can understand. She has no way to circulate any written sort of advertisement. In my case, she uses either the language of dreams or a language using direct experience that I can interpret based on my geomantic perceptions.

The first and—for the idea of earth transformation—decisive communication of this sort occurred in several phases between February and April 1998. During the night of the full moon of February 10th, I suddenly awoke and was intuitively led out of the house and into the surrounding meadows. To get an insight into why I was awakened, I began to test the quality of the ground radiation.

My method of measuring the general quality of the earth organism in a particular place is to let my hands feel the ground radiation. To do this, I bend down to the ground and stretch my hand out into the stream of ground radiation. Then I release it to be freely raised by the "upward stream" of ground radiation, observing what kind of quality is working on my hand, with what type of movement it is drawn upward, and how high.

Until the night of the full moon mentioned above, the ground radiation was recognizable by the dominant quality of the earth element. This was easily understandable since the everyday space in which we live is characterized by its close relationship with the particles of matter. We live in a materialized space that is defined as such by the vibration of the earth element.

Since that night of February 10th the ground radiation has felt quite different. Its vibration did not correspond with the normal, previously established pattern that linked it with the earth element. Now it was bound to the water element and expressed properties that were soft, watery, and feminine. Its pattern was not drawn up into the heights but spread out horizontally to both sides, as if someone were stretching a hand over a water surface.

For about a month there was no change in the new set-up of the planetary aura. Then, on March 9th of the same year, there was a fresh, radical transformation, and the radiation took on a rhythmic, fiery quality. Afterward, a further change followed in the night of April 19th–20th. Now it was the turn of the quality of the air element. The ground radiation showed itself crossing spirally and feather-lightly.

What did the Earth Soul wish to share through this three-month-long process of communication?

First, she shared with me and my readers that within the familiar (to us) physical planet Earth, the concept of a new planetary space is in the process of formation. Its structure is no longer based primarily on the elemental particles of matter. The air element has now become the dominant element of earthly creation. From now on, physical processes will not be in the foreground, and their place will be taken by the processes of consciousness. The air element represents the power and creativity of consciousness.

Second, the fact that the ground radiation ran through all four elements—earth, water, fire and air—in the course of three months means that in the new earth space characterized by the air element, we are dealing with a synthesis of all the elements. In fact, the new epoch of earth and humanity's evolution in the sign of Aquarius will be seen as the one in which the essence of the whole cycle of the last 24,000 years of the continuing Platonic Year comes to expression.[5]

A second way in which the Earth Soul can share her messages is through the picture language of dreams. They are suitable to convey of complex content, because they preserve the multidimensionality of the message. One can interpret dream pictures in various ways to suit the nature of the messages, which tell of possibilities and circumstances beyond the logic of comprehensible reality. Multidimensional reality is many-layered, like the picture language of dreams.

I deal with dreams carefully and respectfully. Each dream is written down with care, and its content meditatively considered. There are dreams that help me to understand specific personal situations and take necessary steps for my own evolution. There are also dreams related to my geomantic or earth healing projects that are already underway. They help me discover specific, hidden connections affecting the place where I am working. Perhaps I was not sufficiently aware or sensitive enough to perceive them myself.

There are dreams of a third kind that tell of the world's destiny and her future pathways. I can recognize these by the complexity of their message and the special fateful feeling that accompanies them. I have selected some of these dreams that have to do with the general theme of current earth changes and placed them in the first part of this book.

1. Synonyms for life force are: vital energy; bio-energy; "chi" in the Chinese tradition and "prana" in the Hindu.
2. The various phenomena of the visible and invisible dimensions of Earth and her landscapes are described in my book *Sacred Geography*, Lindisfarne Books 2007.
3. I address the phenomenon of crop circles in my book *Christ Power and the Earth Goddess: A Fifth Gospel*, Findhorn Press 1999.
4. The evolution of elemental beings is discussed in detail in my book *Nature Spirits and Elemental Beings*, Findhorn Press 2010 (New Edition).
5. Further comprehensive material about the new epoch of the air element (which is identical with the Age of Aquarius) is to be found in the above-mentioned book *Nature Spirits and Elemental Beings*.

1. *I am walking along the edge of the shore with my fishing rod over my shoulder.*

2. *Its small, sparkling eyes are fixed on me with unprecedented love.*

2. *"How should I do otherwise than cast my fishing line with its tightly tied hook into its wide open jaws?"*

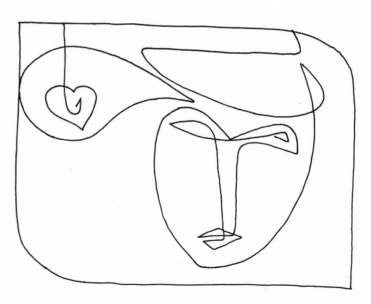

4. *In that moment I am first conscious of the insanity of what I am doing.*

Dream 1: The Earth Soul's Invitation

1   *This dream has me living the life of a simple fisherman. I am walking along the edge of the shore with my fishing rod over my shoulder.*

2   *I suddenly notice that a giant fish has raised its head above sea level. Its jaws open up, bigger than a garage door. Its small, sparkling eyes are fixed on me with unprecedented love.*

3   *Instead of rejoicing, I begin to worry and ask myself what I should do. Since I am a fisherman, I think along the following lines: "How should I do otherwise than cast my fishing line with its tightly tied hook into its wide open jaws?"*

4   *I can feel in my own body how the tiny hook makes its way down the giant fish's endlessly long gullet until it finally attaches to something soft. In that moment I am first conscious of the insanity of what I am doing.*

(Matutu, Brazil, August 30, 1998)

THE GIANT FISH symbolizes the Earth's inner being, the planet's soul aspect—the Earth Soul. She was revered by the ancestral peoples as "Mother Earth" (in Greek, *Gaia*). There are actual traditions that do in fact represent the Earth Soul as a giant fish. In the Slovenian tradition the giant fish that carries the disk of the world on its back is named the "Fish Faronika." The giant fish Faronika is responsible for the well-being of all the life that it carries on its back. As an incarnation of the Earth Soul, it can release earthquakes and floods if life on the earth's surface gets out of balance.

The fisherman, on the other hand, represents the modern human being who believes blindly in our technology that is apparently highly developed but, measured against the multidimensionality of life, is unimaginably limited. Supported by the instruments of modern technology, the current civilization functions only on a single, physical level of existence. All the other extensions of reality, which are very significant for life on earth, are hardly touched. The fisherman with his simple fishing rod could, quite surprisingly, be an appropriate symbol not only for modern technology but, even more, for an associated measure of the consciousness of humanity in its attitude toward life.

There is a glaring inconsistency in the relationship between the fishing rod's little hook and the giant fish's powerful jaws. Looking at humanity from an everyday perspective, we see ourselves concentrating exclusively on earth's physical level and completely disregarding her potential for consciousness, her (vital-energetic) life powers and her spiritual core.

However, the dream's second scene points to an epoch-making change in the huge relationship gap. The giant fish, as symbol of the Earth Soul, is on the point of leaving her "hiding place" in the belly of the earth. The emergence of the giant fish on the surface of the sea indicates the Earth Soul's decision to end her exile, deported to the earth's core, and reveal herself anew to humanity. Her loving eyes allow us to intuit that Gaia, like a loving mother, will not leave humanity in the lurch during the current dramatic events on the earth's surface.

And how is humanity reacting? In the first place it has lost the sensitivity to perceive the Earth Soul's loving offer. Second, it has allowed itself to be engulfed in a rationalistic thought pattern in which nothing like the Earth Mother can exist—except as an anthropologically backward concept embraced by primitive peoples.

The tiny hook that is cast into the jaws of the archetypal fish symbolizes humanity's reaction to the earth changes that are falling down upon us. Instead of opening ourselves at heart level to the Earth Soul's offer of help, we ponder the possibility of diminishing the emissions of propellant gases responsible for the greenhouse effect. Instead of admitting that we as a civilization have found ourselves in a situation that mirrors our complete alienation from the loving consciousness of the living earth and the divine universe, we want to promote a further distancing from the essentials of reality as our hope of salvation.

The dream informs us that the present earth transformation represents such a fundamental process that there is no practical possibility to finally resolve the emerging problems through technological initiatives on the physical level of being. The premonition is gaining weight that there will soon be no other solution than to open ourselves personally and collectively to the Earth Consciousness and its potentials on various levels of being. We should prepare ourselves consciously and psychically in good time.

To be able to communicate with the Earth Soul and her dimensions of consciousness, we should first fundamentally change our preconceptions of the role of the Earth Soul and, secondly, renew our sensitivity toward the spiritual-soul dimensions of being.

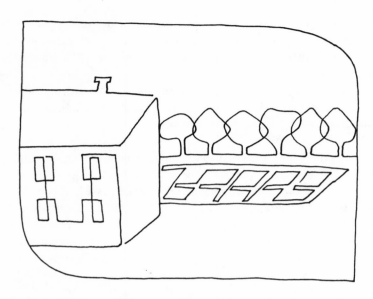

1. *My wife has asked our neighbor to plow a part of our garden.*

2. *I think, "My neighbor is certainly busy plowing, but why is he taking so long?"*

3. *As far as the eye can see, there is only the freshly turned and fragrant earth.*

Dream 2: Unforeseen Consequences of the Earth Changes

1   *My wife has asked our neighbors, who have a small tractor, to plow a part of our garden that lies behind our house. She wants to plant something new there.*

2   *I am sitting at home writing on the computer. For some tine I have been hearing the roar of the tractor outside. I think, "My neighbor is certainly busy plowing, but why is he taking so long?"*

3   *I go out to take a look. As I come to the corner of the house, I feel as if I have had a stroke. My neighbor has plowed through everything! There is no garden any more, no meadow, all the trees are gone. As far as the eye can see, there is only the freshly turned and fragrant earth. My neighbor sits proudly on his tractor and carries on plowing.*

(Osoppo, Italy, November 28, 2007)

IN INTERPRETING the dream vision at Osoppo, one should be aware that we are looking at a planned change. Because a specific part of the garden was to be planted afresh, the neighbor was asked to bring his little tractor and plow up the ground in a defined place. This parallels the way in which the current earth changes are perceived in the public consciousness.

The results of the worldwide scientific research were interpreted such that the earth changes confirmed during the last several years had to do with changes in the areas of climate, warming of the earth's surface, weather patterns, etc. Using the logical principles of reductionism, the often dramatic aftereffects of earth changes were dismissed as isolated occurrences. Relatedly, there was discussion of appropriate measures to be taken in the affected areas.

The dreamer sitting in his room, cut off from the freedom of nature and working on his computer, represents the logically structured consciousness that controls the earthly world today and holds it in specific tracks. He actually knows nothing of what goes on in multidimensional and transrational reality. Most modern people are completely engrossed in their job-related fields and their dreams of wish-fulfillment, which they see as their unique and exclusive purpose in life. Only a distant roar in their ears informs them that there is a process happening of which they know nothing within extensions of reality that their intellect ignores as non-existent.

It is significant that the dreamer must run round the corner of his house to comprehend the true measure of the processes of earth change. The area at the back of the house symbolically represents the realms of multidimensional space that are invisible from the intellect's viewpoint.

Arriving for the first time behind the logic of perceivable reality, the human being can have a presentiment of how comprehensive and fundamental are the processes of the present earth change. The disconcerted intellect no longer sees the world structure on the basis of which it had oriented itself until now. The everyday scenes that modern humankind takes for granted have vanished. There is no longer any landmark to give a sense of direction. Life appears to be over.

This is contradicted by the strong and fertile fragrance arising from the newly turned furrows. As far as the eye can see there is fresh brown earth that promises the birth of a new cycle of life. The manifested natural forms that we recognize have certainly vanished, but not the potential for life.

The dream message directs our attention to the insufficiency of a partial model of earth and climate change. If we overlook the cosmic extent of the change, we deny the possibility of a positive outcome for the change processes. The last dream image leaves no doubt that the earth change involves no partial alteration, but a fundamental process that will create a whole new basis for manifested life on the earth's surface.

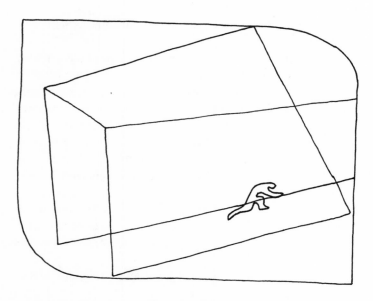

1. I climb down into a cellar excavated deep into the bedrock.

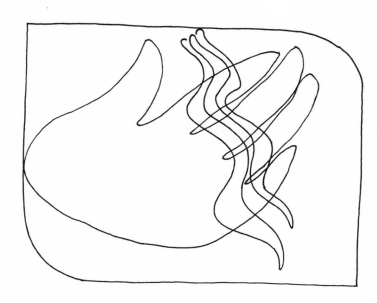

2. Crystal clear spring water is spouting from a single place in the cellar's stony wall.

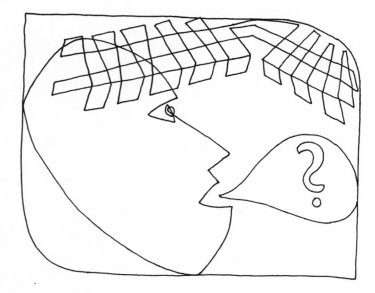

3. Before I have recovered from my surprise, I notice that the other side of the cellar is much more spacious than is usual.

4. I leap across and drag the pile of cages into the middle of the cellar, so that the fire does not overwhelm the entire house.

Dream 3: Unknown Forces

1 *I climb down into a cellar excavated deep into the bedrock because a waste pipe is thought to be leaking. I am filled with apprehension that I must break into the entire wall to find the faulty pipe.*

2 *However, when I get into the cellar and look at the suspected damage, I see that the problem has nothing to do with dirty waste water. Crystal clear spring water is spouting from a single place in the cellar's stony wall.*

3 *Before I have recovered from my surprise, I notice that the other side of the cellar is much more spacious than is usual. Stacked up along the wall there are cell-like cages made of massive iron bars.*

4 *But look out! From one of the "cages," flames suddenly spring up, spontaneously alight. I leap across and drag the pile of cages into the middle of the cellar, so that the fire does not take over the whole house.*

(Sempas, December 15, 1998)

ONE SHOULD CONNECT the message of this dream with the destructive, often remarkable, events that have shaken the natural world again and again during the last decade. We are looking at unusually powerful hurricanes, floods and tidal waves, uncontrollable outbreaks of fire, earthquakes; all four elements appear to tremble in an increasingly chaotic uproar. It has been suggested that this could be nature's revenge for the environmental destruction that is being driven by our global civilization.

In contrast to the negative value put on events connected with climate and earth changes, the invisible and undervalued side of these threatening events is affirmed by the vision of the dream. What the dreamer earlier believed to be stinking wastewater turns out to be the purest spring water.

This warns us not to envisage specific concepts for what happens in and around us in the circumstances of the current earth change. Because of it, a surprising occurrence is approaching. Its sources are unknown to our logical thinking, on which account we tend to give it a negative stamp.

The images in the third part of the dream give further clarification why the intended positive effects of earth change may appear really threatening to human beings.

One should conceive of the iron bars of which the cages are made as the consciousness cells of the human intellect. Like the memory cells in a computer, they are piled up in the cellar of our consciousness. The fire that was lighted there as if of itself represents the cosmic inspiration that seeks to encourage people to abandon the rationalistically conditioned narrows of our evolution and open up to heart consciousness, that is, to put our trust in the path of holistic thinking.

Instead of people following their intuition and giving themselves over to the breadth of the multidimensional kinds of consciousness, a defensive instinct is activated that renders the straitened beliefs of humanity's attitude toward the earth and cosmos more acute. In the dream, conforming to this narrow ideology, the consciousness cells that spontaneously caught fire were dragged into the middle of the room away from the all-embracing fire, to isolate them from the remaining consciousness potential. Those fires could, in fact, completely alter people's attitudes toward the meaning of life.

Millions of people, at every moment, probably experience this unconscious reaction to cosmic inspiration. The consequences are quite devastating. The direction of earth change, which should be understood as a kind of earth-initiated self-healing process, is reversed toward self-destruction.

The dream vision seeks to make us conscious of our unreflective reactions to the phenomenon of earth change. On the one hand we are called to come to grips with the phenomena of the present earth change in a sufficiently deep and penetrating manner. On the other hand we are warned against panic attacks, to which people may easily become subject if the causes of the earth change phenomena are insufficiently explained. If a mass of fears should be projected onto the screen of world events, it will be difficult to mitigate the negative consequences that will unavoidably burst back upon us.

1. Not far from our house, the ground has fallen in.

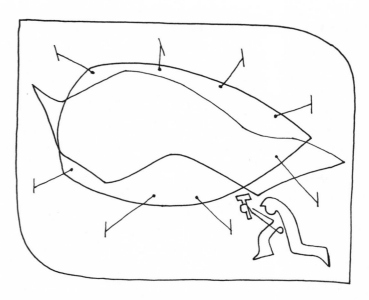

2. The gaping crevice is covered with a plastic sheet, made fast with cords.

3. This time the chasm is so deep and wide that our neighbor's house has been entirely swallowed up.

4. A state commission made up of three men arrives to examine the phenomenon.

Dream 4: It Can Get Quite Dramatic!

1   *Not far from our house, near our neighbor, the ground has fallen in. I run over to look at the hole that has just appeared in the yard. Our neighbor does not know what to do.*

2   *I have finally covered the gaping crevice with a plastic sheet, made fast with cords. But three days later, the earth collapses again.*

3   *This time the chasm is so deep and wide that our neighbor's house has been entirely swallowed up. The collapsed area looks like a grim pit of broken stone, abandoned by all living things.*

4   *A state commission made up of three men arrives to examine the phenomenon and seek a solution. All they can do is peer at the newly formed abyss and bemusedly shake their heads.*

(Quito, Ecuador, November 24, 2003)

THE QUITO DREAM VISION sounds almost like a sarcastic mirror image of the human reaction to the exterior events that accompany the process of earth change. It is characteristic that one seeks first to conceal the consequences of the changes or, if it were possible, get rid of them (see the first dream image).

In its concealment fantasy, the intellect makes a great effort to find logical explanations for the natural catastrophes and cultural breakdowns that are occurring. Attempts are made to bridge the bottlenecks that have arisen in the areas of ecology or financial institutions, and at the same time introduce specific improvements to prevent future catastrophes. The controls directed against the powers of nature are made drastically more acute. Immense sums are wasted on new protective measures. Foes of the established order are sought and appropriately discovered. If people do not wish to submit to the drive for general control, they run the risk of being labeled "terrorists."

But one thing is not done: no effort is made to seek the original causes that lie beyond the logically prescribed ways of thought.

The second dream image shows the consequences of this attitude that seeks to silence the deeper causes of earth and human change. The environmental breakdowns, political catastrophes and financial crises will be heightened to such an extent that the rational intellect goes astray. It is obvious that human beings will be ready to listen to the true causes of world events only when the voice of rational logic has been reduced to silence. Only after all the possibilities of mitigating the current situation have been exhausted can one hope that the truly reasonable person will lend an ear to the actual truth of the world situation.

However, it is unwise to wait for the moment when the intellect is completely darkened. This is the circumstance portrayed by the three officials in the fourth image who, confronted by the chasm, shake their heads in dismay. Pinned against the wall with no way out, the intellect can show its diabolical side and brutally advance against life itself. Similar tragic events are known to us from countless wartime situations.

The message of the dream calls on us men and women who share specific insights into the cosmic meaning of the earth changes to challenge the rational domination of the world. One should develop a mediating role. Supported by the accumulating experience of the processes of earth change, we should be able to explain to people's common sense—which resides in each one of us—that we are not destined to be sacrificed to a planetary collapse but to be witnesses of a unique cosmic Quantum Leap. We are dealing with a mysterious act of renewal that affects the earth as much as humanity.

It is merely demanded of us that we change our negatively angled slant and get into line with the transformative activity of the earthly cosmos. Then there will emerge the positive aspects of the event, which seen from outside (and the intellect can only see world events from the outside) presents a hopeless face.

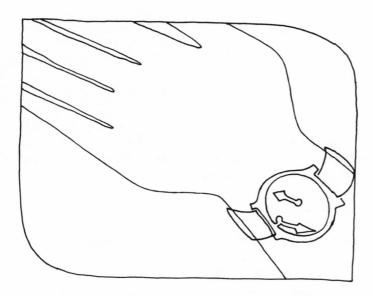

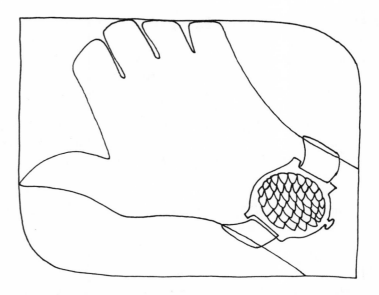

1. *This cannot be my watch! It looks as if it has lain for a long while at the bottom of the sea.*

2. *The watch face can scarcely be seen because it is covered with several scale-like layers.*

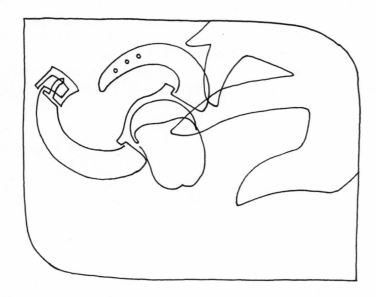

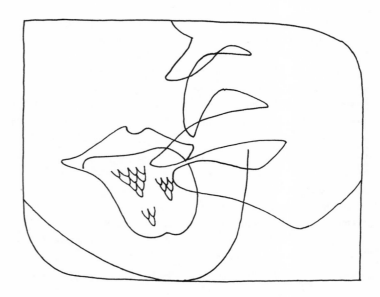

3. *No watch face appears beneath, but a life-like model of a tongue.*

4. *I can now clearly see that I am dealing with a living tongue.*

20

Dream 5: A New Principle of Time Is Born

1   *I peer at my wristwatch. It looks quite strange to me. Why is that? Now I notice that a hand has broken off. This cannot be my watch! It looks as if it has lain for a long while at the bottom of the sea. Where then is my watch?*

2   *As I look at my watch again, I am even more bewildered. The watch face can scarcely be seen because it is covered by several scale-like layers. I start at once to clean the scales off and blow the rest away. I have an uneasy feeling that there is no way that such a dirty watch can still work.*

3   *When I have blown away the remainder of the scales, there appears beneath not a watch face but—a new surprise—the life-like model of a tongue.*

4   *The tongue, too, is covered here and there with scales and I start immediately to get rid of them. Then I shudder with the fear that by picking off the scales, I may wound the tongue. In fact, I can now clearly see that I am dealing with a living tongue.*

(Sempas, Slovenia, February 10, 2004)

THE WATCH IS NOT a symbol of space but an indicator of time. The earth change process is transforming not only the basic quality of space but also the quality of time.

The first dream image informs humanity that the former principle of time's failure to function correctly has passed us by unnoticed. We still look at the time, just as we used to do. Time is still pedantically measured and deployed. However, it is questionable whether the time that we automatically follow is still, in general, a time that is alive. Or is it merely a remembrance of a time when it was still healthy?

The length of time that the old watch spent at the bottom of the sea can be seen as a symbol of time that was smothered in the depths of the subconscious: time drowned in the hectic rush of the profane epoch. Only the way that time is automatically measured allowed it to continue to function as time.

The second dream image leads the dreamer's attention to real time, which reveals itself to him as a future time, a time that is not yet functioning. This is why the watch face appears hidden under a scale-like layer.

The dreamer however was impatient and wanted to acquaint himself with the new time immediately. Thus he takes action to remove the scales and consequently experiences uncertainty whether or not time will function in the future.

The third dream image finally makes it all clear. The quality of the future time is essentially different from the usual concept of time. It can no longer be represented by the wristwatch symbol. Translated into logical language, this means that there is no longer any linear time, counted in a sequence of seconds, minutes, hours, and years. So it happens that the watch is replaced by the model of a tongue. A very mysterious change!

As a symbol, the tongue can be seen as creativity. Words are formed by the tongue, and they may be understood as a symbol of creative action. In the newly birthed concept of time, we are consequently dealing with a time that is not guided by rigid linear patterns, but is determined by the quality of creative input.

The fourth image first warns us that the new concept of time is not to be taken for granted. For the newly formed time to function fully, its legitimacy and laws must first be established. It is for this reason that the tongue, as an icon of creative time, first showed itself covered with scales.

Secondly, one's attention is drawn to the fact that within the framework of the fourth dream image, there is no objective structure representing the new concept of time, but it is just as alive as the subject through which the time is created within a specific creative process. One can hardly describe the depths of amazement that overcame the dreamer when he perceived that time was alive.

Within the framework of earth change, one can see the newly forming time as being no servant of human needs, but rather as a co-creative partner. Time will extend or abbreviate itself in conformity with the quality of love and creative power invested in a specific project. Time will, so to speak, become co-created through the creative process. Or, to put it the other way, if the person involved is incapable of aligning his or her activity with the cosmic cycles, the relevant project will not have any time put at its disposal. For our automatically disposable linear time, it is time to say goodbye!

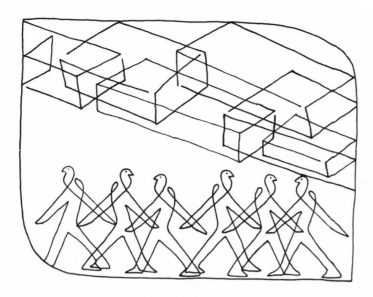

1. *The people do not notice what kind of dynamic is taking place above their heads.*

2. *Now follows a chaotic situation of falling roof plates and confused people.*

3. *The urge to look for my parents is overwhelming.*

Dream 6: It Can Get Quite Bewildering

1   *A wide space appears whose structure reminds me of a Neolithic dolmen, in which the vertically piled blocks of stone are roofed with giant stone plates. Within, people are running to and fro as they go about their tasks. But, strangely, the dolmen's mighty roof plates are not lying still but are moving uninterruptedly and at great speed from left to right and back. The people do not notice what kind of dynamic is taking place above their heads.*

2   *I shudder as I sense the danger that these movements involving tons of heavy stone plates could present for the crowd of people. In fact, there is a dramatic incident. One of the roof plates crashes against the upper rim of a vertical block of stone. There follows a chaotic situation of falling roof plates and confused people. The dreamer was just able to escape from the collapsing space.*

3   *When I am outside, I think of my mother and father who must have remained behind in the ruined space. I face the decision to wend my way through the narrow crannies between the fallen stones that in the meantime have almost completely filled the "dolmen's" space. The urge to look for my parents is intolerable.*

(Findhorn, Scotland, December 1, 2004)

THE CROWD OF PEOPLE who are running to and fro about their tasks in the first dream image represent contemporary humankind who have no presentiment of the lively vigor that is ruling time on the invisible levels of world-space. Connected with the present process of earth change, a new foundation for the environment is arising within the etheric dimension of reality. Although, from the physical level of reality, one can see nothing of this at present, one must believe that one day the impact of the intensive spatial change will also be felt on the physical level of being.

This forecast is confirmed in the second dream image. Two blocks of stone collide in apparently meaningless fashion, and this is followed by a mighty tangle "below" on the physical level of reality. The crash of the falling blocks of stone mingles with the panic of the people, who have no idea what is happening to their environment.

It was no accident that the dream occurred three weeks before the catastrophic tsunami in Southeast Asia, where more than two hundred thousand people lost their lives. The scientists have calculated that the cause of the earthquake, which released the fateful floods of water, was a shift in the earth's axis of "only" two percent.

The third dream image puts the dreamer's reaction in question. In the dream he acts as if the focus of his interest in the epoch of change is his own survival. He simply runs away to save his own skin.

One should be thankful that one can sometimes experience these catastrophic images through television. If such a convenience is not available, one should nonetheless be aware that our common environment will be fundamentally overturned by the action of earth change. It is already true that the old space structure is already collapsing in various parts of the world, just not on our own doorsteps. These events are however part of a general process that affects every person and every living being on the earth, not only those located on the actual site where the old space structure has collapsed. Like time, space represents a uniform category in which we and all living beings participate.

This is why the dreamer feels so strongly urged to look for his parents. Belonging to a preceding (older) generation of humankind, they symbolically represent their unwitting colleagues who have been drawn into the turmoil of the earth changes without understanding the causes of the cosmic transformation.

The dream makes it clear that it becomes very difficult to help one's colleagues after the structure of space has essentially changed already. The dreamer who wants to look for his parents finds himself facing a space structure that has been radically compressed, and he sees it is practically impossible to creep in and rescue his parents. This means that the changing structure of space will, after a certain point in time, be no longer capable of functioning on the level to which the intellect-oriented consciousness (of the parents) is accustomed.

The dream vision confirms that the transition period, in which the earth changes are not yet invading our immediate reality, represents a gift and not an unwanted delay. We should use this blessed, still relatively protected period to join in with the changing force fields of life. We should use them to exchange our experiences of the change processes in our own bodies and in the landscape with others. The transition period represents a very valuable opportunity to communicate and publicly declare the theme of the knowledge and the causes of the earth changes that are overtaking us.

1. *My house stands high above a small lake whose waters pour out in a gushing waterfall to flow into the valley.*

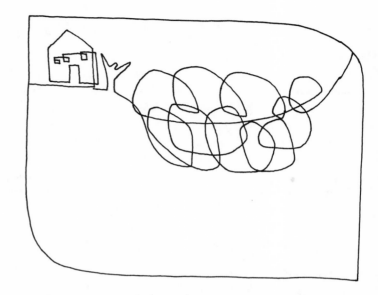

2. *Masses of earth and stone have closed the exit to the valley.*

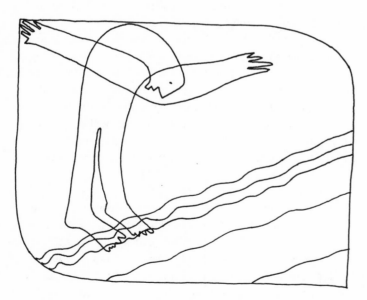

3. *The gush of water, finding no outlet, begins to rise quickly.*

Dream 7: Don't Be So Arrogant!

1 *My house stands high above a small lake whose waters pour out in a gushing waterfall to flow into the valley. In the face of the many water-related catastrophes, I think to myself that elevated as we are, a flood would never endanger us.*

2 *However, the following happens: because of an endlessly long rainy period, the slope opposite, overgrown with bright green grass, becomes so severely loosened that a landslide occurs. Masses of earth and stone have closed the exit to the valley.*

3 *The gushing water, finding no outlet, begins to rise quickly. The flood waves have already reached my feet.*

(Sempas, Slovenia, October 10, 2007)

The dream tries to make clear to us that there is really no way to mitigate the coming earth change. Even if our logic has a hundred times assured us that because of our position in society or other advantages, we are well protected from the consequences of the change process, the opposite can happen. The logical intellect functions wonderfully well, but exclusively in the linear fashion that once allowed it to calculate. However, in the case of the present earth change, we are faced with cosmically triggered processes, whose resolution cannot be assessed from the perspective of the logical intellect. We are dealing with cosmic cycles that guide the evolution of the universe and which can in no way be slowed by anthropocentrically conceived reservations.

For this, the second dream image provides especially clear evidence. Shortly before the unfortunate landslide occurred on the slope of the opposite hill, the dreamer's glance is turned in that direction. The whole slope is overgrown with fresh green grass. In the very next moment the earth begins to split open and the dirty mass composed of stones and earthen clots tumbles toward the waterfall.

This means that even though our physical environment looks so bright and luxuriant today, the whole biotope can suffer a total collapse tomorrow. With earth change we are looking at processes that primarily affect the invisible, etheric plane of reality, of which our modern human consciousness has no concept. The only parts of the cosmic process that the intellect can perceive are the secondary effects of the change processes on the physical level of everyday reality.

It may happen that our world unexpectedly overturns, because, for example, certain fundamental sources on the etheric plane have matured to the point that they must ground themselves (that is, earth). Then the newly constituted space impulse extends to the physical plane. However, it is structured according to the rules of the "old" linearly conceived space. If the new etheric structure alights on the physical plane, the intellect and its perceptive apparatus will experience it as a more or less destructive event. Intellectual logic has no creative tools by which to install the newly arrived impulse positively in our everyday physical reality. Thus this impulse can, unfortunately, manifest itself only in a destructive fashion.

Why should impulses with destructive effects nevertheless alight in our brittle reality?

The physical plane of being cannot be sundered from the process of earth change. If it did not experience a renewal, an important part of the universe, together with us human beings, would remain behind, relative to cosmic evolution, and eventually dissolve into nothing.

This is the problem: the domination of intellect separates the physical plane of space from the wholeness of multidimensional reality and divides it from the other levels of being. Every touch of the cosmic impulse—let us say every touch of eternity—is therefore experienced as a shock, or even as a catastrophe.

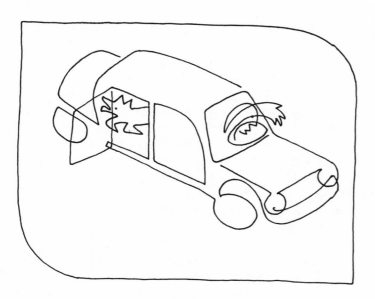

1. The driver, who is obviously very drunk, is asleep, and slumped over the steering wheel. A dog is lying on the rear seat and is howling with pain.

2. The driver climbs out of the car, walks with uncertain steps to its rear door and bends over the dog—which just then has birthed a shaggy pup.

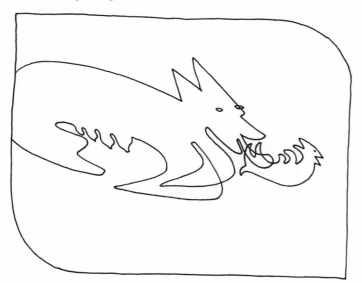

3. At that, the dog opens its jaws as if she is going to swallow her pup. Instead she begins to lick it lovingly.

DREAM 8: NEW BIRTH

1 *I go down a steep street to the river and see an old car parked against the curb of the opposite side of the street. The driver, who is obviously very drunk, is asleep against the steering wheel. A dog is lying on the rear seat and is howling with pain. I think to myself, "The driver should do something about the dog. Her life is finished. He should at least take her to the vet to have a lethal injection."*

2 *While I am saying this to myself, the drunken driver climbs out of the car, walks with uncertain steps to its rear door and bends over the dog. At that same moment I am amazed to see that she has birthed a shaggy pup.*

3 *At that, the dog opens its jaws—I am shocked—it's as if she was going to swallow her pup. Instead she begins to lick it lovingly.*
(Wasmuthhausen, Germany, October 8, 2005)

ALREADY THERE IS a characteristic stamp to the setting of the dream. As in a beat-up car, the present civilization's support structures begin to fall apart. Today one can already see deep rifts in all realms of public life: corrupt financial institutions; hostile religious communities; an ever more manipulative democracy; for example, the suppression of human rights, or the catastrophically unequal division of the goods produced by prosperity…

Further, there is a widening gulf between human culture and terrestrial nature, which is pictured in the dream by the separation between the two beings occupying the front and rear seats.

On the one hand, modern humans are not consciously awake. Drunk on the attractions of the consumer society, they sleep, slumped over the steering wheel, instead of guiding their life intelligently toward a spiritual goal.

On the other hand, nature's representative appears, exemplified by the howling dog on the back seat, suffering horribly. The ecological problems increase to such an extent that the planet, irretrievably sick, is drifting toward its supposed collapse. The comments expressed by the dreamer mirror the current opinion, widely held and silently accepted, that there is no saving life on planet Earth.

Now look at the second picture: it takes an unexpected turn. The man begins (unfortunately still only half conscious) to care about the situation of nature, the atmosphere and the biotope. This gesture, which one can compare with the selfless initiative of the ecological movement during the last decade, is acknowledged from a part of the earth by the creation of a new life-space. A shaggy pup is born.

The third picture confirms the dream's message: do not be afraid of the approaching changes! The events that are then let loose may often assume a highly dramatic appearance. However, no one should despair! Through this process Mother Earth is renewing our planetary home in an unexpectedly loving way.

The dream warns us against unconsciously negative attitudes in regard to our planet's situation. The negative pattern is represented by the dreamer's reaction to the scene of the drunken driver and the howling dog—and the birth of the puppy is characterized as senseless. The silent acceptance of the thought pattern of a "sick earth" is not only false but extends to destructive action.

What we are seeing here is the collapse of a world structure that has lost its function of projecting the future. We should also learn to see this process of collapse through the lens of renewal, by which the pristine health of the inner earth comes to expression anew. Both these faces are relevant to the same future-oriented process.

To nourish and support the birth of the renewed living space, one should consciously abstain from all doubt, no matter what dramatic circumstances arise in the course of the earth changes. Courage and trust are the two qualities that are called for here and now.

Exercises on the Theme "The Earth Is Changing"

An exercise to strengthen the force field of trust in one's environment

The unforeseeable twists and turns in the ever approaching earth-change process will often put us in a situation where we feel completely helpless. At such critical moments, the force field of trust should be strengthened.

- *Be fully present in your silence.*
- *Incline yourself gently toward the earth's center to deepen the relationship of mutual trust between you and the Earth Soul.*
- *Lean gently backward to open yourself to heaven and give reverence to the relationship of mutual trust with the Spirit of the Universe.*
- *Now unite both streams in your heart-realm.*
- *Allow the quality of the archetypal trust that has arisen to spread out around you on all sides, taking the form of a subtle force field and anchor it in space—as far out as possible.*
- *Turn back to your center, which at the same time represents the focus of trust.*

An exercise to renew the relationship with the Earth Soul

This exercise follows the last image of Dream 1 that tells the story of the fisherman and the giant fish. It centers on a positive reversal of the story. Instead of the fisherman casting a fishing line with a hook on its end, an impulse of love is sent "down" to the middle of the earth.

- *You start with a conscious inbreath, where you imagine yourself drawing the breath direct from the earth's core—and understanding that the earth's core is the seat of the Earth Soul.*
- *The inbreath from the earth's core is led to your own heart center. There follows a pause while the breath is laden with the loving quality of your heart.*
- *Now it is the turn of the outbreath, which leads the heart's impulse deep down to the earth's core. There follows a short pause so that the impulse can be perceived by the earth's soul.*
- *Now follows the next inbreath, in which you again imagine yourself to be drawing the breath from the earth's core.*
- *You breathe in this way for some time, exchanging breaths between your own heart center and the earth's core, which is the seat of the Earth Soul.*
- *Attention is gradually withdrawn from the breathing cycle. Instead, you concentrate your feelings on the relationship that has thereby been created between you and the Earth Soul, which knows no "above" or "below." Enjoy it for as long as you want.*

An exercise for entering voluntarily into relationship with the changing earth

To enter into relationship with the self-changing earth, you should take yourself into your back-space, like the dreamer in Dream 2 who "went round the corner of his house." That is one of the possibilities in any case. In this case, the back-space represents the invisible and as yet not outwardly manifested form of the changed Earth.

- *Take yourself into your back-space and focus your attention on its far distances until you feel that you have reached the point of infinity.*
- *You should take your own heart center as the journey's starting point and then glide through the so-called "back of the heart" into the backward space. The corresponding area in the physical back is located in the middle beneath the two shoulder-blades.*
- *When you have arrived in your imagination at the point of infinity, stay present there for a moment to link with the dimension beyond space and time.*
- *Afterward you begin to take yourself quite slowly in the opposite direction, the direction leading back to your own heart center.*
- *As you go back, this time you should consciously (and naturally, still always imaginatively) move through the landscape that lies behind your back. It can be the real landscape where you are at present, or it can be one that you already know and which seems to you important for your experience.*
- *While you are "on the way," you are still staying where you are so that you can sense what is happening on the earth's invisible plane. This means that you move back toward your heart space, but none-theless remain always present in a subtle sense at specific points of the "real" landscape behind your back.*
- *Last, return to your center to examine the experiences you have gathered.*

An exercise to open you to the experience of earth change

The earth change processes run their course beyond the usual dimensions of time and space. They are usually unconsciously perceived as qualities through our emotional fields. How can one translate this sort of nonlogical experience into the logical structures of our consciousness? This exercise suggests how you can arrive at inner insights into the process of earth change.

- *Tune to your emotional field, which constantly receives information about the earth change processes without usually having to be conscious of it.*
- *Imagine the emotional field to be like a lake that lies in the neighborhood of your abdomen and spreads far beyond the boundaries of your physical body.*
- *The next step is to imagine (and feel) this lake rising up like a waterspout, moving through the heart and head areas and finally reaching the center of your head—which symbolizes conscious awareness of the change processes.*
- *You will find there a field of thought patterns and imaginations, which people cherish respective to what is happening with the earth and themselves. This field also creates a force field that circles like a tornado around the head area.*
- *This force field should be led downward to bring the tornado toward your own belly center.*
- *In this way the imaginations and thought patterns will be brought into relationship with the relevant direct experience and appropriately grounded.*
- *After this exchange has taken place, you should concentrate on the region of the heart center, which is the cross-over point of the two opposing streams from head and belly.*
- *What has arisen out of these two movements? Does there need to be a repetition of the exchange between head and belly?*

Chapter 2

The Birth of a New Earth Space

We take the space in which we move as a matter of course, although that simplistic vision is in crass opposition to the reality understood by modern physics. Actually, we have around us "only" a wild tangle of vibrations with no ordered structure of time and space. That wonderfully ordered space-time structure is to be understood as secondary.

Before there can be a space-time structure, there must be a specific pattern that is a template by which the chaotic, archetypal vibrations can be ordered in such a way that a specific time and space structure can, in every moment, come into being.

As the ancient Greeks would say, originally there was Chaos out of which a finite cosmos could finally arise.

If we pursue this way of thinking further, it would mean that the way in which the chaotic vibrations are put together to form the cosmos is not laid down in advance. The particular assembly of the space-time structure and its unique quality are dependant on the pattern according to which the vibrational sea is ordered. And how is the pattern decided, which is the foundation out of which cosmos of our space and time structure arises from the vibrational chaos?

Here we are touching on the secrets of creation, about which scarcely anything can be said in logical language. However, one could imagine that the Earth Soul would have a clear vision of the sort of spatial setting that would be optimal in a given epoch for the further evolution of the wonders of earthly creation. This is the vision through which the corresponding space-time pattern comes into being and is translated into reality with the help of the countless units of earth's intelligence.

The decisive role in translating the spatial patterns into concrete form is played by the invisible intelligences of nature, which are usually described as elemental beings.[1] Of these, the most important are the beings of the Air element, which have been woven into legend as fairies and can be understood as creators of the space-time extension of earth's surface. Humankind also participates in the creative tasks of earth's intelligence, and helps maintain the specific space and time patterns. The specific pattern is projected onto the vibrational sea. It is based on our perception of reality, and is reflected back from every person at every second. We are all helping in this effort (except those who are asleep at the relevant moment) to maintain reality in a specific form. This specific pattern is passed on from generation to generation by teaching it to our children as we bring them up.

Our present space and time structure can best be described by its close relationship to matter. This means that there was a time in earth's evolution that called for a living space in which creation, including humankind, could be settled on the physical plane. This spatial pattern, which still rules today, has enabled the plants, minerals, fishes, insects, animals, landscapes and humans to develop their existence on the level of form. It is almost beyond description what a multitude of forms and motions were thereby incorporated in matter and brought to their highest flowering.

Yet the materialized space in which we live today represents only one possible spatial structure. Parallel to it there exist further spatial dimensions about which modern human beings do not want to know, although these dimensions play a decisive role in the extensions of life on earth. Together they assemble the multidimensional space through which all living beings, not only humans, are given all the necessary conditions for life.

For example, let us touch on the emotional dimension of space. Its structure is not supported by physical particles, as is the case with our traditional space, but by water crystals. The subtle particles of water are distributed everywhere in us and around us. Drops of water hang in the atmosphere, and our bodies are mostly composed of water, to say nothing of rivers, seas, and oceans. However, the watery-emotional space comes into being not from physical water, but with the help of the information stored in each single particle of the countless drops of water.

The sensitivity of water is almost beyond belief, as is the capacity that water crystals possess to store especially subtle information—above all, cosmic information, and specifically the qualities of different star systems.[2] This kind of information is kept by water in the terrestrial sphere, and is constantly renewed. Because of this, the space surrounding the whole earth is so sensitive that the consciousness of the Earth Soul can best express itself through it. We may picture the elemental beings (the consciousness cells of the Earth Soul) as also existing in this watery dimension of space. Thus it may be described as "elemental space" or "fairy space." The unbelievable beauty of the physical world exists mainly because the physical dimension is penetrated by fairy space's much finer, watery dimension.

And why have I called the watery, fairy space also the emotional space? Because this is the dimension of space in which we humans participate through our emotions. I am thinking not only of our emotional reactions, but also of deep heart qualities, when they are lived and expressed.

In addition, the space structure has a little-known protective function. If it happens that a specific evolution has gone so far off the rails that it begins to endanger the development of the earth cosmos[3] as a whole, then it is possible for the Earth Soul to alter the basic pattern on which that reality is structured. Wholly new life circumstances arise, which do not allow the relevant destructive processes to proceed any further. The newly structured space will create a completely new page in the Book of the Life of the earth. Evolution continues, but on a differently structured plane than hitherto.

Myths tell, for example, of a similar spatial collapse in the epoch of Atlantis.[4] In the later years of their civilization, Atlanteans are said to have learned to control and manipulate the then-ruling time and space connections in a terrifying manner. The story goes that social elites had become capable of extending their life span by several hundred years, at the same time forcing a host of men and women to lead a slave-like existence. It came to an unbridgeable polarization between the so-called powers of good and evil, and was followed by highly dangerous wars.

The dramatic change in the codes of time and space that followed is described in the Biblical story of Noah and the Flood. It is said to have rained for forty days, "And the waters prevailed exceedingly upon the earth; and all the high hills, that were under the whole heaven, were covered."[5]

Behind those "forty days," when it is said that the whole earth up to the highest mountain peaks were submerged, is hidden the complicated transformational process that the Bible does not know how to describe. We can imagine that through this puzzling process the old space was dissolved on the one hand, and on the other, a new space structure created. The basic vibrational pattern of reality was structured anew. Behind the scenes of Noah's Flood (or should we say, the destruction of Atlantis?) arose a living space, which is basically the same one that we enjoy today. Its core character can be described—as mentioned above—as the capacity to manifest living forms in matter.

We should admit that the circumstances of life on earth today are sufficiently dramatic that a similar life-preserving, spatial somersault may be thought possible. People have learned to manipulate the inherited spatial structure in dangerous ways in their uses of atomic power and the manipulation of the genetic codes of plants, animals, and possibly, humans too. The conscious mutilation of the atmosphere through so-called "chemtrails" should not be underestimated. It is also suspected that research on the earth's magnetic fields will be conducted in order to control them; and then there are the dangers of nanotechnology....

One might say that humanity has outgrown the conditions that the old space can offer us for our further evolution. Our intellect is capable of so basically changing the life processes on the physical level that there is little possibility of the further spiritual-soul evolution of our civilization. I am of the opinion that the time is ripe for a fresh change through which not only human beings but all living things can be offered a new foundation for the conditions of life.

One should not be frightened by the comparison with Noah's Flood. The Biblical report makes it clear that care was taken in the transformational process to ensure that all living beings could withstand the confusion of the change. The symbol for this is Noah's Ark, in the belly of which all kinds of living beings, humans included, found a safe and protected haven. The Earth Cosmos obviously has at its disposal certain energetic systems that enable the fabric of life on earth with all its beings to be transferred from the dimensions of the old space to the expanses of the new.

In no way does this mean that the passage will be simple for us all! I have chosen the following dream visions because they permit specific glimpses into the future process of spatial change.

1. For information on the evolution of elemental beings, see *Nature Spirits and Elemental Beings*, Findhorn Press 2010 (new edition).
2. Because of its ability to store the cosmic information of the stars, the watery-emotional space is also called "astral space". The word comes from the Latin "astrum" for star.
3. I developed the idea of the Earth Cosmos in *Sacred Geography: Geomancy: Co-Creating the Earth Cosmos* (Lindisfarne 2008) to emphasize that the separation between the terrestrial and spiritual dimensions of being has become untenable. The earth is an autonomous subject of the universe, which contains both the spiritual and terrestrial dimensions.
4. See Plato's T*imaeus*.
5. The story of Noah's Flood can be read in Genesis, The First Book of Moses, Chapters 6-8.

1. *I am running madly hither and thither among a crowd of people who, deep in their own concerns, are crossing a spacious city square in every possible direction.*

2. *I am continually crying out with all my strength and repeating a single sentence to which no one listens; no one even notices me.*

3. *This is the sentence: "We are still thinking that Reality remains as it once was; but it's no longer true—what you are seeing is only a memory of it."*

4. *I scream the words even louder, and the sound wakes me up.*

DREAM 9: A SHOCKING MESSAGE

1   *I am running madly hither and thither among a crowd of people who, deep in their own concerns, are proceeding in every possible direction, to cross a spacious city square.*
2   *I am continually crying out with all my strength, repeating a single sentence to which no one listens; no one even notices me.*
3   *This is the sentence: "We are still thinking that Reality remains as it once was; but it's no longer true—what you are seeing is only a memory of it."*
4   *I scream the words even louder, and the sound wakes me up.*

(Sempas, Slovenia, November 4, 1997)

THE DREAM SEQUENCE IS presented in such a way that the dreamer is instantly aware that it concerns a message, the content of which no single person, himself included, has any inkling. It comes as an absolute surprise. People are running here and there, deep in their tasks, and are not even able to hear what the dreamer is shrieking. Obviously, they do not have the knowledge that would enable them to understand the message contained in what the dreamer is announcing.

And yet that sentence is a logical sentence. Its logic is so precisely expressed that is not really suitable to be shouted aloud. That such a grammatically complicated sentence should be shouted means that what it is saying is so important that it must, quite unconditionally, reach human consciousness.

The sentence is stating that something essential has changed in the foundations of our everyday reality. We humans take it to be untrue only because we have never thought to examine the state of reality. The crowds of people that run uninterestedly past the dreamer's message symbolize the attitude of contemporary humankind which believes that the spatial conditions of their living space are unchangeable.

The shouted sentence maintains a quite contrary opinion. The established spatial structure in which we move is doomed to extinction—that is to say, it still exists only insofar as humans believe in its existence.

However—and this is the essential point—the construct of reality in whose existence humans still believe is no longer identical with the shape of reality itself—which is the core statement of the sentence that people are ignoring. In consequence there is a chasm opening between the reality in which we think we are still living, and the true reality space that is anchored in the essence of earth and heaven.

Does this means that we humans, together with our environment, live in an illusory world that no longer has any direct relationship with the reality of multidimensional life? If one believes the statement of the dreamer who is running madly hither and thither, the answer is without doubt positive.

The dreamer himself did not believe the statement after he was awakened by the loudness of his own voice on that morning of November 4th 1997. He ran out in his pajamas to feel out the radiation from the earth floor.

He was amazed! The quality of the ground radiation was quite different from his remembrance. It felt as if the body of radiation had flipped by 180 degrees. What he knew previously as rising from the ground, now felt as if it would radiate from the earth's surface downward toward the earth's depths. And various power points on which he focused were also reversed.

The upside-down position of the vital energetic body in the dreamer's environment can be interpreted to mean that there are actually two worlds that do not fit with each other. The physically perceptible world is standing on its feet as always, but its etheric complement is on its head.

The drama of the situation that morning soon abated, but recurred repeatedly in the years following—an experience that pointed to the last part of the shouted sentence: "What you are seeing is only a memory of it"—with the words "of it," referring to the nature of the living space as we know it from our previous experience.

Once again, this means that we humans are presently staying in a spatial dimension that is only perceived as existing, because the capability of our memory reproduces it in every moment. However, what is reproduced is no longer co-essential with the reality of the vital energetic space in which we live. This has in the meantime already changed its nature. We do not notice this because, with the help of our intellect, we remain fixed in our habitual spatial dimension, which in the meantime no longer exists.

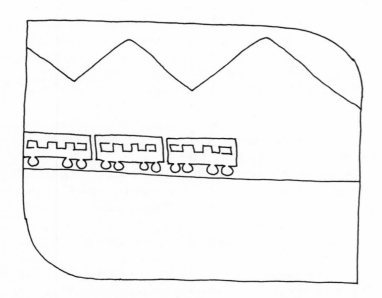

1. We are traveling through the countryside in an old-fashioned railway train.

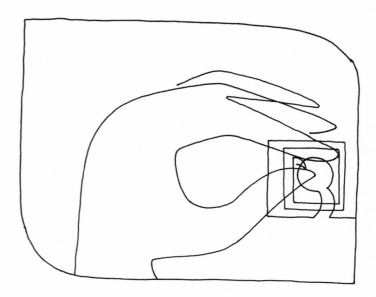

2. I am looking at a wooden lever that can be activated, provided that one is inwardly prepared to dive into a mysterious trance.

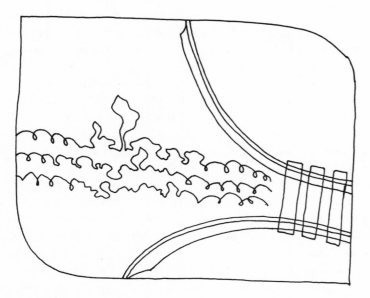

3. Our whole train is tearing along at tremendous speed over sticks and stones where the rails have given out.

Dream 10: The Usual Spatial Structure Is Vanishing

1   *We are traveling through the countryside in an old-fashioned railway train. I am engaged in earnest conversation and miss my station. I want to let the guard know at once that I still want to get out, and I look for the usual alarm system.*

2   *In the old trains there was a cord which ran the length of the whole train, and which one could pull to ring the driver. But this time I cannot find it. Instead, I find a different sort of emergency signal that could be used to bring the run-away train to a stop. I am looking at a wooden lever that can be activated, provided that one is inwardly prepared to dive into a mysterious trance.*

3   *By the time I have activated the emergency lever, we are a long way past my station. I peer through the window and see to my horror that there are no railway tracks ahead of us. Our whole train is tearing along at tremendous speed over sticks and stones where the rails have given out. Here and there the railway embankment is dangerously broken up. The situation is extremely demanding, because the driver must constantly make way for trains that are traveling in the opposite direction…*

(Seeland, Switzerland, May 25, 2003)

THE DREAM TELLS in picture language what is currently happening to our traditional living space. The first picture, showing the express train running on predetermined rails, characterizes today's usual living space in which we live and move, and which prescribes the framework for our various activities. Our intellectual capacity has structured the space through hundreds or even thousands of years, such that every useful function can find its appropriate "rails" and be set in motion. In support there are corresponding laws, regulations, moral criteria, and religious precepts.

Naturally, the opposite is also true: those things that intellect cannot digest are either pushed onto the side rails or else excluded from civilized intercourse. This relatively strongly constructed spatial structure becomes unsteady when there is some incident that does not coincide with the usual order. This is what happens in our dream story. When the dreamer misses his chosen railway station, it shows that the old spatial order is no longer functioning correctly.

Translated into logical language, this means that the inadequacy of the old spatial structure will be made obvious through crisis situations, such as we have seen quite often lately. The functions of the space, as they existed but a short time ago, appear in specific situations to have been extinguished.

The second image informs us that in the meantime new counterparts to the old, habitual functions have arisen. But look! Their function is entirely different! Where previously one could pull an outwardly perceptible cord, one must now grasp inward and activate a lever made of natural material. The inward action is blatantly contrary to the organization prescribed by logic. It is a symbolic representation of humankind's inward, spiritual transformation that enables us to see and grasp how things stand in a different manner than previously.

After this inner transformation has been set in motion, a new, holistic viewpoint comes into being, through which reality is perceived quite differently than before. There follows the third dream image, which delivers a sequence of new, astounding information.

The railway lines, which should deliver the passengers safely to their chosen destination, are no more. They still exist only in our imagination, which is constantly ready to reproduce the accustomed reality although it no longer exists. In the meantime the spatial transformation has advanced so far that life is now being guided by new legitimacies, although these are not perceptible to the linear consciousness. Instead of moving along a rigid railway structure, the train travels directly over the earth floor. See, it is in contact with the earth!

In contrast to the old spatial structure, on whose rails the human intellect can help you move without paying any attention to the signals from earth, the new structure demands cooperation between nature and humankind. Nature's patterns as prescribed by Earth Intelligence are transposed, in cooperation with human imagination, into a multidimensional spatial structure, which will further the future development of life on earth.

Secondly, the train driver must put his own creativity to work to avoid colliding with the trains running in the opposite direction. The railway lines laid down previously are no longer there. Human individuation is so far advanced that personal responsibility for the well-being of all life can no longer be evaded. One's personal ethical attitude, inner clarity, and individual creative dedication are preconditions for inhabiting and working in the new multidimensional space.

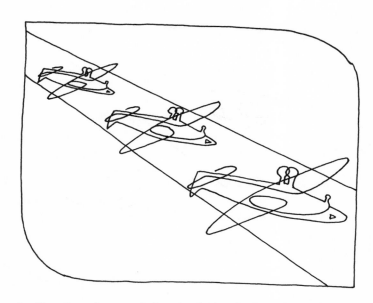

1. *Suddenly I see a dark blue airplane floating on its back as it approaches the runway.*

2. *Then I see the second plane land on its back on the same runway …and then another and another.*

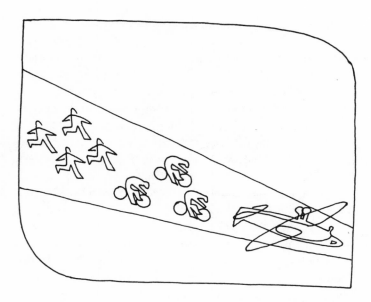

3. *After the succession of planes, a pack of sporty looking bicyclists ride onto the runway.*

DREAM 11: SPACE TURNED UPSIDE DOWN

1   *I am riding my bicycle past a modern airport. Suddenly I see a dark blue airplane floating on its back as it approaches the runway. I am horrified: there is about to be a serious accident! It is a passenger plane; I cannot decipher the name of the aircraft company. I am on the point of phoning a rescue service, but I cannot remember the telephone number.*

2   *Then I see a second plane land on its back on the same runway... and then another and another—at least twenty in all. And during all of this, nothing dramatic is happening. They all move past me, whole and sound.*

3   *After the succession of planes, a pack of sporty looking bicyclists ride onto the runway. They are bent far over their bicycles, so one cannot ignore their straining backs. Their clothing is a bright and pleasant mixture of colors. Behind them march a whole crowd of people characterized by their upright bearing.*

(Sempas, September 26, 2004)

THIS DREAM IS CONCERNED with the essential difference between the linear development of earth mutations and the process of earth change. We can see various outward mutations that alter our environment, such as atmospheric warming, higher levels of flooding, unstable financial markets, etc. We get the feeling that these mutations can escalate still further, but have no idea where all this is heading. The case is quite different for earth change!

The concept of change indicates a nonlinear process that foresees the quantum leap involving similar somersaults. The dreamer is witness to just such a somersault, which he plainly believes to be a catastrophe in the making. As he sees a passenger plane landing on its back, he is prepared for the worst and ready to phone the rescue services.

The second dream image lets us know that we are not looking at an accident but at a somersault that will occur repeatedly in the course of the current earth changes. Not only does the first plane land on its back successfully, but the next twenty also. The message means that the somersault procedure is indispensable to the process of earth change. Instead of becoming upset each time, we should accept the somersault process as an unavoidable part of the present changes, which will guarantee a secure future for life on earth and humanity.

The gist of the third dream image is to clarify the concept of "'somersault." First, we see planes landing on their backs as a symbol of the initial phase of the somersault, which is when the dramatic reversal takes place. The normal patterns of reality are turned on their head. For a moment, we lose the ground under our feet. Socially or energetically conditioned situations arise that are capable of spinning us out of our accustomed ways of thinking, feeling, and handling business.

The sportsmen who follow represent the next phase of the change process. They sit on their bicycles, upright and not upside down, but showing their backs bent far forward as they push at the pedals. Also, they are dressed in bright colors.

They symbolize the decisive middle phase of the somersault in which cosmic rays work to transform the rigid patterns. The sportsmen operate their wheels like a centrifuge—a centrifuge that spews out the old and injects the new. The colorful clothing stands for the cosmic rays whose positive impacts are drawn into the change process.

The men who march upright behind them represent the third phase of the change. The experience of the somersault is now integrated into the wholeness of the being of humanity. The outcome of the whole process is symbolized by their upright attitude. They are to be understood as an expression of the newly won inner clarity. The reversal has achieved its goal; humanity stands upright once again.

The dream vision of planes landing upside down should encourage us to meet the unfolding earth changes in a bold and steady way. A process is coming upon us that is hard to understand and deal with. However, the changes that follow from it carry a deep meaning for our personal and planetary evolution. Thus, it pays to remain calm in the face of unusual spatial somersaults, cope with the resulting physical difficulties and remain confident.

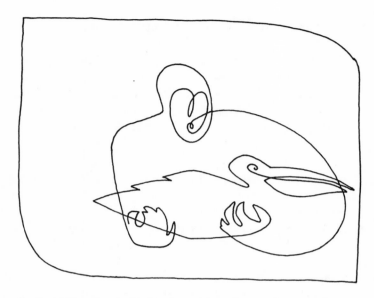

1. *A number of people try to teach the bird to take food, but without success.*

2. *I quickly take the bird in my arms to carry it home and care for its nourishment in my family circle.*

Dream 12: A New Space Is Born

1 *A pelican is born. It radiates an unbelievable beauty. There is, however, a grievous problem. The pelican does not know how to feed itself. One after another, a number of people try to teach the bird to take food, but without success. In view of the unsuccessful attempts, I decide to take the task in hand myself.*

2 *From the time in my life when I was farming my land, I remember the danger that threatens newborn lambs. I know that if lambs do not learn to suckle in a timely fashion, their esophagus seals shut and they die. I quickly take the bird in my arms to carry it home and care for its nourishment in my family circle.*

3 *With the help of a sort of X-ray, I can see that its esophagus is already nearly completely closed. It resembles a closed, transparent tube. I feel the urge to hurry. To my great astonishment, the bird itself comments on its serious situation, saying, "It's already too late." The words are spoken in a calm voice whose tone is unusually deep.*

4 *Though still quite a long way from the house, I call to my wife to make a thin soup for the pelican. An inner voice tells me that the soup should be free of hard vegetable pieces, so that the liquid can slide down through the pelican's esophagus. However, I cannot speak the wish out loud. I feel as if my voice is crippled. I can only hope that, despite the desperate situation, the nourishment will bring success.*

(Sempas, January 31, 2002)

ONE SHOULD SEE the image of the newborn pelican in the context of the dramatic earth changes, which are already in progress. Some very meaningful symbols are contained in this image, and they should not be overlooked.

For a bird to be born and not hatched from an egg means that, in the course of the earth change, an event is happening in which its essence surpasses traditional logic. Assuming that the newborn pelican represents a symbol of the spiritual "emergency rescue plan" for earth and its life forms, it means that the conception of this plan is completely different from what we humans would expect.

In what sense would the newborn pelican be seen as a symbol of the "emergency rescue plan" for earth and its living beings?

Revealing its perfectly white presence, the pelican represents the renewal of the etheric body of earth. It symbolizes the new living space, which is presently being created by the creative intelligence of the earth and the spiritual world in order to make it possible for earth to take the mysterious leap from one developmental plane to the next. This quantum leap will simultaneously take earth out of the danger of destruction.

In addition, the pelican, as a symbol of Christ, confirms the elevated spiritual lineage of the above-mentioned "emergency rescue plan" for earth. Why is it a symbol of Christ? In the Middle Ages, travelers returning from Africa told that the pelican, in a time of famine, would tear open its own breast and give its heart's blood to its young. Thus the pelican became a symbol of the universal love that Christ taught.

Through the feeding problem that overshadows the first dream image, it is made clear that we are not capable of doing anything with the above-mentioned spiritual "emergency rescue plan." Earth's newborn etheric space, which will ensure a future for the planet, will in the best case scenario be accepted by specific spiritual movements as a mental abstraction, which can in no way set in motion any practical follow-up.

The numbers of people who flock around the pelican and seek a solution for its feeding problems represent groups and institutions who try, each in their own way, to prevent the anticipated collapse of life on earth. The dream conveys the message that their well-intentioned efforts are unfortunately unsuccessful, because they are based on human thinking of what is best to do for the fate of the world. There is talk of decreasing the output of harmful gases, of the battle against earth warming, and so forth. Completely lacking from the discussion, however, is the necessary sensitivity to discover, in any given situation, where the unique potential that needs activation lies.

The criticism directed at politicians, environmental activists, and the standard-bearers of spiritual movements means that one should first make the effort to listen to the voice of the Earth Soul, to grasp what are her plans for resolving earth's dramatic situation before making any attempt to help earth and her living beings.

In the second image, the dreamer has chosen to embody an alternative to the traditional rescue ideas. As a first step, he takes the pelican away from the public space to take him to "his home." "Home" means "within." The problems initiated by the earth changes cannot

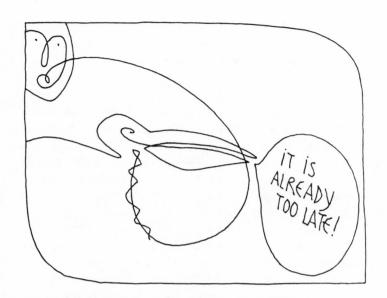

3. *The words are spoken in a calm voice whose tone is unusually deep.*

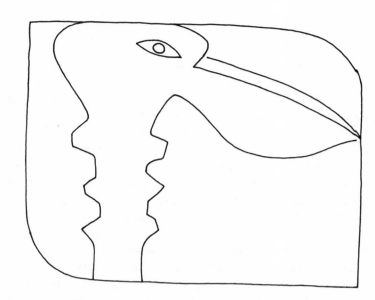

4. *An inner voice tells me that the soup should be free of hard vegetable pieces, so that the liquid can slide down through the pelican's esophagus.*

be satisfactorily resolved by measures in the physical sphere. One should first experience oneself as part of the cosmic life-family, put down strong roots therein, and only afterward enter into action.

This rescue idea, which is totally reliant on personal spiritual change and the individual's impact within the framework of so-called personal ecology, is rejected as unrealistic by the pelican's own statement: "It is too late (for that)!" The concept of personal ecology embraces efforts toward sustainability, as for example in areas such as ecological dwellings, introduction of sustainable technologies, biologically healthy food, a fairer economy, and so forth.

The process of earth change is obviously much too far advanced for its course to be diverted by such "sustainable measures." One would have to have much more time at one's disposal for the results of these sorts of praiseworthy efforts to have a discernible effect at the planetary level. We must not risk missing the cosmic moment that enables the change of course after the lookout calls, "Rocks ahead!" The pelican's shocking message, "It is too late," should direct us back to the circular courses of the cosmic cycles. If we were to follow the plans thought up by our human colleagues, we would miss the cosmic moment that assures us a safe passage to the new evolutionary level.

In this phase of the dream, the white pelican is obviously transformed into a spokesperson for the Earth Soul herself. The specific nonanthropocentric accent in its deep voice indicates that here is no human being, but the united consciousness of earth and nature is speaking.

The mysterious concept of the "thin soup" that is to be cooked for the pelican indicates a further possible way in which people can successfully support the process of earth change. However, there emerges another problem, which is indicated by the dreamer's fear that the soup may contain hard vegetable pieces that could lodge in the pelican's esophagus and stop the soup's free flow.

This last dream image can also be seen as a criticism, this time directed at those persons and movements who are entrusted with the cosmic context of the current earth changes and yet cherish their own ideas of how to react.

Here too are a number of very informative symbols bundled together. The dreamer wants to know precisely what can help the pelican heal and what can hinder it. It should be a "thin soup," but contain no "hard vegetable pieces". And yet he loses his voice when he wants to express his clearly defined knowledge in a message to his wife.

The expression of his message should be likened to spreading the consciousness of the spiritual background of the earth's change among the general public. We have to ask, why can such an undertaking have had so little result, although, relatively speaking, much has been published on the subject over the last ten years?

Can the reason be similar to the panic that seized the dreamer when he thought he was seeing the pelican's esophagus closed tight like a hose pipe? Indeed, is it even tolerable to think that the health of the earth can be dependent on humankind when it is caught in such a dramatic situation, engaged in an epochal change conditioned by cosmic cycles?

And that may be the mistake! Instead of imagining that one must do this or that to help the process of earth change, one should concentrate on maintaining one's inner peace, even when one knows about the drama running behind the everyday world scenery bearing the signs of intensive change. The pelican's perfect shape—which tells of the divine presence within the processes of change—is a guarantee that nothing can go awry. It is from this fact that we derive our trust that nothing, not even the most dramatic twists and turns, can throw it off course.

Founded on our fundamental trust in the cosmically perfect completion of the earth changes, humankind will at last be free to interact with the processes contained therein, either on a personal or public level.

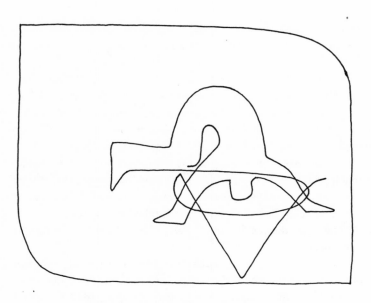

1. *I am a craftsman and am getting ready to start a job that requires me to bend deeply into a well of water.*

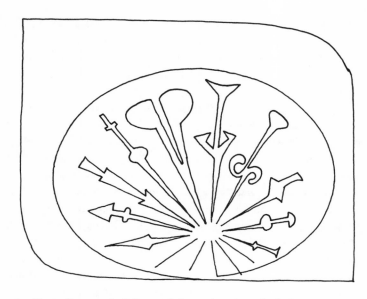

2. *Now all my tools fall out of the pockets into the hole.*

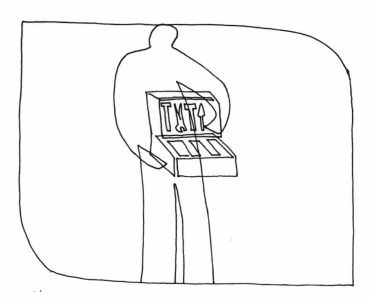

3. *If I had had my toolbox with me, all my tools would be arranged in their proper places.*

Dream 13: A New Creative Set of Tools

1   *I am a craftsman and am getting ready to start a job that requires me to bend deeply into a well of water. The well lies in a cylindrical hole.*

2   *In bending down, I forget that my jacket pockets are packed full of fine tools. Now all my tools fall out of the pockets into the hole. However, when I look down after them, I am surprised to see what sort of tools are now lying in the hole. The shapes of the tools are plainly eerie, and I have never seen the like before.*

3   *At the same time I am thinking what a pity it is that I have lent someone my toolbox. If I had had my toolbox with me, all my tools would be arranged in their proper places. The present mess would never have happened.*

(Sempas, Slovenia, February 25, 2002)

It is best to take the last image first, because one can grasp the dream's message better by going through it backward: "If the man has put the tools of his consciousness in the toolbox of his intellect, he will simply not notice the subtle changes in earth space." This statement is a logical translation of the dreamer's thoughts in the third dream image. If a man is present exclusively on the intellectual level and its "objective distance," he cannot perceive the change processes that play themselves out on a deeper level of being. Apparently, everything remains exactly as it was.

This explains why, for most people on earth, nothing essential has altered, although the Earth Consciousness has in the meantime made giant advances toward changing the foundations of life, indeed toward changing space.

If human beings remain stuck fast in the logic of intellect, they rob themselves of the possibility of gathering experiences of the cosmic process of Earth Change and integrating them into their own bodies and lives.

In contrast, the first image provides an example in which an unforeseen event catapults the man out of the firmly laid tracks of reason. In consequence, he comes in contact, albeit unwillingly, with the burgeoning power of earth change.

The action of bending deeply into a well of water means that you are picking up the spiritual relationship of your own archetypal origins. This is reinforced by your deeply inclining into the depths, which is a symbol of an energy reversal through which the firmly ordered ranks of your consciousness are reduced to chaos.

Now the preconditions are created through which you can come to the experience of the new life stream that has been working in the background to change the crumbling structure of the world. The second dream image shows eerie tool shapes, such as have never been seen before, which symbolize the operations of the cosmic earth forces in reconfiguring earth's body. This brings to mind the springs of archetypal force, interdimensional portals, transformed elemental beings, and other phenomena of the newly forming earth space, which are described in my book *Sacred Geography*.

In contrast to the linear arrangement of the traditional tools lined up in the toolbox of the intellectual consciousness, the "new" tools are arranged, mandala-like, in a circle. Here, the circle stands as a symbol of the holistic consciousness.

The dream regarding the lost toolbox directs the attention of those who are thirsting for the future to the scarcely noticeable somersaults, which represent a unique chance for them to free themselves from the old patterns and open up to the new. Spatial somersaults are a kind of pole reversal that are set in motion by the Earth Consciousness, either in the personal or collective life of humankind, to advance our preparedness for the new conditions of life.

They often occur as unwanted or even fearful reversals in our way of life. One should meet them with an open consciousness, trusting in the wisdom of universal life, and then they can be a blessing as we approach the intact side of the earthly cosmos.

1. *I am standing in a long line in front of a sales kiosk where I can buy travel tickets for myself and my companion.*

2. *When it comes to my turn and I bend down to the kiosk, I see to my astonishment that the travel tickets are being sold by a seven-year-old boy.*

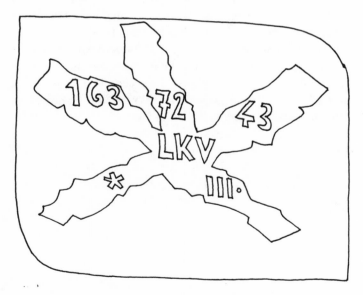

3. *The travel tickets were torn open so perfectly that all the dates to ensure their validity were undamaged.*

Dream 14: Reality Pulsates on Two Levels Simultaneously

1   *I have been asking for a place where I can buy travel tickets for myself and my companion. I am sent to a nearby shop called "Manufactures." Now I am standing in a long line in front of a sales kiosk.*

2   *When it comes to my turn and I bend down to the kiosk, I see to my astonishment that the travel tickets are being sold by a seven-year old boy. With his nimble little fingers he tears open every one of the tickets so expertly that it makes a five-pointed star.*

3   *I was deeply disturbed that the travel tickets would lose their validity by being torn up, but then I noticed that they were torn open so perfectly that all the dates to ensure their validity were undamaged.*

   (Sempas, Slovenia May 7, 2002)

THE MESSAGE OF THE DREAM about the torn travel tickets relates to the prerequisites of life on our earth. The story tells of two completely different dimensions of living space, which exist simultaneously in our time and can both affirm their own validity.

The usual opinion is that the possibility of living and working on earth is a given, because we were born on the planet Earth. No thought is given to the fact that the reality of the form of a specific spatial dimension must be constantly maintained so it can operate as a vessel in which life can find the possibilities for multifold evolution.

To be more precise, by "vessel" is meant the spatial structure through which the life processes can be brought to completion. We are looking at a specific cosmic pattern through which the living space is appropriately structured in every successive moment. If there were no such cosmic pattern, a general vibrational chaos would rule on earth and in the universe itself.

In reference to the first image of our dream, one could compare the presently viable spatial structure with a street, and the traffic running through it with the life processes of the individuals and culture. The travel ticket that the dreamer plans to buy would thus represent his decision to use the traditional spatial structure for his life's journey.

The traditional spatial structure is a mentally created linear (one dimensional) structure that can best be compared to a one-way street. The relatively simple spatial structure is appropriate to the strictly limited capacity of our intellect to find the right path through the multidimensionality of life. Because of our current dependence on rational decision-making, we move nearly exclusively on the materially conditioned level of being.

In the second dream image, the unprepared dreamer is confronted with a completely differently configured spatial structure, represented by the seven-year-old boy who is seated in the place of the expected salesman. The boy, with his incredibly nimble little fingers, represents the so-called "indigo generation" of children who, although still young, are capable of leaping over the linear intellect and opening themselves to the cosmic dimensions of being. In fact, the boy demonstrates the creation of a new spatial consciousness by skillfully reshaping the square travel ticket into the form of a five-pointed star. In so doing, two important details come to light.

First, the travel ticket's five-pointed form is reminiscent of a multidimensional spatial structure in which, proceeding outward from the general (divine) middle, its five spatial dimensions spread out like a mandala. This is essentially different from the static shape of a usual travel ticket related to the "old" space's linear structure.

Second, the five-pointed star represents the archetypal image of the perfect space with the four manifested dimensions which can be linked to the four elements:

   1. Air element—linked to the level of consciousness,
   2. Water element—linked to the emotional level of being,
   3. Earth element represents the physical level,
   4. Fire element—the vital-energetic (etheric) level,
   5. and the fifth dimension, which portrays a spiritual character.

However, the third image makes a decisive statement as to the dream's message. It emphasizes that the "old" linearly extending reality still stays in power, although the new multidimensional spatial structure of the future already exists parallel to it.

And further! Just as the travel ticket, transformed into a five-pointed star, has not lost its validity for traditional public transport, so people can still move with a good conscience along the old tracks. The society, which is not yet entrusted with the new spatial dimensions, desires us to do this. Thus, we are currently still summoned to pursue our old roles and duties.

Nonetheless, we are simultaneously free to enjoy the multidimensional spatial structure and get closer and closer to its rules and rhythms. Gradually, we may build our nest in our future home.

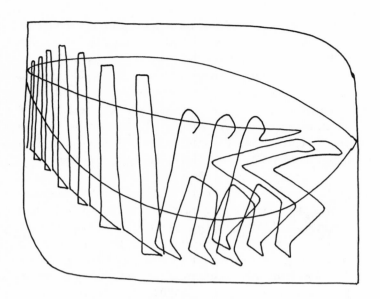

1. We are with a group of men who are pulling a barge over calm water toward the ocean.

2. We gather excitedly on the high bank and look down into a giant hole. The ocean has vanished!

Dream 15: Tasks of the Transition Time

1   *We are with a group of men who are pulling a barge over calm water toward the ocean. The direction in which we tow the boat is precisely prescribed by two rows of strikingly tall stones. The exceptional clarity of the water is remarkable. It has the quality of liquid crystal.*

2   *When we come to the rim of the ocean, our advance is abruptly interrupted. We gather excitedly on the high bank and look down into a giant hole. The ocean has vanished! Its mighty bed is empty. Its floor has dried out!*

3   *Looking more closely, I see that there are some people industriously working on the floor of the ocean bed. Narrow canals are being dug as part of a widespread network. But why dig canals when everything down there is dry? Then I notice that the water from above has in many places flushed holes in the dam wall. Narrow runnels are forming through which water is beginning to flow to fill the giant ocean bed anew. But oh, horrors! The water that is streaming down is abominably dirty!*

4   *Our group is forced to wait until the dry ocean bed is sufficiently full that we can sail on it. To pass the time, I look at a wooden table where an elderly man is sitting and selling sweet confectionery made from pressed dried fruit. They are molded in unusual archetypal shapes. I fancy a "step pyramid" to furnish me with provisions for the long journey. At that moment, a female voice calls out the name: "Marco Polo Piccolo."*

(Hanover, Germany, November 18, 2001)

THERE ARE THREE PARTS to this dream. The first dream image represents humankind's present situation, seen in the midst of a transition between present and future. The "barge of life" is moved along a preordained path that is marked by a double row of posts. The issue is about how our intellect-oriented culture adjusts to its own evolution. Instead of opening itself to the inspiration of earth and heaven, and deciding here and now, on the basis of the insights so gained what further steps to take, the evolutionary path is laid out in advance. So what is the problem? Because the coordinates of reality have been defined in advance, evolution has been transformed into an object that cannot be guided by one's will, but only according to the rules of logic.

One should also notice that, instead of the barge carrying the group, it must be pulled. This is because human beings are always there, adapting the threads of evolution to their own ideas, so that it is they and only they who must provide the motive power. The intelligence and powers of heaven and earth have been granted minimal possibilities to help civilization develop.

In consequence, one is surprised by the observation that the water across which the barge is being pulled is extraordinarily clear, even crystalline. This confirms that the powers of earth and heaven —in the framework of the current planetary transformation—have already changed the circumstances within which our evolution takes place. A new living space is arising whose quality is essentially different from the old space, which is closely tied to physical existence.

Instead of moving through physical water, we move through a liquid crystal. The processes of earth change have sensitized substances; in other words, matter is being subjected to the process of etherization.

To return to the first image: ever since the start of earth change, people have been living "like amphibians." On the one hand, we are forced to abide by the laws of the "old" materially oriented civilization. Its ways are prescribed by a science that is based on the knowledge of the physical world. At the same time we are unconsciously bathing in the subtle frequencies of new spatial qualities, which have meantime been flooding through the invisible dimensions of reality.

Returning to the dream, the image of the empty ocean bed forces the dreamer to confront the challenges of the near future.

One must first state that there can be no linear way of passing from the present state of reality to the multidimensional quality of the future living space. The difference is like comparing the present day's flat body of water to the deep ocean. The first phase of the alchemical kind of change, which alone can lead from one state of reality to the other, is represented by the dried out pit of ocean that first must be filled up so that one can sail upon it. In other words, the ocean of being must first be emptied before being filled anew, in order to make secure the new epoch for the evolution of the foundations of life on earth.

The third part of the dream relates to the practical tasks that are to be finished so that humans can contribute their share to the epochal transformation. We have mentioned the people who are working

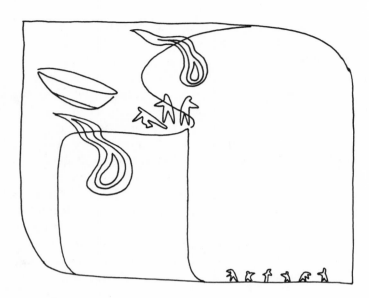

3. *Looking more closely, I see that there are some people industriously working on the floor of the ocean bed.*

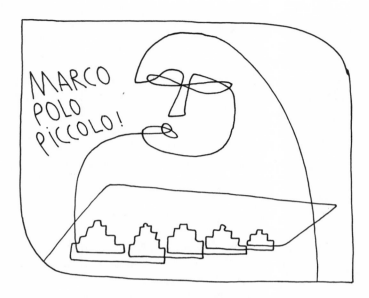

4. *To pass the time, I look at a wooden table where an elderly man is sitting and selling sweet confectionery made from pressed dried fruit.*

industriously on the future ocean floor. However, the network of narrow canals that they are constructing looks too fragile to be of practical value in the future filling of the giant ocean bed. Rather, one can see here a symbol of ongoing work at the level of consciousness. There are many individuals and groups world-wide who are actively working on the formation of the so-called new paradigm. To ensure that forward-looking changes in society, religion, philosophy, and so forth, are thoroughly considered and publicly communicated, humankind is being prepared for the approaching epochal transformation. A praiseworthy activity!

However, the image of dirty water discharged from above (where the dreamer is standing) makes the success of that praiseworthy activity rather doubtful. It is here that we find the salient point of the dream's message: the effort to bring about a real change in consciousness can come to naught if one neglects to work at the same time on the energetic purification of existing trauma and blockages. The wild water streaming downward can all too easily destroy the fragile channels of consciousness.

The closing image specifies the kind of purification that is required on the threshold of the future ocean. The key to it is expressed in the witty name, "Marco Polo Piccolo" (the little Marco Polo). Since the dreamer is called "Marko," one can identify the "little Marko" as his outward personality, the dreamer's so-called ego. It is this aspect of the human identity that most needs clarification.

And why "Marco Polo?" Because the issue concerns the personal clarification and purification of human beings currently alive, who are about to prepare themselves for a long journey into the future. It can be compared to Marco Polo's journey to China in the Middle Ages.

The image of the old salesman addresses the issues of purification and clarification. He offers sweet confectionery compressed into archetypal shapes reminiscent of bygone cultures. Also, they are made of dried fruit; not from fresh fruits bathing in the sun of the present day, but from the preserved memory of an abundant life, now past.

The sweet confectionery symbolizes antiquated psychological patterns and established dogma. They may originate in the long ago past, but are nonetheless capable of grievously inhibiting our progress along ways that point to the future. They are anchored deep in our subconscious, preventing us from taking the joyful journey into the multidimensional future.

In the wake of earth change, countless such patterns can be expected to come to the light of consciousness, in our personal lives as well as in the lives of religious communities, nations, and cultures. Resulting conflict situations are unavoidable, because nobody is happy when they are having to deal with their old stuff. This process should not be hindered, for dependent on it is the success of the coming spatial reversal through which the empty ocean bed is filled with fresh crystalline water. What is now needed is to work busily at freeing one's own powers which have been frozen under the burdens of the past.

Exercises on the Theme "The New Earth Space

An exercise to free oneself from old patterns

We are usually unaware of how strongly we are influenced by the preconceptions that shape our reality. Hence, our perception of reality, as it actually exists at any given moment, tends to be clouded. This exercise should help provide momentary freedom from all this ballast and give you a valuable chance to see the world new and fresh.

- *You should spend some time in silence and then become conscious of your own figure, your outward shape: let your attention slowly travel over the whole surface of your own body.*
- *Then you begin to imagine that your own body surface is drawn inward and concentrated in the region of your own heart center.*
- *While you are drawing yourself inward and together, a change process comes into being through which the outer I-consciousness returns to the I-essence.*
- *At the same time that the drawing together process is happening, an expansion process is also occurring. The spirit of Yourself, loosed from the limits of your corporeal surface, spreads freely through the space around you, far, far…*
- *While you are simultaneously concentrated inward and expanded outward, certain things about the true shape of reality, which are otherwise obscured in clouds, will become clear to you. Take a little time to enjoy the blossoming freedom that ensues.*

To make you familiar with the principle of Change by Somersault

This exercise follows the three phases of the transformation process. You begin with the descent into the personal "underworld" that leads through the back space. After that, follows the "laying in the grave" that is comparable to the new beginning in the womb. In the third phase you experience the ascent to a new level of being.

- *You should seat yourself for meditation in the usual way and become present in your heart center. The exercise can also be done while lying on your back.*
- *First you should imagine that you move out of your body through the crown chakra and take yourself down to the back space.*
- *Go slowly downward through the length and breadth of the back space and through various layers of your own "underworld" until you arrive in the dark space of the belly.*
- *You have now arrived at the second phase of the change process and made it through to lie, so to speak, in your own mother's womb. Take time to savor the experience.*
- *Next, you should inwardly rise upright and gather all your inner strength to climb up to your own heart realm.*
- *Take time to experience yourself anew. Look closely to see whether any extensions of yourself, hidden until now, are newly awakened.*
- *You should let the quality of your new being spread out through your whole body, right down to the last cell.*

A somersault exercise

This exercise enables you to experience the unrecognized dimensions of your own inwardness by causing your chakras to somersault. By chakras, we mean here the seven best-known power centers of the human body positioned along the spine. Each one is marked by a specific color that is traditionally sequenced from below to above as follows: root chakra (red), sacral chakra (orange), solar plexus (yellow), heart chakra (green), larynx (blue), third eye (violet) crown chakra (white).

- *For purposes of the somersault, you had best choose two chakras whose functions are related, for example, the second (sacral) chakra and the fifth (larynx) chakra, both of which have to do with creativity although they operate on two different levels.*
- *For this example, you should imagine the sacral chakra in the form of an orange ball and the larynx chakra as a blue ball.*
- *Now you should exchange the positions of the two balls within your own body. The blue ball is led downward through the back space and the orange ball upward through the body's anterior space. This is the somersault.*
- *After they have found their new places, hold them there for a while, and be consciously present.*
- *Next, forget about having done the somersault, and concentrate fully on observing what is happening in your own inwardness after the somersault.*
- *Finally you should allow both balls to glide back to their original places.*

An exercise to adjust yourself to the new spatial structure

The reshaping of earth's living space is a nonlogical process that is highly bewildering for the intellect. This exercise with its many threads was formed to accustom the consciousness to the nonlogical bends and spirals that will accompany our daily lives in the near future.

- *Place yourself in your favorite meditation position and become still.*
- *Imagine yourself bound by thin threads to various points in your environment around you.*
- *Now imagine yourself bending forward and doing a somersault— and still remaining bound to your surroundings by all the many threads.*
- *Now sit back into your earlier position. And ask yourself, what happened to those many threads when you turned over? Were they perhaps all twisted together into a single chaotic rope? Or did a new order arise in the space?*
- *It would be a good idea to repeat that somersault several times to get a better sense of the process. You should not try to follow it logically.*
- *How does your relationship to the space feel now? Get a sense of it every time you do it!*

Chapter 3

THE DRAMATICS OF EARTH CHANGE

THE DRAMATIC CHARACTER of the present earth change can hardly be better illustrated than by the tragic events of September 11, 2001. Like the majority of people worldwide, I felt shattered in an unprecedented way by the fate of the twin towers of the World Trade Center in New York. I felt so struck in my own core being that for three days afterwards I ran around as if headless.

This is not logical behavior! I had already written and published my first book on the theme of earth change[1] and was aware of the deeper reasons for climate and earth changes. I was thus prepared for possible fluctuations in the terrestrial structure. But I had not expected such a powerful invasion of events on the physical level of reality. It is true that quite violent change processes had taken place between the years 1998 and 2001, but they played themselves out on the subtle etheric and consciousness conditioned levels, hidden from the public eye.

The events of 9/11/01 were quite different. Several thousand people died simultaneously in the middle of the world's great metropolis, seat of the United Nations! New York's two tallest skyscrapers were smashed down one after the other in a secretly prepared terrorist action. We do not know even today who actually conceived it. Was it radical Muslim terrorists alone, or was there also some manipulation by powerful Western elites who were drumming up war?

A year earlier I had had the good fortune to stand with my daughter Ana on the terrace of one of the Twin Towers and enjoy the breath-taking view that spread out before us. And it happened that three weeks after the catastrophe I was in New York, standing before the ruins of the Twin Towers, "astounded by a gigantic heap of wildly woven iron bars, crumbled steel beams, and concrete rubble. A flock of yellow excavators was circling hectically around, intent on removing the stigma as quickly as possible."[2]

Looking back, I realized that from the beginning of August 2001, I had had a series of dreams, preparing me for a special event without my suspecting in what form it would emerge on the physical level of being a month later.

The essential part of the dream messages can be summarized as follows. The transformation of earth's subtle body is far advanced, and the planet's new etheric mantle is largely prepared so that the new disposition of the earth cosmos can manifest itself on the plane of life. In contrast, the great majority of humankind is delaying inside the old mental structures, which totally suppresses any sensitivity to the epochal transformation of earth and nature.

The resulting tension between the upwardly striving force fields of the self-renewing earth and the sluggish mass of hesitant humanity has become so acute that the life-field common to both worlds is in danger of complete collapse. For earth, this would mean that it would no longer be possible to preserve the richness of life on the physical level of being. Humanity would thereby be delivered over to the danger of the "second death."

The concept of the "second death" alerts us to the danger that the identity of humankind's spiritual soul may be completely extinguished. The "first death" means our natural passing from one dimension to the other. The dead lose their physical body, but their life goes on at the level of the spiritual soul. The "second death" would result in a much more fundamental dissolution of the human being, such that, in the extreme case, the cosmos could no longer remember that a specific person had ever existed.

This cannot be allowed to happen to humankind. To protect us in this desperate situation and to deliver earth and humanity from the abyss, the terrorist plot of 9/11 has planted a very powerful and positive seed, a seed of mercy.

I could perceive this when I stood in front of the ruins, and it was also perceptible in the following years when I investigated the positive effects of the catastrophe on the force systems of Manhattan.[3] By the operation of divine grace, the pole of the destructive impulse has been reversed at its core. Thousands of people have unfortunately lost their lives: that could not be changed. Yet, through the sacrifice of their lives, a deeper sense has arisen and become incorporated, which can best be described by the ancient Greek concept of catharsis.

In Greek tragedy, the person who represents the dying hero or heroine, of course, does not really die. Despite this, the audience experiences their dying as a real encounter with death's abyss. The deeply moving encounter with death works in such a way that an inner change runs through the audience. This experience is called catharsis. The people who have experienced it come out of the theater as if newborn. In this, we should visualize the "abyss of death" to be identical with the pulse beat of eternity. Catharsis comes about because, by the imagined encounter with death, one has really touched into the archetypal space of eternity.

In relation to the tragic event of September 11th, this means that millions of people worldwide were experiencing the proximity of death under conditions of great shock and amazement. The thick layers of mental consciousness, into which we are forced as into a strait jacket, were lifted for a few moments. In those moments we all looked on the face of eternity. Although for most of us this happened unconsciously—while our waking consciousness, shocked and disbelieving, was glued to the television screen—it was perfectly anchored in our bodies and can nevermore be dissipated.

Just as in classical tragedy, we did not all need to die in order to experience the healing catharsis. Similarly, a relatively few people sacrificed themselves so that the masses of humankind could make the required reconnection with the archetypal ground of being. To them, we give our eternal gratitude! The danger of the "second death" and the collapse of living systems were successfully overcome.

A further event, which is related to the drama of the current earth change, happened seven years later in Wall Street, New York, only a few steps from the tragic site of the twin towers. This was the collapse of the financial market in October 2008, which was followed by the dramatic fall in stock markets worldwide.

It was thought at first that this collapse was a passing crisis that could be turned around by giant investments of cash. However, within a year this was followed by the general contraction of the world economy, the collapse of some industrial giants like General Motors, and quickly spreading unemployment. What have these unpleasant processes to do with earth change?

The primary question has to do with grounding. The unimaginable masses of money, which have traveled around the planet in the last few decades, represent a serious threat to the stability of earth. For the most part this is not money grounded in real goods or creative actions, or, at least, in gold bars lying in the cellars of the national banks, but instead represents a giant amount of mental energy that goes by the name of finance. Finance has no relation to the reality of life and yet is the cause of many things on earth, among others the highly dangerous developments in weapons production, the unlimited enrichment of individuals and elite groups, etc.

Seen in the context of earth change, the apparently catastrophic events, whether in the realm of finance or the economy, have a positive face. One can really say the same for the natural catastrophes that have been affecting various parts of the earth—outbreaks of fire that take weeks to extinguish, mega-typhoons that can smash whole cities… So how can one find a positive aspect in the avalanche of dramatic events that are continually shaking terrestrial nature and human culture?

The key lies in the concept of transformation. Transformation is not a simple linear change. Transformation demands that something must die for something new to be born.

The classical example of transformation is the change that turns the bristly caterpillar into the wonderfully beautiful butterfly. For the butterfly to emerge, the caterpillar must spend a certain time enclosed in a cocoon as in a sepulcher. It must die as a caterpillar in order to be reborn as a butterfly.

By analogy, this means that earth and human culture are enclosed "in the sepulcher of a cocoon" during the epoch of their transformation. We may visualize this epoch as a transitional hemisphere, with the caterpillar at one end and the butterfly at the other. The apparent decay in our cultural and natural surroundings belongs to the demolition arc of the change process. Are we ready and do we have the strength to perceive the results of the constructive arc of planetary change?

The events of the demolition arc really "only" appear to be negative. They involve transitional processes through which something new and wonderful comes into being. If our sight was also schooled to see the etheric positive of the change processes, we would, in my experience, be amazed at how beautifully conceived is "the butterfly" that arises from the dramatic events of earth change.

I have selected the following dreams to enable certain insights into the processes of earth change that are already in progress. I hope that the dreams I have chosen will enable you to experience the meaning of the demolition arc of earth change as well as the gift of the constructive arc.

1. *Earth Changes, Human Destiny,* Findhorn Press 2000.
2. My experience in connection with the 9/11 disaster is more precisely described in my book *Turned Upside Down,* Lindisfarne Books 2004.
3. See the Chapter "New York: The Megaliths of Manhattan," page 14 of *Touching the Breath of Gaia,* Findhorn Press 2007.

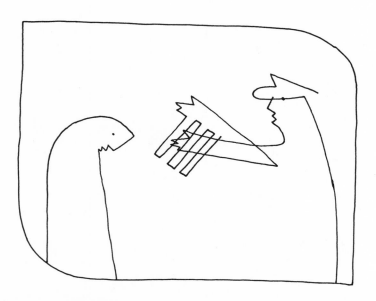

1. *To my astonishment, I am stopped by the police because sticks of dynamite have been found in my baggage.*

2. *Having arrived back home, I continue brooding over how the dynamite could have gotten into my baggage.*

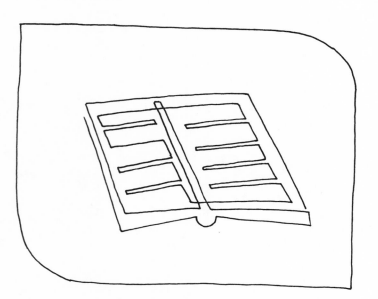

3. *When I open the book, I am horrified to find that are no printed pages inside but, instead, some neatly arranged sticks of dynamite.*

Dream 16: Dynamite in the Baggage

1   *I have just arrived on an airplane and am going through baggage control. To my astonishment, I am stopped by the police because sticks of dynamite have been found in my baggage. I have no idea where they came from and feel deeply ashamed.*

2   *Having arrived back home, I sprawl in my armchair to recover from the stress. I continue brooding over how the dynamite could have gotten into my baggage.*

3   *Seeking another train of thought, I take a book from my bookshelves. When I open it, I am horrified to find there are no printed pages inside but, instead, some neatly arranged sticks of dynamite.*
(Villach, Austria, April 29, 2004)

THE DREAM FROM VILLACH lets us know that when we imagine ourselves to be free of destructive patterns, this may be a lie.

The dreamer is obviously no terrorist, or the police would not have let him go free after finding dynamite in his baggage. This means that the dream is about an average person who will threaten no one. And yet within him he obviously carries destructive patterns of whose existence he is ignorant. They can operate at two different levels.

Since the first dream image happens in a public place where the unknowing smuggler has been caught, the thought occurs that we are dealing with a general thought pattern that hides brooding in the human subconscious. As members of the present civilization, alienated from our own true being, we have united the thought pattern to ourselves without being aware of it. It is simply carried on from generation to generation.

However, the pressing need to free oneself from general thought patterns is well known. Every serious spiritual movement preaches increasingly on the subject. If one remains hanging in the stream of the general thought patterns, one must renounce any prospect of advancing oneself on the spiritual path.

But if something is already well known, why should a dream make it a point of emphasis?

The next two dream images provide the answer to this question. The dreamer now finds himself in his own private home, which means that he is in the intimacy of his inner being. He is surrounded by his trusted bookshelves, which represent his spiritual potential. And behold! Once again he comes across dynamite!

This time, the dream message points to a culturally conditioned pattern that each of us individually, whether or not we want to, is carrying in our subconscious. It is these patterns that now and then drive us to become aggressive (perhaps over unimportant incidentals), although we are firmly resolved to live in peace with all beings. These same patterns can lead to a raging war if political maneuvering activates them simultaneously among masses of people. Fresh examples from modern history need no retelling.

The dream from Villach emphasizes the need to transform the deep underlayer of culturally-conditioned patterns. One could classify them as negative archetypes. If they remain ignored in humankind's subconscious, they present a potential danger that could upset the successful conclusion of the global earth change.

The message of the dream is primarily addressed to those people who have advanced on the spiritual path and perhaps think that they have long been free of the patterns of power. The message of the dream opposes this concept, asserting our participation, willing or unwilling, in persisting destructive patterns through our membership over many thousands of years in a power-wielding civilization. In consequence, each one of us is co-responsible for their transformation.

There is more. The development of the global earth change is so configured that the hidden patterns of power—in our case symbolized by sticks of dynamite—are continually driven to the surface of daily life. They manifest through specific unpleasant events, not to punish humankind but to point to their existence, with the hope that they are perceived and a transformation process initiated.

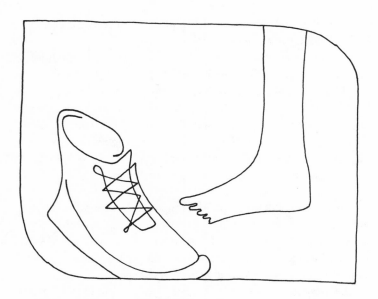

1. *Before we get out, I take off my shoes because I suspect that we will watch rituals, for which one should go barefoot.*

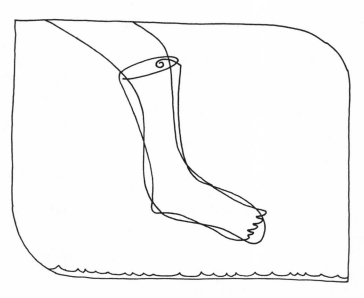

2. *Now I am standing in black knee socks, and I know they will get wet if I go any farther.*

3. *I am now among a crowd of people and feel unsettled as they eat and drink and dispute violently among one another.*

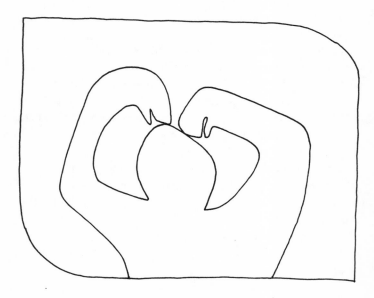

4. *But, oh horrors! The vehicle has meantime been driven off, taking my shoes with it....*

Dream 17: An Obstacle to the Soul's Relationship with the Earth

1   *Our group has just arrived in a bus to visit a Tibetan temple. Before we get out, I take off my shoes because I suspect that we will watch rituals, for which one should go barefoot. We are led through various buildings, each of which represents single initiatory steps. In the course of this, I am left somewhat behind because I have been very thorough in my performance of the rituals.*

2   *Now I find myself alone on the threshold of a broad temple court. In the meantime it has become dark. In the shimmering moonlight I perceive that the court ahead of me is somewhat marshy. Because I took my shoes off in the bus, I could get wet crossing the court. This would not be so bad if I had taken off my socks at the same time as the shoes. Now I am standing in black knee socks, and I know they will get wet if I go any farther.*

3   *If I want to keep my feet dry, I must go back and fetch my shoes from the bus. On the way, another solution comes to mind. I turn into the temple canteen to wait for my colleagues to finish their tour of the initiatory sites. I am now among a crowd of people and feel unsettled as they eat and drink and dispute violently with one another. Much time has gone by, but the rest of my group has still not arrived.*

4   *I now decide to fetch my shoes. I shall put them on and go to look for the rest of my group. Although the night is now black as pitch, I am in good spirits as I go to the place where we left the bus. But, oh horrors! The vehicle has in the meantime been driven off, taking my shoes with it...*

(Ljubljana, Slovenia, February 22, 2003)

To go barefoot on the earth means you are keeping a free and direct relationship with earth and nature. The shoes are a symbol of the culturally conditioned (alienated) relationship that human beings have with earth and nature. Taking my shoes off means, in this case, a wish to return to the original connection with earth and nature.

The action of taking off the shoes can be compared to the ecological stance that currently inspires countless people. We are proud of the quick development of eco-friendly technology, we buy biologically raised food, trash is carefully sorted, and we interest ourselves in the well-being of plant and animal species.

The first dream image compares the development of the modern ecological attitude to an initiatory walk through a temple site. However, one feels a breath of criticism. The walk through the temple site is over too quickly, which can be interpreted as a sign that the current ecological attitude lacks something essential in its attention to earth and nature.

The second dream image attempts to characterize what is missing. The relevant symbol takes the form of the socks which are still on his feet. It is obvious that the symbolic action of taking off one's shoes is insufficient to enable a new relationship with earth and nature. Our generally accepted and highly admired ecological attitude does not suffice to bring one into contact with earth and nature, which are not mere biological forms but a conceptual intelligence (being) that is constantly changing.

To clarify the symbols, it must first be said that socks are in no way shoes. This is not a symbol of the conceptual relationship with earth and nature, but of a much more transparent level of relationship. If you decide to tread in water, your feet get wet even if you have socks on. The socks' transparent weave points to an emotional relationship that rests midpoint between spirit and matter.

We should also notice that the dream is explicit about knee socks and specifies that they are black.

Knees are a traditional symbol of our relationship with the soul. They mean that the presence of the soul cannot extend as far downward into matter as does the physical body. Seen symbolically, her presence reaches only to the knees, not to the floor. This means that when we are kneeling, we are standing on the feet of our soul. This is why we kneel to pray.

In this we are to understand the concept of the soul in a spiritual and not a psychological sense. Whether in reference to the earth or human beings, the soul indicates an extension of being, one that vibrates beyond time and space. It refers to the individual spiritual core of earth or people. That these exist beyond the physically perceivable world is symbolized in our dream by the color black. It is a symbol of the absent presence.

Accordingly, the black knee socks, which the dreamer will not allow to get wet, represent humankind's relationship to the Earth

Soul, which is traditionally called Mother Earth, or in Greek, the Goddess Gaia. This relationship is a heart to heart connection between humankind and the Earth Cosmos.

We can best grasp the message of the second dream image through the symbols of marshy ground and shimmering moonlight. To reconstruct the flawed relationship with the ensouled immanence of earth, intellectuals must open their emotional, or feminine-spiritual, potential to earth and nature. Why feminine-spiritual? Because the silvery, shimmering moon is a symbol of the Goddess, that is, of the feminine aspect of spirituality, which is based on the quality of love.

This idea is a stumbling block for us moderns: the idea of surrendering ourselves to a deeply passionate relationship with our home planet. A destructive pattern of fear lies anchored there: rather than give oneself over to an emotionally fraught relationship with an earth supposedly put together out of dead matter, the intellectual human flees—like the dreamer in the third image—to the canteen of forgetfulness. One concentrates on consuming the multifold gifts of earth, far distant from the "danger" of engaging with her in a spiritual love relationship.

The fourth dream image finally confirms that there is no possibility of a return to the old distant kind of relationship with earth and nature. After the processes of planetary change have run their course, the earth is no longer a place where a person can shuffle around in thick shoes and still have a good conscience. The bus with the shoes that the dreamer took off has driven away. Changes are already happening.

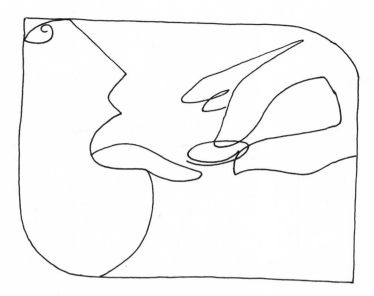

1. I am being fed with gold coins. While I hold my mouth wide open, the first gold coin is laid on my tongue.

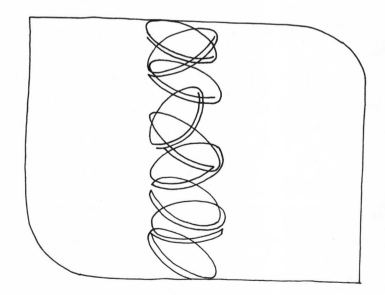

3. As if in an X-ray film, I watch the coin slide slowly and laboriously down toward my belly.

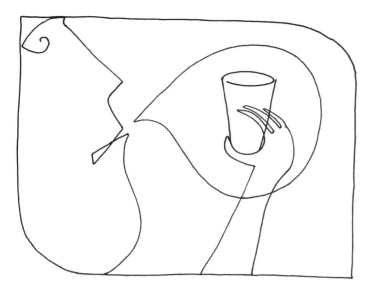

2. It is extremely difficult for me to swallow the glittering coin. How I wish for a drink of water to help the gold piece go down!

Dream 18: The Exaggerated Yang

1   *I am being fed with gold coins. While I hold my mouth wide open, the first gold coin is laid on my tongue. The ceremony reminds me of the ritual taking of the Host in the Christian communion service.*
2   *It is extremely difficult for me to swallow the glittering coin. How I wish for a drink of water to help the gold piece go down!*
3   *As if in an X-ray film, I watch the coin slide slowly and laboriously down toward my belly.*

(Sempas, Slovenia, February 14, 2003)

There is an oft-repeated saying that one cannot eat money. One might also say that there are more important things than money if one's life is at stake.

In this dream, the story is precisely that money is eaten—and not any sort of money, but gold coins.

Gold coins are a symbol of the masculine (Yang) power. The color of yellow gold is an extreme Yang color. The glittering brightness of gold represents the Yang power of the sun in contrast to the silvery Yin power of the moon.

Money, which rules and controls the whole world, is a symbol of the over-mighty power of masculinity, that is, of the Yang forces, in our civilization. The symbol of the gold coins doubles the effect of the masculine force. The Yang color of yellow gold potentizes the masculine character of the concept of money.

 The dreamer's burning wish for a drink of water is a clear sign that he lacks the feminine Yin power. The cool water is the feminine counterpoint to the burning heat represented by the Yang forces.

Eating, seen as the intake of organic nourishment from the surrounding natural world, is a Yin process. That the gold coins were eaten in ritual fashion symbolizes the absolutely unbalanced might of the masculine Yang principle that is leading straight into a cataclysm. It is disgustingly perverse that a ritual significance should be ascribed to the eating of gold.

The dream of swallowing the gold coins points to the exaggerated might of the masculine power in our present civilization, an abomination that cries to heaven for redress. It is a compelling admonition to all of us to work actively to renew the Yin-Yang balance, both at the personal and global levels.

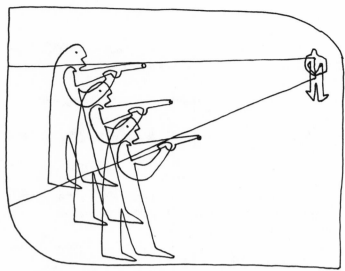

1. *I cannot see the firing squad with their loaded weapons because I must keep my back turned to the soldiers.*

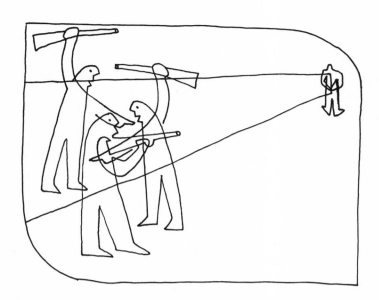

2. *The death volley does not happen. Instead, I can hear the soldiers engaging in a violent dispute over something.*

3. *Thus I decide to make an enormous concentration of my spiritual powers, and let them radiate to reverse the dangerous situation.*

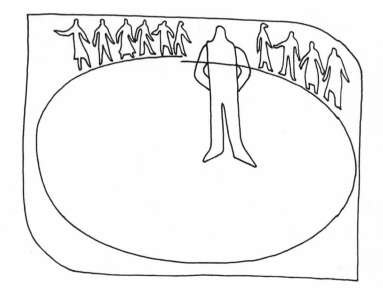

4. *After turning myself around, I am surprised to find that there are no soldiers present, and in general no threat to my life.*

Dream 19: There Are Contrary Powers

1   *I am standing with my hands bound, about to be shot. I cannot see the firing squad with their loaded weapons because I must keep my back turned to the soldiers. But I can feel the tension in the air and know that my situation is bitterly serious. I wait on the death volley.*

2   *The death volley does not happen. Instead, I can hear the soldiers engaging in a violent dispute over something, but I cannot understand what it is about, although I am burning with interest.... The distance is too great.*

3   *It is clear that the squabble in the firing squad represents some hope for me. So I decide to make an enormous concentration of my spiritual powers and let them radiate to reverse the dangerous situation. It is not easy to create a light aura around me because the available space is so narrow.*

4   *The death volley has still not happened. I take courage and begin to turn around slowly to see what is really happening. In an unprejudiced fashion, I talk with the people who are standing around to observe the execution. I wanted to discover what move I should make. After turning myself around, I am surprised to find that there are no soldiers present, and in general no threat to my life.*

(Sempas, Slovenia, September 16, 2005)

THE FIRST DREAM IMAGE portrays a conflict between two opposites, which is characteristic of the astrological Piscean Age, now vanishing. On the one hand stand the soldiers armed with weapons who are representatives of the ruling social elite; on the other hand stands the dreamer for the forces of opposition. The dualistic pattern of the old epoch with its constant wars and social polarization is here taken to extremes. It is a matter of life and death.

As in a theater, the climax of a transformational process is presented in a highly dramatic way. The goal of this process is to change the separative and divisive pattern of the Piscean Epoch into the cooperative pattern of the Aquarian. In the transitional epoch, in which we are now living, there pulses on one side the polarizing pattern of Pisces, and simultaneously on the other the universally connective pattern of Aquarius. We can clearly recognize the steps of the transformational process in the structure of the dream, in which the divisive pattern is gradually changed to a connected pattern.

The first step of the transformational process is portrayed by the squabble in the squad of soldiers. The dominant elite lose the advantage of a philosophically and ideologically united group. The symbol for this is the rumored split in the firing squad itself. Society's globalized systems slump in ecological, financial, economic, religious, and political crises. In the course of these, the polarized pattern that was previously dominant is weakened from within.

Contrarily, the other, weaker pole, represented by the condemned dreamer, is strengthened. (See the third image!) This reinforcement arises through the foundation of various new spiritual movements in the second half of the nineteenth century. More and more people are deciding to go on their autonomous spiritual way, to meditate and join themselves to the powers of heaven and earth's center, independent of the existing religious systems.

Both the above processes lead to a decrease of the polarity's tension pattern. The danger of death appears to be over. To finally conquer it, only one more conscious step is needed, and this is suggested by the fourth dream image.

Following his intuition that the danger of death is past, the dreamer begins to turn around to evaluate the situation. In this process, we should take heed of three symbols. First, the turn is carried out gradually while he is communicating with his fellow humans. Communication involves the conscious clarification of the true state of affairs and some mutual understanding.

Second, turning around symbolizes an attitude that runs completely contrary to the linear concentration of weaponry. Linear concentration shuts out, the circular turning draws in.

The third symbol is decisive: after the dreamer turns around, it appears that the death squad never existed. The thought arises that the dreamer's bitterly serious endangerment was "only" a thought pattern to inspire fear. This pattern tells people that their heart's desire, the way to find their true self, to anchor themselves directly (without religious intermediaries) in the core of the Godhead and to seek for their own inner freedom—all these may be different facets of an "offence." There are powers on this earth that will pursue and punish a person for such an offence.

1. *I am standing on the edge of a landing with a small naked child in my arms, watching the waves of a rather rough sea.*

2. *Suddenly, an unknown voice tells me that I can throw the child into sea without causing it any harm.*

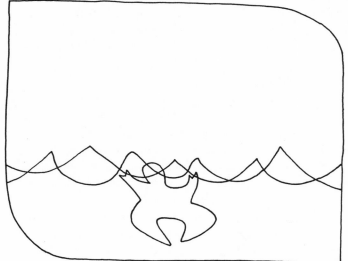

3. *When it does come up, the child can get no air because the waves are continually splashing over its head.*

4. *As if I were the prisoner of an unknown power, I cannot decide to jump into the sea, although the need is obvious.*

Dream 20: The Voice of Intellect

1   *I am standing on the edge of a landing with a small naked child in my arms, watching the waves of a rather rough sea.*

2   *Suddenly, an unknown voice tells me that I can throw the child into the sea without causing it any harm, because the principle of buoyancy will bring it back to the surface. This seems to me enlightening and, unworried, I cast the child into the deep water.*

3   *For a long time the child does not come up, and I become afraid. When it does come up, it can get no air because the waves are continually splashing over its head. Besides, it is in danger of being thrown onto the rocks.*

4   *I begin considering whether to leap into the sea to rescue the child. As if I were the prisoner of an unknown power, I cannot decide to do it although the need is obvious.*

(Sempas, February 12, 2003)

THIS VERY SHOCKING DREAM addresses the voice of the intellect and the dangers run by modern humans who run headlong and heedless to carry out its suggestions.

The little child who is held in the dreamer's arms represents humankind's inner self, the inner core. The child, "born seven days ago," still carries the memory of an existence beyond space and time and has therefore become a symbol of the eternal aspect of humankind.

The unknown voice that sounds in the dreamer's inwardness is clearly the voice of his intellect. One can recognize the voice of the intellect by its logically based arguments which first exclude the feelings of the heart.

The argument using the principle of buoyancy may indeed be correct. One cannot object to it. But then where is the fatherly feeling hiding? It must ruffle any indwelling paternal feelings to resign the fate of one's child to an experiment that is logically correct but thrusts the little child into unimaginable danger!

The third dream image testifies to the inner battles that are constantly waged in the psyches of intellectual people today. Reason dictates the contemporary forms of life, the way we interact with nature, and the ways in which we mix together in various social groups. At the same time, we sense in our heart that the activities, prescribed by our intellect, are often destructive.

The consequences of those actions that are based on rationalistic thinking can be seen in the shape of dying nature, religious quarrels, and warring nations. One would certainly prefer to abstain from all of that. At the same time however, one can sense the logic of an intellect pledged to be included in "normal" society.

In the end, all of this can be swept under the carpet as being a personal psychological problem. Not so the message of the last image. It confirms how disastrous the human involvement in intellectual patterns is for the fate of life on earth. Instead of taking the immediate steps needed in light of the dramatic upset of the earth changes, the dreamer broods over the logical consequences and wrestles whether or not to make the necessary decisions.

The dream's message is not directed against intellect, but in favor of the plural dimensionality of human thought. It goes without question that intellect is a valuable asset that is reserved for humans among all the beings of the earth. The problem arises if the intellect takes the dominant role within the human consciousness, so that other levels of intelligence are suppressed or even mocked as immature. This problem is addressed by our dream's message. In such a case, one may clearly leave rational logic behind and practice thinking in a way to perceive the impulses of the heart and draw them into the thought stream.

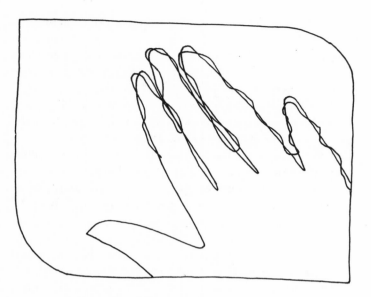

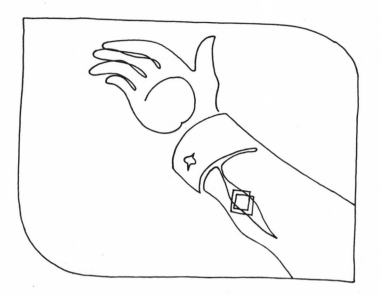

1. For some days now I have been looking at my right hand, which is badly swollen and covered with an unknown kind of ulcer.

2. Through the slit in the sleeve of my shirt I can see a photographic slide lying on the surface of my arm.

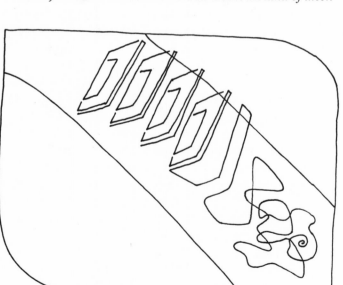

3. When I take the slide out of the pocket in my skin, another one immediately appears, and after that another—and so on.

Dream 21: The False Inborn Pattern

1   For some days now I have been looking at my right hand, which is badly swollen and covered with an unknown kind of ulcer. Its ugliness gets worse day by day. Before going to sleep on the third day, I pray for an enlightening dream.

2   In the dream that follows, I turn my right arm slowly around. Through the slit in the sleeve of my shirt I can see a photographic slide lying on the surface of my arm. What is a slide doing on the underside of my arm? How can it have come there?

3   Looking for an answer, I pull up the sleeve. I am surprised to see that the slide is placed in a small pocket that has been skillfully impressed into my skin. When I take the slide out, another one immediately appears, and after that another—and so on. After the slides, I start pulling out of the little pocket, broken pieces of plastic, crumpled paper…. Each of the objects that follow appears related to an organic substance. The first slide's relationship to my blood was impossible to ignore.

(Sempas, August 6th 2004)

THE COMBINATION of the physical experience and the dream points to a fateful pattern that the story of humankind has impressed in our genetic code. Some of the dream's symbols carry clear and relevant statements. Let us begin with the symbolic role of the photographic slide.

Since a slide, if projected onto a wall, creates an image of reality, a slide can be seen as a symbol of the archetypal pattern that arranges our reality. The many slides that the dreamer pulled out of the pocket on his arm represent the endless series of archetypal images that are inscribed in his blood—or should we say in his genetic code. These are archetypal images that are not relevant merely to the course of a single human life such as are relationship patterns. They are relevant to archetypal patterns that belong to the being of all humans. They are native to us, and it is for this reason that their relation to the dreamer's bodily substance is especially emphasized.

The problem addressed by the dream has to do with those patterns inscribed in our genetic code that are foreign to our true spiritual core, our divine-human identity. It is believed that they were impressed on humanity through certain conscious manipulations.

The dream's message gives no information in respect to the culture responsible for these manipulations. This may be unimportant. To look on the positive side, one can view these implanted foreign patterns as a challenge that forced human beings to express certain qualities that otherwise would have vanished in the evolutionary dynamic. In this way we were forced to wrestle with certain contrary powers and thereby work out our own clarification. This does not mean that we are bound to carry these falsehoods with us through eternity.

In the dream, the false genetic patterns are symbolized by the various foreign substances that are alien to the body's internals. The broken pieces of plastic and crumpled paper are distinct from the perfect series of photographic slides, which represent the positive aspect of the genetic code.

The dreamer has also noticed that the foreign, chaotic-seeming objects that were pulled out of his arm have had a bad effect on the substance of his body. The organic fabric, which has obviously been in touch with humankind's evolution over a long period, appeared rotten with ulcers, as if attacked by a fungus. This must be eradicated.

The message of the dream pleads for the dreamer to become conscious of the foreign genetic pattern and to work on its transformation. It is time for humankind to be free of false genetic patterns. What does it mean, that "it is time"?

It means that the epoch of planetary change is the ideal moment to free oneself from these manipulatively impressed patterns. Who knows when another such opportunity will recur? If one does not take care to uncouple the false genetic patterns, one cannot expect any further great advances in human evolution.

Because this is an emergency, the horrific effects of false archetypes operating in the epoch of change will appear again and again in the form of irresolvable conflicts. They come in all their force not to punish us, but to gain our support for their eradication.

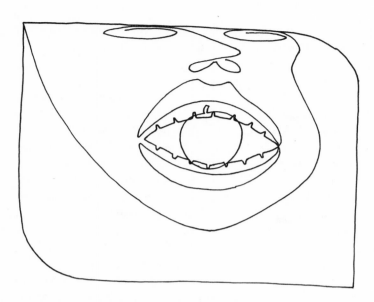

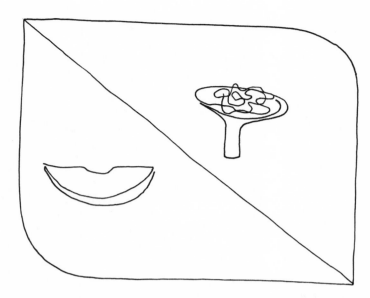

1. The arrangement states that the monthly rent for my room shall be paid in the form of a golden yellow apple slice.

2. Then I have the idea that I could pay the rent with the material that collects in the drainage sieve.

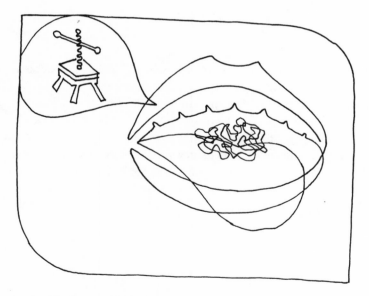

3. I wish that I could have a little press to get the stiff material into some simple form without having to put it in my mouth.

Dream 22: The Life Force Is About To Disappear

1   *We are looking at an unusual rental contract. The arrangement states that the monthly rent for my room shall be paid in the form of a golden yellow apple slice. I have paid the rent a few times without a problem, each time breaking off a slice of apple with my strong teeth.*

2   *However, the slices get thinner. Finally, the apple slice is so thin that I feel deeply ashamed when I am ready to hand it to the landlord. Rather than do that, I take it back. Then I have the idea that I could pay the rent with the material that collects in the drainage sieve. This is a ball that consists of hair, dirty grease, and other small pieces of waste.*

3   *To get it into shape and use it as a means of payment, I stick the ball in my mouth and begin to chew it. It tastes horrible and I do not succeed in getting the stiff, dead material into any sort of shape. I wish that I had a little press that would get the stiff material into some simple form without having to put it in my mouth.*

(Sempas, Slovenia, January 20, 2003)

THE UNUSUAL RENTAL CONTRACT refers to the "rental contract" between humankind and the guardians of earth. The planet Earth does not belong to us humans. We only rent it, so to speak, to complete our evolution upon it. The web of life, which the Earth Soul has created here over billions of years, is ideally crafted to enable us to develop our human creative power in a physical, that is, material, environment. It would be hard to find another planet better suited for this purpose.

Since the room (planet) does not belong to us, we must pay a specific rent. The rent is the symbol for that which we, as people of the earth, give back to the guardians to close the circle of giving and taking. The message tells us that the cycle of exchange between humankind and earth no longer functions. Has it come to this, that we are to be thrown out of our house?

In the symbolic language of the dream, the rent is paid with a slice of apple. An apple represents on one hand the incarnate power of life, and on the other, as the apple of paradise, the perfection of the earthly creation. This means that the rental contract is such that the rent that we humans should pay for our planetary dwelling place is the same living value as that which honors the living systems of earth. Translated, this means that our terrestrial creativity should not deviate from the guidelines that lead earthly creation toward the image of its paradisiacal origin.

However, it has turned out differently and people have forgotten the requirements of the rental contract. What we construct on earth and organize in the sense of evolution has become so strangely constituted that the earth receives almost nothing more "in rent". Human creation is beginning more and more to chase its own tail. What it is giving back to earth is merely human waste. This change has reached a danger-point, symbolized by the dreamer's retrieval of the over-thin apple slice and his attempt to pay the rent with the ball of waste.

The dream tells us that humankind is being warned that we are approaching a point at which the negative potential of our relationship with earth and nature will have the upper hand. After that things can only get worse. In the language of the dream, the rental payment will in future be made mechanically, without the necessity of any human touch. The touch of the mouth—although rated negatively in the final phase—will in future be replaced by a mechanical press.

It is not by chance that the method of rental payment involves the touch of the mouth. It is through the mouth that we take in nourishment, which is a requisite for our life on earth. If we did not take in nourishment, the usual consequence would be that we must die as terrestrial beings. The same would also happen, according to the message of the dream, if we were to eat the detritus which, in the framework of our alienated civilization, we give back to the earth.

The dream tells us that, based on the broken circle of giving and taking, we are approaching the point at which the life force of the human environment is so far depleted that it can no longer sustain us.

What makes this difficult to understand is, first, that the average person can have no knowledge of the absence of the life force, because we modern people generally lack the capacity to perceive the inner quality of food or of the environment. Second, it is hard for us to confirm the catastrophic failure of the life forces in our usual living space, because the natural world in us and around us already vibrates in the frequencies of the transformed living space and confronts us as healthy and full of life.

1. *After the Austrian monarch Maria Theresa dies, she does not completely depart.*

2. *Her son, the Emperor Joseph II, takes incredible pains to open the bamboo pod.*

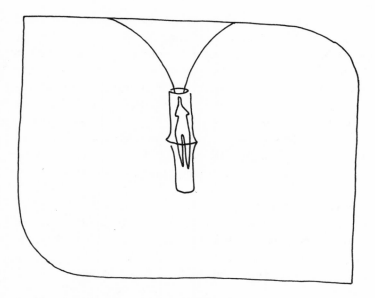

3. *Then he takes some water and fills the pod with it.*

Dream 23: The Code of Life Is Endangered

1   *After the Austrian monarch Maria Theresa dies, she does not completely depart. Much reduced in size, she still exists, remaining enclosed in a bamboo pod that is composed of two pieces. The two pieces are so securely coupled together that it seems impossible to pry them apart.*
2   *Her son, the Emperor Joseph II, takes incredible pains to open the bamboo pod. He tries again and again. Suddenly he succeeds.*
3   *Then he takes some water and fills the pod with it.*

(Klagenfurt, Austria May 7, 2006)

WE SHOULD POINT FIRST to the historical difference between the reigns of Maria Theresa and Joseph II. They ruled what is called the Holy Roman Empire in the eighteenth Century. Maria Theresa ruled throughout her forty years (1740-1780) like a mother who tried her best to care for her kingdom. Joseph II, who reigned for the ten years following, was in contrast a representative of pure reason. He had reformed his empire along the guidelines of intellect.

Now we turn to the symbol of the dead Maria Theresa who still exists, much reduced in size, in a bamboo pod. We are obviously dealing with a mysterious aspect of the life after death. People are accustomed to imagine the dead as formless or, at any rate, without a body. Otherwise they cannot be described as dead.

In the context of our dream, however, it is suggested that the dead live on in their bodily form, though it is much smaller. In this, the symbol of the bamboo pod, which is to be understood as a home for their presence after death, is especially important.

Both symbols, the continued existence of the bodily form and the bamboo pod, point to nature. Is there an aspect of the human being that we might say belongs to nature rather than to the spiritual world, and therefore returns to the wholeness of earth after death?

Yes, there is! Our multidimensional body with all its functions, force structures, and intelligence belongs to the evolution of Nature. Like plants, animals, elemental beings, and minerals, humans are also (seen from this viewpoint) an expression of the living organism of Earth. In this sense, a human (as an eternal spiritual being) does not return only to the spiritual world after death. As an expression of the living organism of the earth, the human being also returns to its original terrestrial plan that makes no distinction between animals, plants, and humans.

Maria Theresa, reduced within a vegetable pod, represents the code of terrestrial life that makes it possible for human beings to incarnate in the earthly world. Not just after our death but during our lifetime, we are connected to the life code of the earth. It is this life code that makes it possible for our spiritual being to "translate" into a living human being.

Joseph II represents the human intellect's capacity to probe into the mysteries of the code of life and even to run experiments there. The practice of gene manipulation is an example. This can put the life of the earth in the utmost danger, not only for the healthy continuance of single animals, plants and humans, but for the continuance of the whole earth as a living organism!

In the narrative of the dream, this danger is represented by the conduct of the Emperor Joseph II who, in the third dream image, fills the bamboo pod with water and lets the living mother drown.

Exercises on the Theme "Overcoming the Barriers"

An exercise to work on transformation of the hidden pattern of power

First, we should be aware that the alienated pattern does not represent a hostile energy but is rather to be seen as an anomaly within one's own power structures. If we know about their alienation and undertake to transform them, they can be reintegrated harmlessly into our wholeness. The exercise that follows is conceived along these lines.

› *As a key to the exercise, you should take the situation in which the alienated pattern has shown itself (or in which it usually shows itself). Sense the vibration of the situation, which is the vibration of the pattern, and place it in the area behind your own back. In doing so, you will be helped by the memory of certain situations you lived through in connection with the pattern—and the accompanying images, symbols and feelings will also be helpful.*

› *Now let the shadow of the pattern that you have manifested in your back space glide slowly through your body and through every one of your cells. The principle of resonance will ensure that the particles of the pattern will be washed out of the consciousness field of your cells.*

› *You should collect the pattern's particles that have been washed out and place them in an expanded sphere, which you visualize in front of your own body. It is filled with the transformational power of violet light.*

› *After all the pattern's particles have been washed out of your consciousness field, you should let the sphere glide toward the earth's center with the prayer for Mother Gaia to purify it and return the transformed forces to you, for they are particles of your being.*

› *Finally, you should give thanks from the depths of your heart for this liberation.*

An exercise to free oneself from the dominating pattern of intellect

One is really no longer aware that one's perception is constantly controlled by one's intellect. This exercise sets out to free you from this control for a short while, and attain a feeling for reality in all its multidimensionality.

› *You should sit down and peacefully concentrate on the outward forms of your body. The body's superficial forms serve as a symbol of the human intellectual level, since the intellect always sees things from the outside.*

› *Now you should move yourself inward into your own bodily form and into your own heart center. In doing so, you will be made so much smaller that you fit in the space of your heart center.*

› *Arriving in your heart center, the outer human (your so-called ego) has become quite small and is embraced by the forces of the heart.*

› *Now use this moment of freedom from the control of intellect. Still keeping your outer "I" in your heart, spread yourself freely out into space.*

› *Experience your surroundings in this way and rejoice in life uncontrolled by intellect.*

An exercise to participate in the elimination of the false archetypal pattern

We people of various races and nations have experienced much during our persistent alienation over thousands of years, which has left deep scars in our being, among them various manipulations of our "genetic codes." It is to be expected that this kind of foreign information will at certain moments reach the surface of our consciousness to be eliminated. Then the following exercise can be helpful.

➤ *First, you should be aware of what you are in your own being and you should also sense it in your inwardness.*
➤ *Next, imagine that a sun is shining with all its fiery force behind your back.*
➤ *Now, in your imagination go slowly backward to put yourself in the center of the sun so that everything shall be burnt up that has to do with the foreign genetic patterns and which does not belong to your divine core.*
➤ *Go further backward until you come upon a watery sphere, which you see as the earth in the shape of her spiritual soul.*
➤ *You should place yourself in the middle of the watery sphere and allow all the genetic patterns that do not belong to your terrestrial being to be washed out of your personal genetic code.*
➤ *Continue going further backward till you reach the point of infinity, that is, eternity. There pray that your true genetic code be confirmed.*
➤ *Afterward, return to your center and let your body participate in the changes that have occurred during the exercise.*
➤ *Give thanks for your liberation and the divine grace afforded you.*

An exercise to help in renewing the life codes of the earth

Dream 23 asks us to notice the mutilation of the life codes of earth, and also the process of their renewal, which is still awaited. This exercise is so formed that you can cooperate as a conscious participant in the process.

➤ *First of all you should get to know the levels in your own organism, where you are connected to the life of nature in you and around you. In a physical sense, they are located between your coccyx and your navel.*
➤ *See how your being, connected to the worlds of terrestrial nature, spreads out on all sides over the above mentioned levels like a broad force field. Sense the presence in it of different sorts of plants, beasts, elemental beings, rocks…*
➤ *Imagine that, with your thumb and index finger, you are touching the middle of this broad field (which is to be found in your own mid-section) and you are slowly drawing it upward. You should also perform this gesture with your hand.*
➤ *Continue to draw the force field upward until it reaches the level of your heart. Wait patiently until the whole field has arrived and established itself on the level of your heart center.*
➤ *Be aware at this moment that your heart center is capable of drawing to itself the cosmic and terrestrial forces that work on the renewal of the life codes of the earthly realm.*
➤ *Allow them to work through you for a while.*
➤ *When this seems complete, allow the field to sink back to its original place and be sure to see how precisely its vibrations now oscillate in time. Please give thanks!*

Chapter 4

THE NEW CREATIVE TOOLS

DURING THOSE DRAMATIC evolutionary periods when the cosmic cycles begin to overlap and shocking upsets occur as the planet Earth's path unfolds, new force systems are set into motion in both the earth and human beings. One scarcely had any notion of these forces during the cycle's upswing; it is clear that Earth holds in reserve certain force systems and beings that for the most part are awakened and put to work in the epochs of planetary change. Otherwise, they rest half asleep and are applied only as needed and in limited ways, to the challenges of the life processes on earth's surface.

Judging by all the signs, we find ourselves today at the threshold of a stormy phase of earth change that requires, in addition, a quantum leap along the path of human evolution. It would be wise to get to know the tools that Gaia has prepared to handle the deepening planetary crisis. We will be more able to overcome the obstacles that the change in the earthly cosmos has heaped along our path if we know some of the transformational tools.

My discovery of the interdimensional portal in 2005 could be an inspiring example. It happened during a Hagia Chora[1] bus journey in Asia Minor, in which we followed the constellation of the seven cities mentioned in the Revelation of St. John, the so-called Apocalypse.[2] The decision to undertake so long a journey was based on my intuition that an important key to the future of earth and humankind was contained in the letters from Christ to the seven early Christian communities in Asia Minor, which are cited in the Apocalypse. In the letters to the communities of Ephesus, Smyrna, Pergamon, Thyatira, Sardis, Philadelphia, and Laodicea, I found statements on which I could make a formulation, the codex of new and suitable ethics for the then still future epochs of earth and human transformation.[3]

Our heart-felt interest in the foundations of the new ethic was not the only reason why we decided to make the journey to Turkey. In addition, there was my eerie but pleasant perception of the district in the middle of Asia Minor that the ancients Greeks called the Lakhmos Mountains.

In the course of my preparations for the journey to the seven cities of the Apocalypse, I used a map of the area to open my inner self to the region. I was very surprised to confirm that in the environs of the Lakhmos Mountains, between the modern cities of Aydin to the north, Yazikent to the east, Milas in the south and Bafa Lake in the west, there is a sort of energetic hole that leads deep into earth's inwardness. I had the feeling that I could use my hands to reach through this gateway into the bowels of the earth. There is a relationship between the gates of Lakhmos and the experience of Dream 31 (an interdimensional portal). I am thinking particularly of the closing sequence of the dream, when the doors of the overturned bus do not open outward, but instead into the inwardness of earth.

We could not unlock the geomantic meaning of the giant gateway into the earth until our travel group had visited the mysterious district of the Lakhmos Mountains and perceived various places in person. After individual participants had exchanged their experiences, it was clear to me that we were dealing with a previously unknown geomantic phenomenon. I spontaneously called it an "interdimensional portal."

The above-mentioned dream, which I dreamt directly after the Asia Minor trip, has helped me understand why the interdimensional portal should emerge at this precise point in time, simultaneously appearing in the etheric fabric of space and in our consciousness. Also helpful was the experience of some other portals of the same sort during the following year.[4]

The most impressive component of an interdimensional portal is its ability to abolish the traditional structures of time and space. It feels as if one is falling into a black hole—hence my experience of the Lakhmos region as a tunnel leading into the depths of the earth. If one climbs into the portal's acceleration tunnel, one loses contact with everyday reality. In some ways the situation is reminiscent of the first moments after death. The person is still present, but not perceptible to us materialized people. The existential center of gravity has moved to another level of existence.

We should imagine ourselves arriving at such a point, and seeing the possibilities opening to move ourselves to any of the various dimensions of the earth cosmos. This is how I had the idea to name such a phenomenon a "portal." I mean by that a combination of several gates on different levels, leading to different dimensions of the earthly cosmos.

What meaning do interdimensional portals have for the developing, all-embracing transformation of earth space? My intuition tells me the following: they make it possible for the Earth Soul to demolish and rebuild the existing structures of space and time without destroying the whole fabric of life and all its beings. They enable the Earth Soul to raise the incarnated living beings into a neutral dimension of being for the duration of the life-endangering turbulence on the earth's surface and later to resettle them on the newly structured surface of earth. In the language of pictures, earth's living kingdoms exit by a different gate than the one by which they entered.

The introduction to the second chapter of this book made it clear that in the process of the transformation of earth space, care would be taken to ensure that all living beings survived through the confusion of change. As a symbol, the Ark of Noah was mentioned, in whose belly all kinds of living beings, including humans, found a safe and protected haven. I suspect that the interdimensional portal involves energetic systems that are identical to Noah's Ark. They enable the temporary extraction of the fabric of life on earth with all its beings from the dimensions of the old space, and the translation of these beings later into the expansiveness of the newly constituted space.

However, now we come to the salient point. The indications of the powerful interdimensional portal in Asia Minor, which I discovered in the Revelation of St. John, are so formulated that it is clear that, in the case of a planetary emergency, there are certain ethical conditions that enable human beings to participate in the advantages of the interdimensional portal. This means that portals of this kind are not pure, energetic phenomena, but also moderately conscious tools of change.

In addition to the energetic function of an interdimensional portal, there is a spiritual component, which really leads us to suspect that a dual light pyramid is wrapped around the portal. This is a geomantic phenomenon in which the apex of one of the two pyramids points to the heavens and the other to the center of the earth. Their rectangular surfaces are set at 45 degrees to each other.

The function of the dual light pyramid is usually seen as joining the powers of heaven and earth together and furthering an exchange between them.[5] In the case of the interdimensional portal, however, I perceive a further role for the dual light pyramid. It has a protective character. This is not easy to describe!

Gates that lead into other dimensions must be guarded, not only against a possible thief (a joke), but to protect the established cosmic order. They open and close themselves according to the rhythms of cosmic changes. It is not a matter of a controlling power that watches over the opening and shutting of the interdimensional gates. Quite the reverse! It depends, so to speak, on the subject—be that a human being or a culture—who stands before the gate, whether or not the portal opens its doors.

Let us examine, for example, the situation of a man who is standing before the entrance of an interdimensional portal. It depends on the quality of his ethical attitude whether the entrance to the various dimensions of being stand open for him or not. However, this is not a matter of observing a specific ethical code. It is much more concerned with a kind of heart-felt dedication in which the person decides to dismantle his egocentricity and follow his own inner voice.

It cannot be coincidental that the interdimensional portal in Asia Minor is situated in the same region as the ancient cities to which were sent the seven letters of Jesus Christ mentioned in the Apocalypse. It is my conviction that they contain the knowledge of the ethical qualities that we should nurture as individuals and also as cultures to be able gradually to join with the high vibrations of the interdimensional portal. My translation, from the language of the Apocalypse, of the seven foundation stones of the new ethic is to be found among the exercises in the last chapter of this book.

Interdimensional portals, coupled with the seven foundation stones of the new ethic, represent only one of the creative tools that Gaia, the Earth Soul, has developed in concord with the spiritual world to handle the tasks of the epoch of transformation. The following dreams present power systems and beings with roles that are just as important to changing the current state of the earth cosmos.

1. Hagia Chora (Greek: "the Holy Landscape") was co-founded by the author during the 1990s as a school for Geomancy, later also as a journal for Geomancy (see: www.hagia-chora.org)

2 The seven letters to the communities of Asia Minor are to be found in Chapters 2 and 3 of the *Revelation of St. John*.

3 Chapter 6 of *Earth Changes, Human Destiny* (Findhorn Press 2000), gives details.

4 In *Sacred Geography* (Lindisfarne Books 2007), there is a chapter on the subject of Interdimensional Portals. In *Touching the Breath of Gaia* (Findhorn Press 2007), I have described the Portals of Geneva (p. 47) and Asia Minor (p. 127).

5 See the chapter on the dual light pyramid of Hallstatt in *Touching the Breath of Gaia*, (p. 79).

1. A tiger is lying in the sun and has taken its body apart so that each separate piece can be fully irradiated.

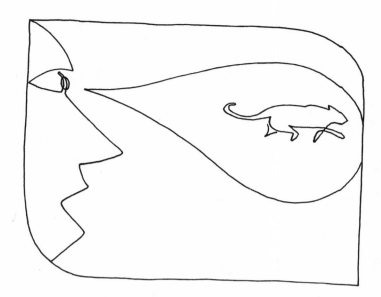

2. My arrival causes the tiger fear and panic. His body parts are drawn together lightning-fast, and he runs quickly away.

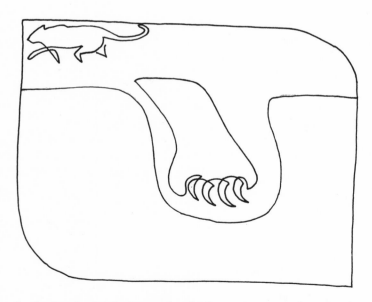

3. In drawing his body together, he forgot a paw. It is lying on the ground: the tiger runs around distracted.

Dream 24: The Phenomenon of Archetypal Forces

1   *A tiger is lying in the sun and has taken its body apart so that each separate piece can be fully irradiated.*

2   *My arrival causes the tiger fear and panic. His body parts are drawn together lightning-fast, and he runs quickly away.*

3   *In drawing his body together, he forgot a paw. It is lying on the ground: the tiger runs around distracted. I consider whether to bury the paw in the earth and forever cripple him.*

(Sempas, Slovenia, May 19, 1998)

THE INTERPRETATION OF THIS DREAM is best begun with the final image, which indicates a relationship to the earth. We should not imagine the dreamer to be so wicked as to want to cripple such a beautiful and currently rare beast as the tiger. Expressed in the language of the dream, this is only a "consideration." But this consideration is an important key to unraveling the message of the dream.

It means that the dream is pointing to a specific relationship with the earth that has nothing to do with the surface, but is "buried in the ground." Secondly, since it has to do with the paw that is a part of the tiger's movement apparatus, we can suggest that we are dealing with the earth's energetic system, through which the life of the earth is brought "into movement."

The tiger, which has laid out his body parts separately in the sunlight, would therefore represent a model of the energetic system. We are dealing here with a tiger and not a lion; the tiger is a beast that appears in Chinese geomancy as the Yin-opposite of the dragon, and thus indicates a geomantic relationship.

Just as the different body parts of a tiger, when put together, make up a complete organism, so too do the energetic (geomantic) phenomena of earth and landscape represent a complete system. For the organism to be capable of life, no body part can be missing. This is also true of the earth's geomantic system: the entire system is responsible for the life of planet Earth, but if one part is missing, the entire system fails.

Now we should ask the question, which of the system's parts, missing in the dreamer's consciousness, is indicated by the dream's uncanny story?

To answer this question, we should be aware of the level of geomantic research that the dreamer had reached before May 19, 1998. In his book *Schule der Geomantie*, [6] we can see that the "three intact paws of the tiger" were assigned to three geomantic systems—the vital-energetic system (power centers and ley-lines of the landscape); the system of the Earth Consciousness (elemental beings, emotional levels of the landscape); and the spiritual-soul system (landscape temples).

However, the dream's message points to a fourth system that has always existed, but has remained unnoticed. After 1998, based on the current earth change, the activity of "the fourth system" was accelerated, or perhaps we should rather say that it became perceptible. Through the intervention of dreams and happenings, which the dreamer describes in his book *Earth Changes, Human Destiny*,[7] the forgotten geomantic system finally emerges in his consciousness. In *Sacred Geography*[8] a whole chapter is devoted to "the fourth paw of the tiger" under the name "Archetypal Forces behind Reality."

This name relates to the system of archetypal forces that nourish the living systems of earth. They nourish the nourisher. The system of archetypal forces nourishes the geomantic system that next, in the following step, nourishes the beings and living worlds on the earth's surface.

We call forces of this type archetypal because they are (still) undifferentiated. They include the whole undivided cosmic spectrum of earth force before it is separated into individual functions as mentioned above. Their gigantic power upheld the life energies of the planet Earth, which is why these archetypal forces were known in mythological language as dragon powers. For this, a scary, fear-inspiring tiger would be an appropriate symbol.

---

6   *Schule der Geomantie* (1996) has been published only in German. However, *Sacred Geography* (Lindisfarne Books 2007) is an updated version.

7   *Earth Changes, Human Destiny* (Findhorn Press 2000).

8   *Sacred Geography* (Lindisfarne Books 2007).

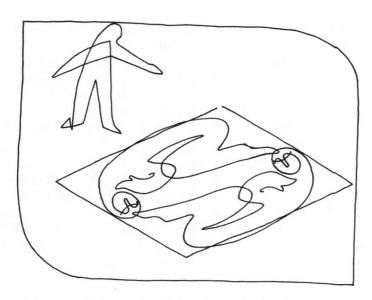

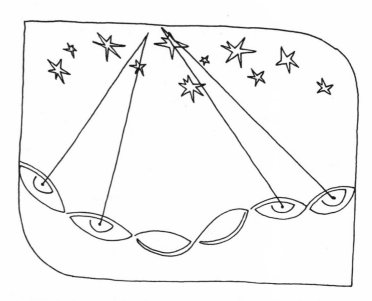

1. *A woman and a man are lying naked in a hole in the ground in such a way that their two bodies complement each other like the black and white fields of the Yin-Yang symbol.*

2. *While they are lying thus in the earth, their gaze glides over the heavens adorned with countless stars.*

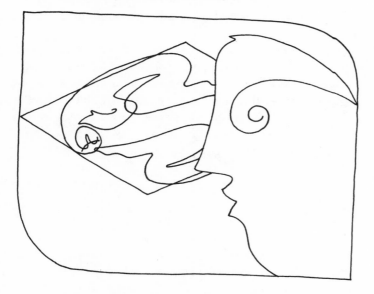

3. *My wife is so greatly drawn to the two otherworldly "Asiatics" that she leans far over the earthen hole to observe them.*

Dream 25: The Archetypal Powers of Heaven and Earth

1   *A woman and a man are lying naked in a hole in the ground in such a way that their two bodies complement each other like the black and white fields of the Yin-Yang symbol. Their skin color is neither black nor white but both at once, so that they seem unearthly. It is night, but nonetheless one can see them as plainly as by day.*

2   *While they are thus lying in the earth, their gaze glides over the heavens adorned with countless stars. There is a masculine looking person nearby who is continually watching over them to ensure they don't fall asleep. And yet it cannot be overlooked that time and again at rhythmic intervals they go to sleep for 10 minutes, without being interrupted in their constant gaze.*

3   *My wife is so greatly drawn to the two otherworldly "Asiatics" that she leans far over the earthen hole to observe them. I feel forced to advise her to withdraw herself and look at them from a distance.*
        (Rio de Janeiro, Brazil, September 1, 1998)

IN THE FIRST TWO dream images, one cannot overlook the many illogical connections. How can skin color be both white and black at the same time? How is it possible to be both awake and asleep simultaneously? How can it be as light as day in the middle of the night?

The nonlogical connections tell us that we are dealing with a power and, linked to it, a consciousness that vibrates on a level of being that lies beyond traditional logic. Obviously, this is a level of being that one may describe as archetypal. We may think of it as precreative.

Before any creative process can come into being, something all-embracing must first be present. If this all-embracing something is to embrace everything, all possible contradictions must exist within it, without giving up any of their contrariness. Such an archetypal state, as sketched in our dream story, was called "Chaos" by the ancient Greeks; Chaos was the origin of all manifested and logically comprehensible things.

And yet this dream message suggests that the archetypal level of being is not just "chaotic" (in the figurative sense of the word). It is at the same time perfectly ordered, as is clear from its second characteristic: the archetypal forces are also the sustaining powers of the universe. Through them all contradictions can be contained in the archetypal state, without their claiming their own polarized space for themselves. They are agreed in their contrariness.

For example, the two "Asiatics" are polarized by gender and yet they are perfectly nested together according to the Yin-Yang principle. They lie in the earth, in an earthen hole, and yet they constantly watch the stars of heaven.

Within the archetypal power—which is identical to the archetypal consciousness—is contained all aspects of the Being of the future, including the contradictory ones, as in a pre-existing seed.

It is fascinating to experience such a power as this. The dreamer found the two people so unfamiliar that he called them "Asiatics." One could recognize their terrestrial forms, and yet they seemed to spring from another star. This mirrors a further characteristic of the archetypal powers, their earthly-cosmic character.

The archetypal powers of life can be classified either as terrestrial or cosmic. Yet they are both, because there is no alteration in their vibrational level as between star and planetary systems. Thus they operate cosmically although vibrating within a planetary system.

We should note that in the dream story there are still two people who cannot be interpreted as symbols of the archetypal power of life. The observant "masculine" has set himself at a distance from the phenomenon, which is characteristic of modern natural science when it has to do with the archetypal power of an atom. The observer seeks to control the monstrous dragon power of the atom and lead it to perform a specific function—good or bad—which is basically contradictory to the essence of archetypal power. To control this contradiction, the distanced human must develop a wholly precise control over the processes connected with the archetypal power of the atom.

By contrast, the woman, representing the sensitive face of humankind, is so strongly drawn to the manifesting phenomenon of archetypal power that the dreamer must ask her to withdraw. Many people have an interest in shamanistic cultures and prereligious rituals in which they sense that the knowledge of archetypal power and the archetypal consciousness of life is still contained. But today it is often quite withered and over-formalized; and in this sense, one can understand the dreamer's rejection of her interest. Thus, this fascination should rather be turned toward an interest in the new manifestation of the archetypal power of life. Fascination with the old is out-of-place within the framework of the current earth change.

1. A couple come toward us and offers the assistant a lovely necklace that has a cosmogram in its center, engraved on a small metal plate.

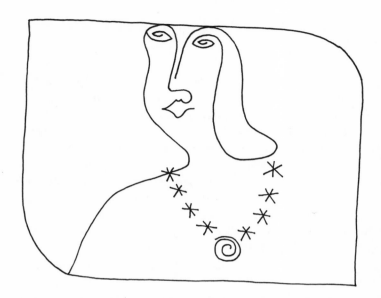

2. I have the sense that she finds the necklace extraordinarily pleasing. I suspect she is thinking that she does not have sufficient money for it in her purse.

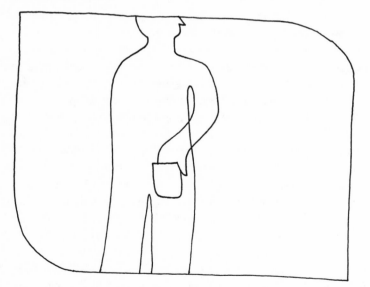

3. Without waiting for her answer, I slip my hand into my hip pocket where I keep my wallet.

DREAM 26: WHERE ARE THE ROOTS OF OUR CREATIVE POWER?

1 *With my young assistant, I have just arrived at our work place. A couple come toward us and offer the assistant a lovely necklace that has a cosmogram in its center, engraved on a small metal plate.*

2 *The assistant behaves as though she has no interest in acquiring the precious object. However, I have a sense that she finds the necklace extraordinarily pleasing. I suspect she is thinking that she does not have sufficient money for it in her purse.*

3 *I decide to be generous and ask her if I may buy the necklace for her. Without waiting for her answer, I slip my hand into my hip pocket where I keep my wallet. I draw it out and proudly open it. To my disappointment, I find it contains only a five-Euro note.*

(Sempas, Slovenia, January 29, 1999)

THE PROCESSES OF THE CURRENT earth change run simultaneously at the micro and macro levels of being. Thus, one can project that our everyday reality, which is thought and lived too much on the surface, will fade away and gradually be replaced by a deeper reality space that is rooted in the archetypal ground of being. In consequence, our renewed humanity will come into contact with the archetypal powers of earth and cosmos, the so-called dragon powers. Their role is to form a spiritual-emotional-energetic foundation anchored in the core of eternity. This is the base on which all the various creative and formative processes of manifested life can be set in motion and constantly nourished.

The dream currently under consideration seeks to clarify the role that the archetypal dragon forces play in the human body. On the one hand it concerns the neck and, associated with it, the assistant's larynx chakra. This is the frontal side of the body, which symbolically represents humanity's creative activity directed externally. The word-forming larynx symbolizes the wonderful human ability to be creative in the physical world and to make things that have not existed before. From this comes the fascinating beauty of the necklace whose attraction is the result of creative human deeds.

The reserved reaction of the assistant, who behaves as though she has no interest in the necklace, is a key symbol. It calls into question the conduct of contemporary humans who are persistent and generous in their making of things and who regard themselves as highly creative, but have forgotten to let their creations evolve from the archetypal ground of being. Because of this, we have become more and more superficial and brittle. We make so much that we allow ourselves to be fascinated, but must at the same time just be observers as our creations are gobbled up by wars, natural catastrophes, and the egocentric excesses of many individuals.

The fateful deficiency of our creative deeds is confirmed by the near emptiness of the boss' wallet: cosmically valued, the results of human deeds have become ever more meager. However, we should note that when the boss draws the wallet from his hip pocket, he is drawing it from his own back space.

Just as the frontal space represents the manifestation of creative deeds in the fabric of everyday, so the back area of the body can be seen as the inward oriented sphere of the archetypal forces. And just as the neck area can be understood as a symbol for communication with the environment, so the buttocks can be seen as an indication of the root chakra and its associated personal anchorage in the realm of the archetypal forces (dragon forces).

The relationship between the boss and his assistant is also significant. Therein one can recognize an indication of the primary function of the archetypal forces in the creative process. The boss represents the decisive factor in the process. Without an active relationship with the archetypal forces of being, there can be no lasting creation. The assistant's reserved reaction to the new necklace could also indicate that the man, in view of his often unsuccessful attempts to create, gradually becomes conscious that his relationship with the archetypal sea of creation is quite absent.

1. *The road becomes so narrow that only half of our jeep fits on it. The driver is not worried and drives on at the same speed.*

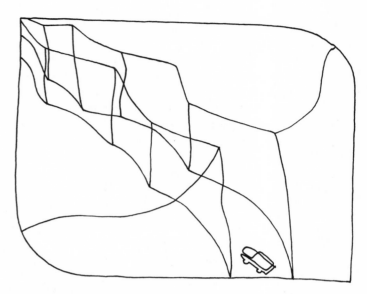

2. *Finally we come to the mouth of a deep, steep gorge. Although there is no road to be seen, the man drives into the dark ravine at the same high speed.*

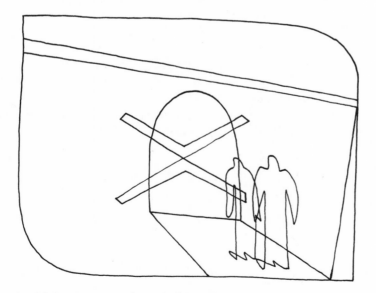

3. *We have come to the end of the gorge. We climb out of the jeep and stand in front of a portal that is completely barricaded shut.*

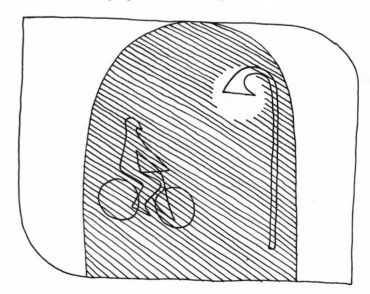

4. *I am disappointed to see that the mighty channel opens into a banal suburb. It is late in the evening and the street is poorly lit.*

Dream 27: Discovery of a Channel of Archetypal Power

1   *A strange-looking man has invited me to take a trip with him in his jeep. We reach a narrow valley and drive along the steep slope. The road becomes so narrow that only half of our jeep fits on it. The driver is not worried and drives on at the same speed, although only two wheels are on the road. The other two are turning in the air.*

2   *At last we come to the mouth of a deep, steep gorge. Although there is no road to be seen, the man drives into the dark ravine at the same high speed. I realize that this mighty gorge is actually a channel carved in stone; but I have no inkling which bygone culture was powerful enough to undertake such a gigantic work.*

3   *My initial astonishment flips into anxiety and fear. Blocks of stone may lie in this narrow gorge and block our path. However, nothing of the sort happens. Instead of giving myself over to the inner serenity shown by the driver, I am overcome by the fear that although we are traveling along a dry river bed, we could suddenly be washed away by a flood wave. Meanwhile we have come to the end of the gorge. We climb out of the jeep and stand in front of a portal that is completely barricaded shut.*

4   *I succeed in peeping through the barricade. I am disappointed to see that this mighty channel opens into a banal suburb. It is late in the evening, and the street is poorly lit. The traffic is not heavy: a man rides by on an old bicycle; pedestrians go about their business…. Obviously, the passers-by do not know that the gigantic gorge exists.*
(Sempas, Slovenia, November 30, 2001)

THE FIRST DREAM IMAGE reveals the source of the message. The driver who leads the dreamer to discover the missing energy channel is obviously not a human but a spiritual being. His jeep runs with two wheels on the earthly road and the other two on the "spiritual" one.

Among spiritual beings, those who dwell in the spiritual worlds and yet cherish a relationship with incarnate earth, are humans who have died, or as appropriate, those who are yet to be born; they are the so-called ancestors. The life of a human being swings to and fro like a pendulum between existence in the spiritual world and incarnation on earth, like the strange man's jeep. Based on this image, we can regard him as a messenger from the spiritual world of the ancestors.

The second dream image clarifies our perception of the phenomenon that the spiritual messenger plans to show the dreamer. It is an eerie mixture of natural and cultural creations. At first, it seems to be a natural gorge. On closer examination, there are traces of the work of the human hands that shaped the channel's final form.

Beyond the symbolic language of dreams, this means that we are looking at a natural river of earth power that was known to certain archaic cultures, which activated its creative power, and developed it further, as necessary. Appropriate rituals could alter the archetypal power that originally flowed along such a channel so it could be of use to the further evolution of humanity and its cultures.

It would have been a channel of power that connected the human body to the ocean of archetypal powers from which it draws its life force, the so-called Hara or Loin Channel that, at the abdominal level, runs from the right-hand corner of the body to the power channel that joins the root chakra to the crown chakra. If the Hara channel is blocked, as in the case of the dried-out river bed, the human being is only sparsely supplied with life's creative forces.

In the third dream image, there are two types of barrier that are symbolized by the dreamer's psychic reactions to the drive through the energy channel. First, he is afraid that there may be rocks blocking the road, and then that they may be swept away by a flood wave.

These two panic attacks are testimony that the mysterious energy channel was made taboo during the later epochs of human evolution. It is even clear that people were severely punished if they dared visit the sources of archetypal power and use the forbidden channel's force potential in any ritual fashion. It is possible that a social elite—priests, for example—continued to exploit the energy channel to reinforce their earthly dominion, and forbade others access to its powers.

The last dream image confirms that the newly discovered energy channel has nothing to do with any esoteric mystery but provides a communication channel through which the archetypal forces of nature and culture can conduct their normal exchanges. These concern our relationship to the fundamental source of life power, which makes possible the paradisiacal beauty and creativity of everyday life. The aura of mystery that surrounds it is based simply on the banishment of any knowledge of its existence from the consciousness of humankind, so that it has become forgotten. The result is pictured in the dreariness of life on the other side of the blocked entrance to the archetypal channel.

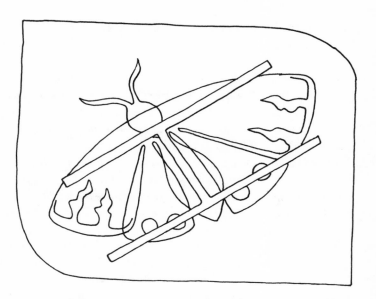

1. *An officer has come to choose those out of a group of men who are to be shot. I am enraged to be included in the choice.*

2. *The moonlight shows a beautiful moth. It is carrying something like the letter 'H' spread over the whole expanse of its wings.*

Dream 28: The Other World Announces Itself

1   *An officer has come to choose those out of a group of men who are to be shot. I am enraged to be included in the choice. Die? For what? I can find no reason for it.*

2   *It is night and the moonlight shows a beautiful moth circling around my hips. Its flight is hindered, and it stumbles so that it can hardly complete its circles. Do I see aright? It is carrying something like the letter 'H' spread over the whole expanse of its wings.*

3   *Regarding it more closely, I see that the moth's wings are also loaded with little heaps of ancient dust. I sense the moth's demand that I at least free it from this additional weight and try to brush them off with my fingers.*

4   *But there is a further problem! The moth seems to be entangled in the dusty threads of a spider's web, which do not let it move its wings freely. The threads are so fine that at first I had not noticed them. My whole body trembles for its fate.*

(Sempas, Slovenia, December 29 and 30, 1998)

THE FIRST DREAM IMAGE, which was dreamt separately from the others, has no apparent relation to the dream story that follows, but offers an important key to it. The death sentence is an indication that the dream's message is concerned with a relationship with the world beyond life. Some of the group of people who appear in the first image are to be sent beyond the boundary that divides the world of the living from the world of the dead; others are to remain on this side.

At the same time, the senselessness of the choice, which also affected the dreamer, indicates that the concern is not with a concrete decision between life and death, but rather with the relationship between the world of the living and the so-called "realm of the dead," which really stands for the spiritual world. One even feels drawn to posit the hypothesis that, in the process of earth change, an essential shift has occurred in the relationship between the two world dimensions. The dreamer knows nothing of this and is therefore much shaken by the experience of the nearness of the Beyond. It is as if death had reached out and caught him.

Humanity is really an amphibious being. By day we live in the materialized world. When we go to sleep, our materially conditioned existence is "frozen," and the focus of our being is transferred to the Beyond. Humanity oscillates daily between this side and the other side. We pass our existence partly in the terrestrial living world and partly in the spiritual world.

Up till now, almost the only meaning of our nightly existence has been to get some rest. Only dreams, which emerge here and there, leave behind the impression that something important happens during our nightly sojourn in the spiritual world. Can it be that, through the epochal world change, this relationship becomes something essentially different and humanity loses its amphibious character? In any case, one can expect that the communication between this side and the Beyond will intensify. And what then? About that, the dream story (still) tells us nothing.

What the dream does tell us about is that there are certain grave barriers that will certainly prevent a refashioning of the relationship between the two parallel worlds.

The problematic moments are demonstrated by a moth which is a being of the night. The dreamer's hips, around which the moth circles, point to the abdomen as opposed to the head area, which would equate with the waking consciousness.

The first barrier to be represented is symbolized by the letter 'H,' which in spoken German often functions as an "unvoiced H," and although written is not pronounced. The symbol corresponds to our culture's basic attitude toward the Beyond. We all know that a world must exist beyond that dread threshold. We see our beloved dead journey thither, and it is from thence that we observe our children come.

But as a modern culture we possess as yet no language and no rituals to call correctly upon the half-world of Beyond and acknowledge its living presence. The creative existence of that living realm from which we originated and to which we will return is reduced to silence.

The following dream image shows little heaps of dust on the wings of the lovely moth. The dust testifies to something that it has given and gives no longer. Therein lies the curse that rests on the World of Beyond: that it is a world of the past that includes the remains of what no longer exists in the present moment! Quite the reverse! The World of Beyond is the living world that vibrates in the eternal Now. Every night we humans slip away to be renewed in the well of life force that knows no past. Unfortunately, we usually think the

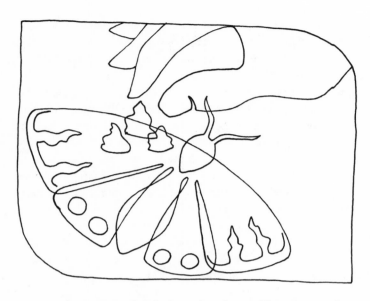

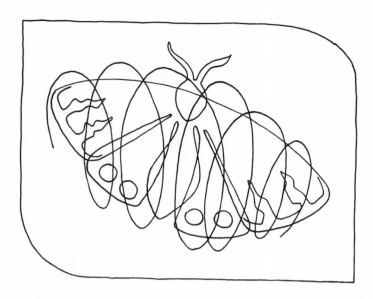

3. *Regarding it more closely, I see that the moth's wings are also loaded with little heaps of ancient dust.*

4. *But there is a further problem! The moth seems to be entangled in the dusty threads of a spider's web, which do not let it move its wings freely.*

opposite: that we took part in the spiritual world of the past before we were born, and will take part again after we have died.

Expressed in a logical way of thinking, it might even happen like that, with the World of Beyond abdicating its eternal presence in our lives. That would be like forgetting a limb of our own being in the soul-imbued core of humanity through which we constantly take part in eternity. One could also take the view that at birth we step out of our own core soul and return to it after death. But the essential point is that, in the time between birth and death, our innermost union with eternity is constantly renewed by the rhythm of sleeping and waking.

The dreamer wanted to use his fingers to brush away the heaps of dust from the moth's wings because he wishes to experience the new way of uniting with the eternal quality of the World of Beyond. To attain this experience, the old ideas about the spiritual world must obviously first be demolished.

And what about those dusty threads of spider's web, which prevent the moth from moving its wings freely? These represent the obstructive power of the thought patterns that humanity projects on the gates of Beyond. The creativity of the spiritual world is chained by the human thought patterns that equate it with the realm of the dead. As a result, the gifts that the spiritual world would constantly like to bring to this world, settled by materialized humanity, are neither seen nor accepted.

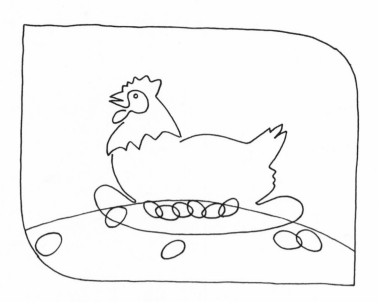

1. *I am horrified to see that some of her eggs are scattered around the nest and others tipped almost completely on the ground.*

2. *Now I notice that the nest is quite lop-sided, and decide I must improve it. So I begin to dig around it and make it horizontal.*

3. *The hen is soon back, obviously anxious: I burrow around in the turned-up earth and cannot find a single egg—and there had been so many!*

Dream 29: The Role of Humanity

1   Our broody hen is sitting solidly on the eggs. I come by to make certain that all is going well. I am horrified to see that some of her eggs are scattered around the nest and others tipped almost completely onto the ground. There is no way they can have been kept warm!

2   Feed is strewn to one side to get the hen away from the eggs and set the nest in order. Now I notice that the nest is quite lop-sided and decide I must improve it. So I begin to dig around it and make it horizontal. I can scarcely believe what hard work this is!

3   The hen is soon back, dancing here and there, obviously anxious that her eggs may be getting cold. I burrow around in the turned-up earth and cannot find a single egg, and there had been so many! It is unbelievable that they have all vanished, down to the very last one…
(Kirstenbosch, South Africa, October 25, 2007)

Let us say that the broody hen, sitting on the eggs, represents the Earth Soul which is incubating a new spatial structure that will make possible a future epoch, and further evolution for herself and us. In other words, the eggs that the Earth Soul is hatching represent a fundamental change in our living space.

The egg can symbolize the archetypal potential of our living space. Such a symbolic egg already incorporates the space's future form, the space in which the various aspects of life and the various living beings can unfold their existential forms. These potentials are developed into a new reality space through the process of incubation.

The dreamer who comes to supervise the nest and finds a problematic situation represents the human beings who have sensed, or learned from various sources of information, that behind the scenes of everyday life a fundamental change is taking place in the living space. The findings of scientific research, which confirm that fundamental changes are taking place in our planet, help us become aware of the serious situation. One feels summoned to do something decisive. But what? The situation in the nest that so horrified the dreamer symbolizes what must be done first to help the Earth Soul easily hatch out the new living space.

In its latest phase, our civilization has concentrated so heavily on the physical level of being that our form of reality has lost its capacity for movement. But movement cannot be avoided if reality is to follow the bends and twists of the change process. That frozen state of immobility is symbolized by the eggs that are stuck too deeply in the physical earth for the Earth Soul to warm them. This is also true for those of us individuals who vegetate, immersed up to the neck in our daily duties.

The other problem is that modern humans have in large measure lost their focus on personal spiritual development. They may follow various religious traditions that lead in various directions or, on the contrary, deny the focus of spiritual development as being non-existent. This dispersal of spiritual focus is symbolized by the eggs that lie scattered around the nest and cannot be warmed by the hen.

In consequence, the dreamer decides that he must demolish the barriers that prevent the Earth Soul from caring for the continuation of life in earth. The hen is enticed out of the nest, and the dreamer starts his task of bringing the nest into an ideal state.

It is at this point that the core message of the dream begins to emerge. Instead of changing the circumstances of human civilization so that the Earth Soul can best complete her epochal "project" of earth change, the man thinks he knows best how to counter the threat of climate changes, global warming and the other difficulties deriving from earth change.

The modern human's materialistic attitude that the basic evolutionary problems of the spirit and soul of the universe can be solved by mechanical measures is symbolized by the dreamer's idea that the nest is not level. He thinks that by physically leveling the nest, he can ensure that the eggs on which the hen is sitting will not slide out. The hatching process can then proceed.

On the one hand, we have human beings' mental projections and scientific measurements regarding what would be good for the earth at this moment. On the other, we have the real needs of the Earth Soul and her geomantic organism, which is actually responsible for the quality of life on our planet.

The dreamer's shock, when he can find no more eggs for hatching, points to the danger that we are gambling away our real chance to renew life through the earth change process by wrongly concentrating on materialistic measures to "save" the earth.

The broody hen's nervous reaction lets us know that we do not have much more time for wrong decisions. We must follow the cosmic rhythms if we are to ride the swelling wave of earth change.

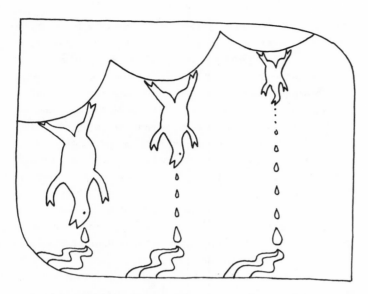

1. At the country's boundary, we see dead animals hanging up in a way that makes clear that they were not simply slaughtered but killed as part of a ritual.

2. In every place that their hooves touch the ground, there arises a spring of crystal clear drinking water.

3. It is said that wherever a drop of human sweat falls on the ground, a spring of water will arise, just as I have seen happen with the animals.

Dream 30: A Change in the Realm of Emotional Forces

1 *Accompanied by a Brazilian shaman, we are traveling to Chile. At the country's boundary, we see dead animals hanging up in a way that makes clear that they were not simply slaughtered but killed as part of a ritual. Their blood, dripping on the earth, works constantly to purify the ground water.*

2 *As we walk on, I observe various animals which I know from Europe trampling around in the forest. In every place that their hooves touch the ground, there arises a spring of crystal clear drinking water.*

3 *Now we are going to run through the woods: we run and run. We run so much that we start sweating. It is said that wherever a drop of human sweat falls on the ground, a spring of water will arise, just as I have seen happen with the animals.*

(Sao Paulo, Brazil, November 28th 2002)

THIS DREAM, which a Brazilian shaman dreamt for me during my workshop in Sao Paulo, is about a shocking change in the emotional realm. Why do I make that claim?

The beasts, in contrast to human beings, are an incarnation of emotional intelligence. It's not that human beings don't know about emotional qualities! But we currently live them at a very surface level. We react feeling-wise with each other or with the environment, or life situations, and so forth. But we have not yet learned to embody these feelings as cosmic forces. There are animals that are capable of that.

The first dream image clearly emphasizes that something much more important is happening on the feeling level than mere emotional reactions. The fact that the sacrificed beasts are hanging from the heavens points to the cosmic dimension of the emotional consciousness, which for long epochs has incorporated the presence of various animal species on the earth. We can think of the zodiac (in German, it is *tierkreis* = animal circle) in the heavens and the twelve cosmic archetypes, which were originally represented by various species of beasts and whose influence advanced evolution on earth. The emotional consciousness has a beneficent outcome, which is pictured in the dream by the beasts' dripping blood that purifies the ground water.

The ground water is a symbol of the emotional world in which all beings take part. This is an emotional power field, also called an astral field, which has the ability to mirror back the cosmic powers of the stars, planets, and galaxies: "astrum" means star in Latin. The agents of this mirror action are the animals, and through them the emotional world of earth and her beings is constantly purified and supplied with new inspiration—as indicated in the first dream image.

The second dream image confirms that the more highly developed animals currently have responsibility to purify life's emotional field and renew its original qualities. Their *simple presence* in various parts of the earth ensures the performance of this valuable service to life. The dream image illustrates this: the animals do nothing special; they simply move over the earth's surface through forests and savannah, and yet thereby offer the valuable possibility of purifying and nourishing the emotional field. As sensitive beings, our existence on earth is enriched and yes, even made possible by the animals.

The lack of feeling that rules on earth today, whether in the waging of war, drug trafficking, pornography, corrupt finance, etc, can be traced back to the repression and decimation of the animals' place in life. This has gone so far that they are no longer capable of caring for the constant purification and renewal of the emotional ocean on earth. It becomes ever dirtier and pervaded with emotional poisons.

The third dream image points to the possibility of solving this most pressing of the world's problems: human beings themselves should take over the responsibility that the animals can no longer handle. How can we prepare ourselves for this task?

We see the dreamer running through the spaces of the world in order to sweat. We remember the sweat lodges through which the shamanistic cultures cared for the emotional health of their participants. Our case, at the beginning of the twenty-first century, is obviously somewhat different. The dreamer does not sit passively in a sweat lodge, but is challenged to develop long distance running.

It is clear that this activity has to do with the shedding of "inner water," which one can see as a symbol of human emotional powers. And so, through a permanently loving attitude toward life, through creative mastery over the contradictions in the environment and one's own inner being, and thus by the activation of one's own emotional field, humans can support the animals in their devotion to emotional purity and fullness of life, even perhaps eventually replace them.

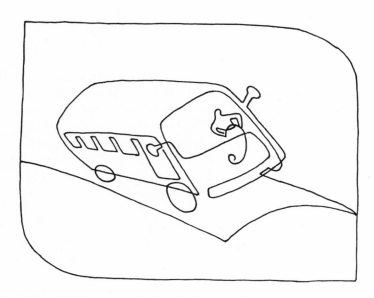

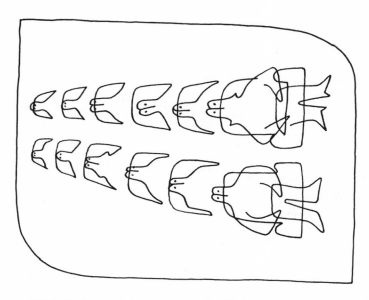

1. *The driver steers too close to the edge and the bus flips onto its side.*

2. *With the bus on its side, we are all still sitting in our seats, waiting expectantly to see what the driver will do.*

3. *The driver solemnly opens the door, which is on the left side near the driver's seat, and jumps out to set the bus upright.*

4. *The little fellow crawls between the bus' side and the road surface to the front door and opens it downward into the depths of the earth.*

Dream 31: An Interdimensional Portal

1   *We are traveling in a chic white bus. The road curves quite sharply and is also arched in the middle. The driver steers too close to the edge and the bus flips onto its side.*

2   *However, there is no fuss or struggle. With the bus on its side, we are all still sitting in our seats, waiting expectantly to see what the driver will do. We cannot get out because the bus with its whole load is lying on the side with the door.*

3   *The only door that can be opened is on the left side near the driver's seat. The driver solemnly opens it and jumps out to set the bus upright. His attempts to lift the bus with his bare hands are of no avail, so he hurries away to look for help.*

4   *We passengers wait, all hoping that the driver will return with a crowd of strong men. Instead, he arrives with a small being who hardly reaches as high as the driver's hip and whose features, moreover, are not at all humanly pleasant. The little fellow crawls between the bus' side and the road surface to the front door and opens it downward into the depths of the earth.*

(Hallstatt, Austria, September 22, 2005)

LET US START with the premise that the passengers in the bus represent the people of the current civilization. The driver would represent the leading political and intellectual elite whose ideas and decisions are presently guiding the development of human society.

The state of the road leads one to suspect that changes in the course of cosmic cycles made it difficult to steer the bus. The dream is concerned with the present situation of the bus, or should we say, of human society? The accompanying symbols make important statements:

First, the bus does not run any more, which means that the developments that are taking place within the civilization have lost touch with the development of the cosmic contact. Second, the bus is flipped on its side, which means that its space coordinates have fundamentally changed. What was previously below is now to be found on the side! Third, we could speak of the fundamental change in the living space, which is now quite unsuitable for human beings. The passengers are still sitting in their seats (in the space) as if the floor were still under their feet. But that is obviously no longer appropriate for the present state of reality. To the passengers, their sideways position seems normal. From the outside however, let us say from a neutral standpoint, they are all wrongly positioned.

Instead of adjusting to the newly established coordinates of space, the passengers project the hope that the elite leaders of the world can turn the situation of the earthly cosmos around and reinstall the old situation. It is a fact that politicians are trying to arrive at decisions which will stop the process of earth change. Ecology and technology are being tasked to develop strategies that can suppress (reverse) the dramatic development so that the old world order can continue.

The relevant symbol is the bus driver who lets us know that he has the situation under control. His unsuccessful effort to lift the bus with his bare hands is a symbol of the failure of the world elite to put the world situation back on its old tracks.

The fourth dream image points to a successful alternative. The associated symbols are important: first, the being who can offer humans substantive help in this dramatic situation is not human. The dream image describes him as if he were an elemental or an extraterrestrial. The message tells us that to get to rights with the upturned world situation, humans must accept otherworldly help. To maintain a simple anthropocentric attitude is plain suicide. Second, the bus is not raised high enough to free the exits. Seen symbolically, this means that the difficult situation is not to be resolved by materialistically inspired power, nor by any method known to us. It means in fact that the bus door is opened in the direction of the inner earth, and thus in a way that contradicts traditional logic. How can it be possible for human beings to enter the inner earth in order to leave the upturned bus?

In fact, geomantic research over the last few years has established that there are interdimensional portals. They are a kind of energetic gate by which one can reach other spaces in the multidimensional reality. Given that the further development of our civilization should run on another level of spatial frequency, the interdimensional portals are the right doorways through which "to exit the upturned bus."

The dream's message further informs us that as a society we waste valuable time seeking solutions to reverse the world situation. There is no longer any way back. The planetary situation has changed irreversibly. It would be wise, in such a situation, to open ourselves to the possibility of radically changing our notions of what is and what is not. It is time unhesitatingly to accept the help of the other beings of the earth and universe when it is offered with pure intent.

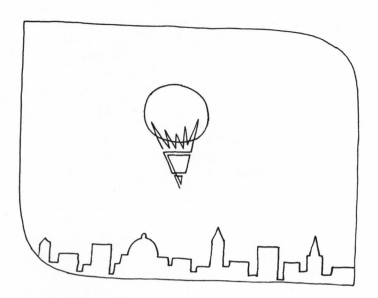

1. *It is said that no one in Zagreb is capable of flying air balloons. But look, there is one floating over the city's panorama.*

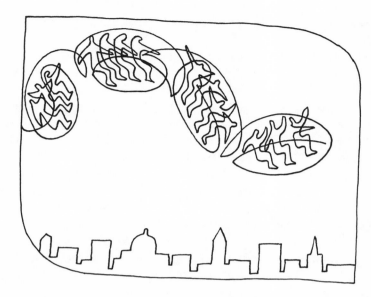

2. *The train's carriages are full of strange looking people who are enormously enthusiastic over the air train's tearing speed.*

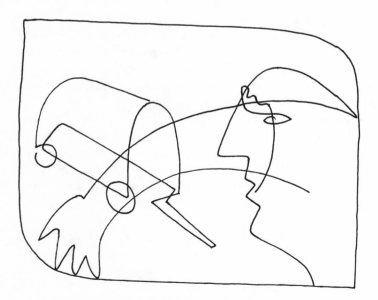

3. *The gypsy wagons standing around are covered with the same material as the curious air train.*

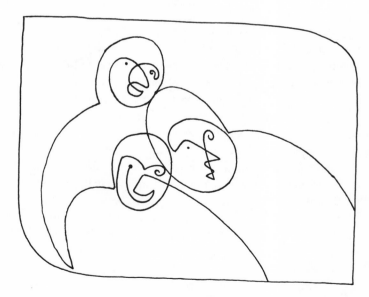

4. *Their rousing music rings out, and I see people who look strange but are full of rollicking joy.*

Dream 32: Cooperation from the All

1   *It is said that no one in Zagreb is capable of flying air balloons. But look, there is one floating over the city's panorama. It looks like an extraterrestrial flying object that has descended from the All.*

2   *Now we are traveling on an air train through the city's atmosphere. There are no railway lines. The train's carriages, made from the same material as the air balloons, are full of strange-looking people who are enormously enthusiastic over the air train's tearing speed.*

3   *My journey brings me to a place where there is a gypsy encampment. The gypsy caravans standing around are covered with the same material as the curious air train. I decide to travel on immediately—but look, at that very moment the gypsy wagons also begin to move in the same direction. I feel myself unwilling to share the road with the gypsies.*

4   *Looking closer, I see some really jocular types among the gypsies. Their rousing music rings out, and I see people who look strange but are full of a rollicking joy.*

(Srakane Vele, Croatia, August 28, 2005)

To put this story in context, I should mention that I had this nighttime dream after a day when the inhabitants of the little Dalmatian island of Srakane Vele had shared a most unusual experience with the dreamer. Three nights earlier a giant light object had landed on the hill above the village. The man who by chance dwelt close to the event had wakened other villagers to provide additional testimony to his vision.

The following dream can be viewed as a commentary on the experience described by the villagers. To avoid conflict with the public consciousness, which finds the existence of the extraterrestrials questionable, the first dream image affirms that there are no extraterrestrials in the city—which is looked upon as a symbol of cultural development. The extraterrestrials wish to play no role in the evolution of human cultures. Their flying object appears in the brightness of day—and in a form that one could easily deny to be of extraterrestrial origin.

In the second dream image, the dreamer is given to understand that groups of the extraterrestrials are present in the planetary space of earth; however, they are still bound to their own spatial structure, which enables them to move freely through earth space. For this they need no highly engineered apparatus or space ships. These might be useful only if they wished to contact humans, locked in their mentally created world of matter.

In the third and fourth dream images, the dreamer is gifted with an inner experience of the extraterrestrial folk. At first he reacts negatively, because he is a prisoner of the many preconceptions that modern humans regularly project on their co-citizens from the All. It is characteristic of this attitude that in the dream they are associated with gypsies.

Gypsies represent a race that does not originate from Europe, but from India. They were driven out, and during the Middle Ages they wandered into Europe. Their lack of homeland and their different understanding of goods and possessions led to permanent doubts about their honesty, and they were treated as unpleasant foreigners.

The fourth dream image aims to sweep away the false projection that sees extraterrestrials as a dangerous race who threaten human beings. In contrast to the apparent technical and racist patterns projected on extraterrestrials, they are shown to be good-natured, joyful, and benevolent, so that previously they were thought to be elementals.

Elemental beings, as an invisible embodiment of nature consciousness and natural forces, are children of the Earth Soul and as good-natured and beneficent as the extraterrestrial folk represented in the dream. The dancing forms of the fairy world come to mind. The intellect of modern humanity has also banished the earthly elemental beings from public consciousness because like the extraterrestrials, they are also not physically perceptible.

The dream images described lead to the conclusion that extraterrestrials are not technical monsters but beings which in their own way also know the elemental level of existence and joy of living. They are not children of the Earth Soul, but co-creators of life on other planets or star constellations, although active not in the physical dimension but on other levels of being. Just as earthly elementals are responsible for all the vital-energetic and consciousness-conditioned processes of earthly creation, so their sisters and brothers from the All are responsible for the corresponding evolutionary processes in the universe.

Because the earth is a part of the universe, it must naturally follow that the extraterrestrials are also currently co-creating in earth space and the inner earth. It could be because they would like to demonstrate their offer to help us through the approaching earth change that they are currently showing themselves to humankind.

1. *I see a young, sportively attired stranger striding across the courtyard toward me. Michael's sheepdog springs forward.*

2. *I want to make it clear to Michael that his help is urgently required, but the appropriate words will not come out.*

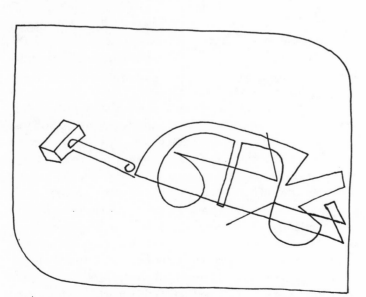

3. *The stranger is trying to flee and comes driving at great speed in his own vehicle, smashing into the tractor.*

Dream 33: The Angel-World's Offer

1 *I am making a visit to Michael. I see a young, sportively attired stranger striding across the courtyard toward me. Michael's sheepdog springs forward. I think he wants to play, but he starts biting the stranger in the chest.*

2 *I try to hold the dog back and at the same time call for his master. I want to make it clear to Michael that his help is urgently required, but the appropriate words will not come out. Fortunately, at the last moment Michael appears. While he is trying to calm the dog, the stranger disappears.*

3 *Michael reacts lightning fast and fetches a giant agricultural tractor from the barn and blocks the exit with it. The stranger is trying to flee and comes driving at great speed in his own vehicle, smashing into the tractor. Now I see for the first time that behind his car he is towing a giant hammer. His intentions in coming here are distinctly dubious!*

(Srakane Vele, Croatia, August 28, 2005)

THE DREAM DESCRIBED ABOVE is a continuation of the gypsy dream (32); the place and date of both dreams, August 28, 2005, are identical. They were dreamed in the same night. Outwardly they have nothing in common; nonetheless, they should be considered as two parts of the same message.

The first dream indicated that the so-called extraterrestrials are not a highly advanced race of engineers but are cosmic elemental beings. They are shown as a cosmic intelligence responsible for the implementation of life processes in the universe—and thus partly for those on planet Earth; only partly, because Gaia has evolved her own consciousness, represented by the unique elemental beings of planet Earth.

In the second dream, the owner of the house is expressly called "Michael." By the name Michael, the Judaic-Christian tradition understands an angelic being. The syllable "el" denotes a being of light. Like the extraterrestrials, angels are also counted among the cosmic beings whose physical appearance has no regular form. Can it be that, regarding angels, as with extraterrestrials, we humans retain certain old projections that do not allow us to accept these beings as our equal-born co-creators of the universe? Is it necessary to rethink this concept in the present epoch?

This idea tends to be confirmed as the story of the dream unfolds. The dreamer who symbolizes modern humanity is incapable of unmasking the stranger's spiteful plans. He lacks the instinctive quality that animals possess—look at the sheepdog's immediate reaction. It is not so much that humans do not have it, but that it is suppressed by the human intellect.

In such a state, the human being is not well-placed to perceive and deal appropriately with the destructive intentions of certain powers, and we need the assistance of the responsible cosmic intelligence. In this sense the dreamer has acted correctly in calling on (the angel) Michael for help. But when he comes to voice his cry, he finds his vocal cords are blocked. He can only call out the name "Michael." Obviously his voice was blocked because his cry for help was wrongly conceived. He thought that the stranger must be saved from the dog. But the true situation is precisely the opposite: the house must be saved from the stranger—the giant hammer tied to his car and shown in the last dream image is evidence that he has come with evil intentions.

As indicated by the symbolism, this would mean that humanity is not capable of dealing on its own with the challenges of global transformation. There are aspects of the event for which we are not a match. To deal correctly with the powers involved in such circumstances, we must call on the appropriate cosmic intelligence for help.

The third dream image demonstrates the ability of the cosmic intelligence to deal with a situation in which, as yet, human beings are overmatched. This is symbolized by Michael's lightning-fast reaction which blocked the way for the stranger. Afterwards, the dreamer was able to see through the stranger's evil plan for the first time.

Dream 33 warns of the shadow aspects of the same phenomenon of Dream 32. It warns us that there are civilizations in the universe, or even in our solar system, that are trying to steal our unbelievably rich creative potential, of which in our current alienated phase of evolution we are not even aware. They may see the treasure of life's eternal fullness embedded in the earth, which we are currently disregarding, and want to carry it off into their own sphere of existence.

The thick hammer tied onto the stranger's car allows us to entertain this thought. Yet one cannot say that there is ultimate evil in the destructive plans of certain extraterrestrial civilizations. It is possible that their attacks will shake us awake and arouse us to our true nature.

Exercises on the Theme "The New Creative Tools"

An exercise to experience the all-pervading presence of archetypal power

The experience of the archetypal power of the universe is an experience beyond the boundaries of logical meaning. Therefore the exercise is composed in a way that will inspire a person to leave the customary ways of logic behind.

> *First, you should seek your own center. Where, at this very moment, do you sense the position of your center within your own body? You should first decide on this.*
> *Be present in your center for a while.*
> *Afterward, stretch your attention outwards on all sides throughout the space that spreads around you till you feel that you are touching infinity all around you.*
> *As you do so, watch continually that at the same time you keep concentrating on your center.*
> *Now, after sensing that you have arrived at infinity, turn your attention back around.*
> *Let the feeling of infinity imbue your center (back in your own body)—and at the same time extend your center toward infinity on all sides.*
> *Now, how does the space feel that has arisen through this somersault?*
> *You can repeat this several times to gather experience.*

An exercise to relate to the archetypal forces of your own body and to their transformation into creative power

This exercise follows the instructions of Dream 27, which deals with the ideational realization of the role of archetypal power in the creative processes. One should not only understand the process but also be able to experience it.

> *Be still and focused in your heart center.*
> *Imagine that you can open your back along the spinal column from the shoulder blades to the coccyx as you would open the two wings of a gateway.*
> *Now transfer your attention out of your heart center, over your head and down toward your back space. You can imagine that you are gliding along this way with the essence of your own body.*
> *Glide slowly down through the back space and re-enter your own body as deeply as possible through the open gate.*
> *You are now in the archetypal space of your mother's womb, bathing in the original power of the amniotic fluid.*
> *You should bind with these qualities in your innermost being and let them penetrate you.*
> *Afterward, you rise from there vertically through the middle of your body, gliding up through the heart region till you reach the region of your larynx.*
> *Now you should look around you and see the wonderful flowers of your creative power unfolding on all sides to bless your surroundings near and far.*

An exercise to activate your own emotional field

This time of transformation is not a time to remain enclosed in our own inwardness. It is time to open up the emotional qualities that we have kept encoded in various bodily levels and share them with the world around us.

➤ *You can sit or remain standing, but in either case the spinal column should be kept erect.*

➤ *Imagine that a crystal-clear watery ball is vibrating in your abdominal area. It represents the emotional power that slumbers inside you.*

➤ *Now develop a wave of power that descends from heaven and another that moves upward at the same time from inner earth.*

➤ *The pressure of the two waves of power, possibly repetitive, works on the ball of water in the middle of your belly to such effect that it gets flatter and flatter and eventually broadens into a horizontal disk-shaped field that spreads out around you.*

➤ *You should take the time to experience the quality of this force field.*

➤ *You can raise this newly developed force field to the level of your heart and let the love in the essence of your spiritual-soul stream through it.*

➤ *You can raise the field still higher to the level of your larynx, or let it glide downward to the level of the coccyx. On each occasion you should observe the changes that take place within the field and your environment.*

➤ *You should remember to repeat the exercise several times a day so that your emotional presence gradually becomes a blessing for your environment.*

An exercise to strengthen contact with the World of Beyond

Here, the concept of the World of Beyond means the dimension of being in which our common ancestors and successors are dwelling, together with the spiritual masters of human evolution. This is not pre-eminently about making individual contacts, but rather about making oneself familiar with this parallel dimension of being.

➤ *For a start, be fully present in your body.*

➤ *Be aware of the stars of heaven behind your back. Every star symbolizes a human soul, pulsating in eternity.*

➤ *Imagine yourself moving backward (in a gentle upward direction) toward the starry heavens.*

➤ *At the same time you should be looking at the stars of heaven in the mirror of your own body. The whole cosmos of stars is present within you. Focus on this. Observe how the different star constellations and galaxies vibrate and radiate within your own body.*

➤ *Now be aware that the real concern is not with distant stars but with the resonance in your body of different focus points of the spiritual world. It is through this that the spiritual world is identified with the world of our ancestors, successors and spiritual masters.*

➤ *Select some of these focus points and submerge yourself in their forces and qualities. Bind yourself to them—acting also in the name of all humankind—and gather experiences of that dimension of being.*

Chapter 5

The Powers that Work Against Earth Change

For knowledge of the future evolution of earth and humanity, I put most trust in the Revelation of St. John, also called the Apocalypse.[1] It is simply my instinct that makes me feel assured that the Apocalypse gives a faithful account of the divine message.

The Apocalypse is also trustworthy regarding the present earth change, because it outlines not just single glimpses of the event but its whole cosmic context, a time panorama that provides an overview covering at least three thousand years.

Yet I remain somewhat reserved about the meaning of the language of this holy writing. A text that unhesitatingly lays bare the frightening consequences of human self-alienation can in no way survive uncorrected for thousand of years. For the purposes of protection, divine wisdom has provided a textual form in which the story is told simultaneously on two different levels.

The surface layer, to which one usually refers to discern the meaning of the Apocalypse, runs linearly from the beginning of the text to its end. Its task is to satisfy intellectual curiosity and offer it symbolically coded riddles on which one can chew forever. Characteristic of the linear level of the text is the dualistic pattern of the division between good and evil, a pattern that reflects an error in human thinking rather than an origin in a divine archetype. The deeper textual layer that lies underneath is composed quite differently.

The text of the deeper layer begins with Chapter 12, precisely in the middle of Revelation, and unfolds "backward and forward" simultaneously. Chapters 11 and 13, which are constructed symmetrically, follow on Chapter 12. In Chapter 11 there is talk of two divine witnesses, and in 13 of two monsters that represent the forces working against the divine plan. The symmetrical construction of the Apocalypse unfolds further with an angelic message in Chapter 10, which is completed by the action of a second angel in Chapter 14. Thus the text's deeper layer is composed spherically. One starts to read it in the middle and thus arrives at the beginning and end simultaneously—which joins the beginning and end together once again.

This unique symmetry appears throughout the book between the beginning Chapters 2-3 and the closing Chapters 21-22. The first chapters define the new ethical code for humanity. This is relayed through the seven letters addressed to the early Christian communities in Asia Minor—which have already been discussed here in the previous chapter. The messages to these seven communities contain the concept of the transformed human being which will be ours to embody when we have worked through the whole process of earth change.

In contrast, the final chapter of Revelation presents the seven aspects of the transformed earth cosmos, that is to say the newly arisen form of earth, which Revelation calls the "New Jerusalem." The seven aspects of transformed humankind outlined in Chapters 2-3 at the beginning of the text are completed at its end in Chapter 22 by the seven aspects of the renewed planet Earth.[2]

The grand compass of the Apocalypse is constructed around a central point contained in its central Chapter 12. In place of the masculine form of God, a woman stands in the middle of the changing universe: "And there appeared a great wonder in heaven: a woman clothed with the sun, and the moon under her feet, and upon her head a crown of twelve stars. And she being with child cried, travailing in birth, and pained to be delivered." (Revelation 12:1-2)

Is this not phenomenal? Without exception, the religions of the world place the figure of God in the center of the universe, but in this case a woman with her newborn child is perceived at the center of the All. But this is not a repetition of the concept of the "Great Goddess." The new world picture is centered in a mystifying partner relationship between the Goddess, Heaven, Earth and the Underworld joined with each other[3] and her son "who was to rule all nations with a rod of iron." (Revelation 12:5)

Does this mean that a fateful change has occurred within the cosmic order, one which centers our universe in a new way that never existed previously? If such were the case, it follows that we would experience the echo of such an earthly somersault in the form of human and terrestrial change. Have the waves of the "cosmic tsunami" that were released by the change finally reached our planet today, two thousand years after the Apocalypse of St. John revealed the new world order?

If we assume that the Revelation of St. John has been handed down to us truthfully, it would mean that the hierarchical world order, until now organized around masculine logic, has been converted into a spherical, rounded-off cosmic order, constituted through the power of love and based on creative freedom. That would cause a powerful upset of the spiritual relationships in the universe and consequently in the life processes of earth. Modern humans, whose way of being is totally alienated from Wholeness, would be deeply traumatized.

Another question is whether it is possible for such a fundamental change in the universe to run its course without resistance. In fact, in verses 3 and 4 of the central Chapter 12 the birth-mother of the new world order is immediately confronted by powerful opposition in the shape of a fiery red dragon: "And the dragon stood before the woman which was ready to be delivered, for to devour her child as soon as it was born." And further in verses 7 and 8: "And there was war in heaven: Michael and his angels fought against the dragon; and the dragon fought and his angels."

Naturally, one must interpret the concept of "war in heaven" as a symbol and not as fact. It refers to a struggle between two differing concepts of world order.

The old, materialistically oriented concept rests on the archetypal power of matter, which, for example, is manifest in the monstrous energy that is stored in every single atom. This is the world embraced by modern astronomy and atomic physics, a world of unimaginable distances, of the mighty radiating power of stars and the information that slumbers within the various incarnate beings in the shape of genetic codes. One faces a world dimension that is absolutely mechanistic and therefore loveless. The image of a merciless fiery dragon that embodies the spirit of the material universe is an entirely appropriate symbol.

The Apocalypse may be saying that earth has been chosen as the planet where the transformation of the material dimension of the universe will first be achieved. If so, we cannot expect to find anything like ourselves on the planets in our galactic environment that are settled with organic or even intelligent life, even though we are continually catapulting our probes into the universe to search for

other life forms. The earth is playing a pioneering role in the process of resuscitating the material universe, a role that has been prepared for billions of years. There may be mighty civilizations on other planets or in various star systems, but they are obviously lodged in other dimensions of the All.

In the language of the Apocalypse, the drama that accompanies the earth's pioneering role is described as follows: "And the great dragon was cast out, that old serpent…he was cast out into the earth and his angels were cast out with him."(12:9) This means that the final struggle of the new cosmic impulse against the old world order is brought to an end on earth. We humans, with the angels and elemental beings of earth, are protagonists in this "cosmic strife."

But this is not about a battle between two parties, one of which embodies the good and the other the evil. We are the same human beings and angels who incorporated the old world order—and were simultaneously inspired to struggle with the disadvantages of the materialized world. Furthermore, the same people who were to be swallowed by the might of the fiery red dragon are predestined to realize the new world order. The battle which consequently rages in every one of us may be identical with what has been called the concept of earth and human transformation—although in this there enter other aspects of change.

The events of Chapter 12 of the Revelation of St. John take place on the cosmic stage. In contrast, the events of Chapter 13 are played out on earth. It is the intention of Chapter 13 to name the forces of the old order that oppose the inspiration of the new love-infused cosmos on earth. They are named as "two beasts," although their description rather points to two monsters: "And I…saw a beast rise up out of the sea, having seven heads and ten horns, and upon his horns ten crowns, and upon his heads the name of blasphemy." (13:1) And the second beast "had two horns like a lamb, and he spake as a dragon." (13:11)

Thus the Apocalypse divides the forces that work against earth change into two categories. One can recognize the first category as an expression of materialistically directed ideologies. They can bind human beings to the rigid structures of the materialized world that have been broken off from multidimensional space. These massive bonds have come into existence through our human fascination with the perfection of the material world: "And he opened his mouth in blasphemy against God, to blaspheme his name and his tabernacle, and them that dwell in heaven." (13:6)

The second category of the opposition exhibits a mental character. One can interpret the two horns as the encapsulated intellectual forces of the heart intelligence and intuition: "And deceiveth them that dwell on the earth by the means of those miracles which he had power to do in the sight of the beast." (13:14) One can recognize—expressed in the symbolic language of the Apocalypse—even the intellectual capacity to create a robot: "And he had power to give life unto the image of the beast, that the image of the beast should… speak" (13:15)

When you read Chapter 13 carefully, you will also find a statement that makes it clear that the unique struggle with the contrary powers does not take place in the outer world, but in the personal cosmos of each individual human being. "If any man have an ear, let him hear." (13:9) In the contrary powers, we are dealing with forces that exist only because we humans have fed and encouraged them. Through our unthinking participation in the binding circle of repetitive causes and effects, we have become a sacrifice to our own decisions and attachments.

The meaning of that key statement in Chapter 13 is emphasized by the sentence that follows. It tells us: "He that leadeth into captivity shall go into captivity: he that killeth with the sword must be killed with the sword." (13:10)

1. The Revelation of St. John, also called the Apocalypse, is to be found among the writings of the Bible's New Testament. The quoted texts are taken from the King James Version.

2. The meaning of the Apocalypse, as reflected in the mirror of the present earth changes, is described in more complete form in *Earth Changes, Human Destiny* (Findhorn Press 2000). Here is my summary of the seven qualities of the New Jerusalem (Rev :21-22).
   › The future earth space will be composed of a refined, etheric material (21:11 and 18}.
   › There are no longer any religious institutions on the new earth, because God is directly present in every human heart (21:22).
   › Instead of being illuminated from outside as at present, the earth will radiate light from its center (21:23).
   › The new state of the earthy cosmos does not recognize the duality of good and evil. The shadow aspects are integrated into the dynamic of the whole (21:25).
   › The many planes of the new earth enable the simultaneous appearance of the different (visible and invisible) spatial dimensions (22:1).
   › Eternity and chronological time will be absorbed together into everyday life. This means that there are no more boundaries separating heaven and earth (22:2)
   › The sharing of the holistic life processes of the new earth cosmos enables the different races and peoples to cooperate creatively (22:2).

3. One should take note of the statement in 12:9 that the red dragon "was cast out into the earth, and his angels were cast out with him." This means that "the dragon" is working on earth together with the spiritual intelligence that ensouls the old cosmic order and is making its own consciousness available to it. One can identify this intelligence as a power that consciously works against the earth changes.

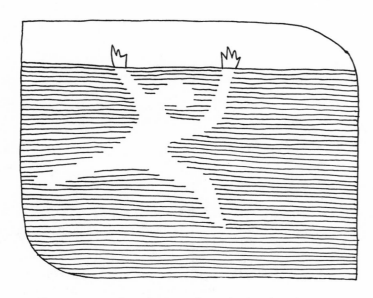

1. *The youngest, who is immersed over his head, is the worst off.*

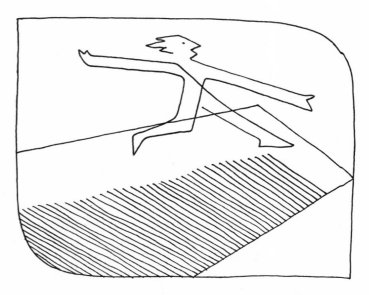

2. *The second youngster is nimble, and by making some acrobatic leaps, has saved himself from the cesspool.*

3. *The third youngster has been deeply upset by the incident. He remains squatting unhappily in the cesspool and will not get out.*

4. *Our paths cross exactly in the middle of the empty square. A part of me remembers I must run off immediately to make some purchases.*

Dream 34: A Panorama of Contrary Powers

1   *My sister comes to visit with her three children. They play behind the house where there is an old cesspool that is nearly completely overgrown. Unfortunately, all three fall in the pool. The youngest, who is immersed over his head, is the worst off.*

2   *The second youngster is nimble, and by making some acrobatic leaps, has saved himself from the cesspool.*

3   *The third youngster has been deeply upset by the incident. He remains squatting unhappily in the cesspool and will not get out.*

4   *It is already late in the evening, and I am walking homeward when I meet their mother in the spacious square. Our paths cross exactly in the center of the empty square. I am surprised to see how deeply she is sunk in sorrow. At the same moment, a part of me remembers I must run off immediately to make some purchases before the shops close. And I am gone at once.*

(Seeland, Switzerland, May 28, 2003)

THIS is a story about a family. One could guess that the brother, sister and three children represent the "family" of humankind and their handling of a specific aspect of earth change. The old cesspool is a central symbol that informs us that this story of earth change will be told from the perspective of dealing with so-called negative forces.

A cesspool stands for waste material that no longer has a task in life. Of course, waste can have a constructive role if it is recycled as manure. However, the dream emphasizes that the cesspool has been left unused for so long that its surface is covered with plants.

The cesspool that is lying unused behind the house can therefore be associated with forces, feelings and thoughts which are produced by human beings, but which are no longer in tune with the spirit of the time. They have separated from the evolutionary process of earth and cosmos and now are concentrated in the human subconscious, forgotten but as active as a time bomb.

In the dream, the old cesspool's influence on the present is portrayed through the story of the three brothers. Each represents a different aspect of human involvement with the "negative forces"— which one should understand to be forces that work against the successful execution of earth's transformation. They are seen as negative, not in any absolute sense, but from an energetic point of view.

The youngest brother stands for the majority of humankind. They are completely unaware how strongly their feelings, thoughts and actions are influenced by forces that have separated themselves from the cosmic cycle. Without conscious reflection, their feelings, thoughts, actions, and repetitive problems persistently reproduce the old brew of negative effects. Without their wishing it, they become an embodiment of the force that works against the epochal transformation of earth and humanity.

The second brother represents the few individuals who have consciously learned how to use "the old cesspool of negative power" for their egocentric well-being. Together they represent a world elite that knows how to use the forgotten containers of destructive force to build capital for their claims to power, cultural superiority, or financial profit.

The third brother brings a whiff of hope to the story. He represents the many individuals who sense how corrupt life has become within us and around us, so that the "old cesspool" persists in circling through cultures and continually creates unsolvable problems, in ecology, politics, health, and so forth. Certainly, he is still squatting in the cesspool, but inwardly he has distanced himself from the poison of the contrary powers.

The last dream image comes to expression in a wide public square, that is to say, in the middle of the earthly universe. The mother, who is now standing in the precise middle of the universe, symbolizes the mother of terrestrial creation. She is sunk in a deep depression. The dreamer notices the mother's sadness (the three children have fallen in the cesspool) but does not react with a question about the cause—something like, "Dear Mother, what is the matter?" Instead, he thinks he must run off at once to the shops to buy something.

This last dream image represents the downside of human involvement with the contrary powers. Instead of worrying about the garbage of human culture and the need to create some better sort of order behind his own house, those pressing necessities are hidden by external recycling measures. The worldly concern is for order that is social, financial, intercultural, environmentally friendly, and so forth, and there is violent criticism if there are any signs of disorder. Who asks about the causes and operational effects of the network of destructive forces that have poisoned the principles of our contemporary society? The dreamer's reaction to this attitude is typical. He runs away as soon as the divine Mother appears to help him.

1. My wife and I have planned to make a bicycle trip to Jerusalem the goal of our holiday.

2. Of course, the thief does not know that I am asleep inside. He attaches the bus to his car and drives quickly away. Help!

3. We drive past people and I try to make myself noticed at the window. No one senses that I am a prisoner.

4. I see a group of people on the curb—but unfortunately they are only dressed up like policemen.

Dream 35: Our Dependence on Alien Forces as a World Problem

1   *My wife and I have planned to make a bicycle trip to Jerusalem the goal of our holiday. On our first day I notice that I have left my wallet at home. I suggest that my wife should go on while I fetch the wallet and catch up with her later.*

2   *Now I am on my way to catch up with my wife. Arriving near an abandoned bus, I want to have a break and slip inside to take a short nap. While I am having my siesta, a thief comes to steal the bus. Of course, he does not know that I am asleep inside. He attaches the bus to his car and drives quickly away. Help!*

3   *We drive past people, and I try to make myself noticed at the window. No one senses that I am a prisoner. I sit at the steering wheel, but cannot steer it as I want: the bus is traveling according to the thief's plans. I try to sound the horn, but it does not work.*

4   *My last hope is to meet up with the police and have them notice my situation. In fact, I do see a group of people on the curb who might be policemen—but unfortunately they are only the retainers of some unknown folk who are dressed up like policemen. How can I ever find my wife who is cycling on the road to Jerusalem while I have been carried off in an unknown direction?*

(Riederalp/Immenstadt, Germany, July 13, 2003)

IF ONE IS GOING TO cycle to Jerusalem on a simple bicycle, one must create the necessary energy for the plan to succeed. Where is this energy coming from? The dream's story indicates the discrepancy between human ambitions and the natural state of things, and suggests this may possibly drive the negative power that works against the transformational processes of earth and humankind. It expresses itself in the form of varying dependencies, both on the personal and cultural levels.

After the first day's journey the dreamer must turn back and fetch the (additional) money, because the goal of the journey is not appropriate to the energy level on which the two travelers are moving. Jerusalem is thousands of miles distant, yet they want to spend their vacation pleasantly cycling there.

A human being is free to want something that far exceeds what is really possible. However, to reach the goal, if it exceeds the real possi-

bilities, additional power must be made available. It is to be found in the cosmic reservoir of archetypal power. That is all well and good. The decisive question is whether the person is also capable of forming a backwash that honors and in a specific way makes restitution to the "cosmic reservoir of archetypal power"—which is the divine source of all Being—from which it was drawn. The cosmos would collapse if the energy balance did not work out in the long term.

The next dream image portrays the consequences of the dreamer's unjustifiable indebtedness. He has obtained sufficient power to realize and make possible his over-exuberant plan, but he must pay for it with his own freedom. When he briefly goes to sleep, and thus loses control over the course of his life, he, who is indebted to power, is taken prisoner by an unknown force.

The manner of his imprisonment is characteristic. He continues to sit by the steering wheel—representing his life—but can no longer guide it as he wishes. He is led hither and thither according to the unknown code of rules set by the alien force. He does not know where he will end up or whether he will ever again see his wife.

In such cases, Western spiritual science speaks of the "Lucifer Syndrome"; psychology calls it the "Pact with the Devil." Both names signify a power that is able to satisfy the human appetites for grandiose experiences, unlimited rule, overflowing wealth, etc. The ruthless and oppressive bondage arising therefrom (which is indicated by the above expressions) should teach the affected persons to take the legitimacy of the cosmic cycles into their future considerations.

The dreamer does everything possible to make others aware of his pitiful situation and save himself from his self-initiated dependency, and yet no one sees his need. Unsuccessful, he hopes for intervention by the police who are responsible for the public social order. But instead of the police, he is driven past a group of men who are only dressed up like policemen and from whom he can expect no help.

At the very moment that earth and heaven need free and spiritually independent co-creators to complete the mighty task of transforming earth and civilization, we are confronted by masses of power-dependent people who are ensnared in their addiction problems. Drug-dependency, against which society and all its institutions are fiercely battling, is only an external symptom of the many fateful addictions that have caught an inconceivable number of "normal" people in their patterns of dependency.

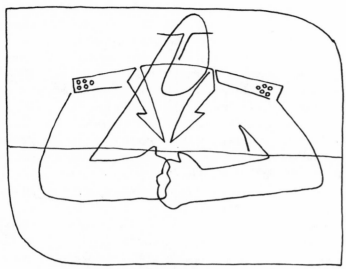

1. *In bidding us farewell, however, the officer says that under specific conditions he has the right to recall us into the army.*

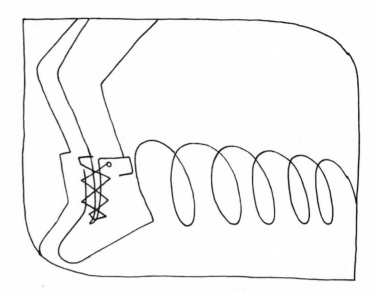

2. *He shows us a sort of spiral cord that still binds us to the army. It looks like a length of black cord twisted in a spiral.*

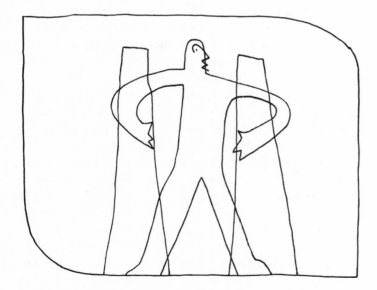

3. *I also inform the officer that I have chiseled two sculptures out of stone for the army, and in this way paid off my dues.*

Dream 36: The Lucifer Syndrome

1 *There is good news! The law was changed. We have obtained the right to leave the army. In bidding us farewell, however, the officer says that under specific conditions he has the right to recall us.*

2 *He shows us a sort of spiral cord which still binds us to the army. It looks like a length of black cord twisted in a spiral, such as are fixed on bicycles to prevent their being stolen. The officer demonstrates a particular rhythm in the individual loops of the cord that would make possible our recall to the army.*

3 *I am furious and firmly determined that I will never return to the army. I also inform the officer that I have chiseled two sculptures out of stone for the army, and in this way paid off my dues. I even threaten to retain a lawyer to fight for my rights.*

(*Riederalp/Immenstadt, Germany, July 14, 2003*)

THIS IS THE SECOND PART of the dream of July 13, 2003, and it was dreamed one night later. It is a likely supposition that the two dreams are linked.

To some extent, the second dream can be seen as an elaboration of the first. The first dream presented the general problem with the "Lucifer Syndrome," which is that human beings lose their personal spiritual freedom when they tap into the cosmic reservoir of archetypal power to satisfy their own egocentric appetites. The second dream informs us of the changes that have occurred in the area related to the present transformation of earth and humans. The new legal edict, of which the officer speaks, is a symbol of this change.

The right to be released from the army can be interpreted as an act of cosmic (divine) mercy that offers individuals the possibility of freedom from the oppressive burden of the alien powers. This means that those who are ready to perceive this cosmic offer can join in the processes of the epochal change without bringing their old baggage with them.

However, the second dream image makes clear that the release cannot happen automatically. It has only a temporary effect, during which humankind, so to speak, is free to catch a necessary breath of air. Seen in the long run, one is still duty bound to "pay back the debt."

This sort of statement can be read into the symbolic language of the Apocalypse of St. John, given that the Apocalypse is understood to be an early vision of the currently unfolding world changes. It is reported there that the Devil will be incarcerated for a millennium, after which he will be let free to complete his work among human beings.

However, the third dream image suggests that one may finally be able to free oneself from bondage to the alien cosmic power. There are two pre-conditions: first, one can definitely free oneself from Luciferic bondage by developing one's own creativity. Since the dreamer's official calling is that of a sculptor, his creative input is symbolized by two chiseled stone sculptures. However, the real concern is not with specific pieces of creative work, but rather with the development of one's own creativity, which works as an antidote to the drugs of the Luciferic power.

A dangerous downside to the alien cosmic energy (the so-called Luciferic power), which is used to manifest one's egocentric purposes, is that one's own sources of creative power, which are carried within ourselves as creative subjects of the universe, are neglected and even forgotten. Instead of using one's own creative potential, one is dependent on an unknown and distant energy source from out of the broad universe. From this there develops an addiction that is only to be finally extinguished by the constant input of one's personal creativity in different areas of life.

The second pre-condition is demonstrated by the dreamer's firm decision to battle for his own complete freedom. In the course of the current world changes, people are offered the unique opportunity to free themselves from the lures and tricks of the Luciferic powers. To realize this possibility, one needs a firm determination to renounce their attraction and to watch persistently over all one's dealings to see that it is one's own center that grounds one and makes one creative.

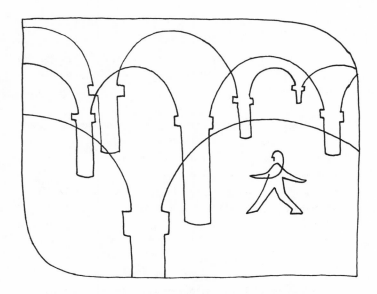

1. I am running to and fro in the area of a Romanesque basilica, but cannot find the sacred church.

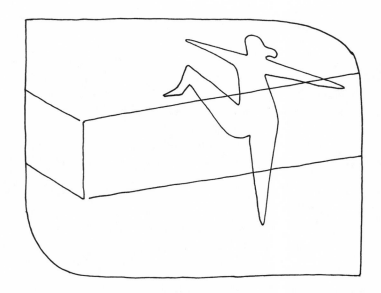

2. I see a woman who has taken a step down with one leg, but whose other remains stuck above.

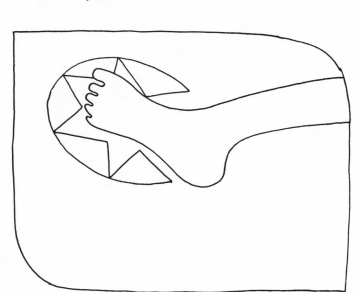

3. Then I look closer and see that her foot is stuck to a red-colored sign, but I can only partly recognize its shape.

Dream 37: Religious Bondage

1   *I am running to and fro in the neighborhood of a Romanesque basilica, but cannot find the sacred church. I still hope to find the famous basilica, but all I can see are subsidiary spaces that are meaningless.*

2   *In searching for the sacred space, I come upon a step that is eerily deep, a sort of threshold leading downward, with which I must deal if I am to go any farther. There is a woman there who has taken a step down with one leg, but whose other leg remains stuck above.*

3   *The situation is quite startling. Her legs are parted so widely that it is obvious she cannot hold out much longer. She has gathered all her strength together to free her upper leg but without success. Looking closer, I see that her foot is stuck to a red-colored sign, but I can only partly recognize its shape.*

(*Prague, Czech Republic, July 24, 2003*)

THE ENVIRONMENT of the dream tells us that its subject is the search for the divine. The dreamer knows that he is close to a famous church, a basilica dating from the Middle Ages. He wanders about but cannot find the sacred place.

Interpreted in the context of the current earth change, this symbolizes the alteration of the sacred standards. If one follows the usual paths, it does not mean that one arrives at the sacred themes. They are now settled on a different level of existence than before. What was once the leading quality of the divine may now appear as something subsidiary. So it happens that the dreamer, in search of the sacred place—that is, the divine space—can find only subsidiary spaces.

The second dream image tells us that one must overcome a high threshold to make any further progress toward the new spirituality. This is obviously a symbol of initiation. The threshold is too high to be accepted as a normal stairway. To pass through a threshold, in the sense of initiation, means to attain specific inner experiences that open the gates to a new insight into the mystery of life.

It is important to note that the threshold leads downward, and thus into the earth. Interpreted as a symbol, it means that the new way of spirituality is more grounded, perhaps even that the Earth Spirit will now and in the future play a greater role, in a sacred sense, than is the practice with present-day religions.

At this point the dreamer is made aware of a difficult predicament. The problematic situation is posed by a woman, which indicates an alternative to traditional religion where men regularly play the main role.

This means that the woman represents the new, unorthodox efforts that are being made in search of the new spirituality. Why is she not free to go on her way in search of the Spirit of Life? Because we live in a civilization where the free choice of spiritual orientation is prescribed by global standards.

The dream's story shows unequivocally that she is determined to go on her way into a more grounded spirituality. She is held back by force, so that she cannot implement her own free choice. However, the force that chains her to the old sacred standards—and herein lies the emphasis of the dream's message—is a hidden force. Its power is covered by the victim's own foot, so that neither the dreamer nor the general public could know its origin.

From the dream we know only that it has to do with a sort of magical (red-colored!) sign that binds the foot of the seeker to the old sacred qualities. What statement can this symbol be making?

One could interpret it such that the traditional religions, be they Muslim, Christian or Hindu, have developed their own magical formulas, agreeable to themselves, by which they can bind billions of people to the sort of spirituality that they maintain is righteous and the only one pleasing to God.

This binding force usually concerns dogma or other sorts of spiritual scriptures that are represented as the only relevant portals to God—and which simultaneously function as energetic shackles. They draw their power, as far as possible, from their believers' fear of being separated from the beloved Godhead if they do not keep to the prescribed dogma, traditions and scriptures.

The cosmic transformation, which is in the process of creating a new order for our epoch and all its institutions—including our relationship with the divine—needs people who are free to perceive the new dimensions of the world and gradually realize them in daily life. To free ourselves from the chains of spiritual bondage is one of the pre-conditions that would allow humanity to participate fully in the present epochal transformation.

1. *I find myself in some oily water watching the duel of two warriors from a bygone era. They are swinging their swords, fighting to the death.*

2. *Greatly flustered, the announcer informs us that one of the warriors is mortally wounded.*

3. *I emerge from the water and see a man in a modern suit, sitting on the bank of the water where the battle took place.*

4. *The man fumbles in his pocket. He gets out his spectacles and puts them on his nose. How surprised he is at what he sees before him!*

Dream 38: Do the Contrary Powers Self-Destruct?

1 *I find myself in some oily water watching the duel of two warriors from a bygone era. Standing up to their knees in the oily water, they are swinging their swords, fighting to the death. A radio announcer is accompanying the battle with his commentary, yelling excitedly as if he is at a football game.*

2 *Greatly flustered, the announcer informs us that one of the warriors is mortally wounded. At that, his name is called out: "Bosko Hodzic." Absolute silence follows. This lasts for a long time.*

3 *I emerge from the water and see a man sitting on the bank of the water where the battle took place. He is wearing a modern suit, which is fresh from the store.*

4 *The man fumbles in his pocket, gets out his spectacles and puts them on his nose. How surprised he is at what he sees before him! There is no trace of the two warriors on the outer level of life.*

(Sempas, Slovenia, September 22, 2001)

ONE THING CAN IMMEDIATELY be recognized from the structure of the dream: the life processes of the modern world run on two different levels. On the outer world level, one dresses in chic and modern clothing, but the two warriors on "the level below" are equipped in antique fashion and fight with swords, as in the Middle Ages.

One can pursue this dualistic structure further. The media persistently reports on specific events that impact the outer world, and for this a football commentator emerges as the symbol. The true causes of world events dwell, however, in the bottom half of the divided world and are regularly disregarded. Modern people, sitting on the bank, know nothing of the causes of the battle that rages in the water, and so are unable to relate and take a stance.

It is typical for the radio commentator to belong to the outer level; he does not perceive the battle between the two warriors, though it affects him. To draw a parallel, if one hears the daily news, one assumes that the catalog of world events is jumbled together by chance. This is not true at all. Yet one is led from news item to news item without catching a glimpse of the deeper causes of the events.

What is really happening—beyond the media commentators— is a power struggle that plays out on the invisible plane, so to speak,

behind the scenes of worldly events. To symbolize this, the second level of reality is represented as an underwater world, in contrast to the worldly level, which is identified by the area of the water's bank. If one sits on the bank of a body of deep water, one knows nothing of what is happening in its depths.

But the dream scene makes clear that the events in the water are not invisible because of its depth but because of the oily substance that contaminates it. The substance is similar to water but does not act like clear water. The oily substance is more reminiscent of that emotional level where human feelings are clogged together. This is a distinct level of the emotional world where humanity's raw negative feelings are stored. One often speaks of this level as the "lower astral." It is a layer of the emotional world that is contaminated by mob feelings like fear, mistrust, power lust, and so forth. Groups of people who seek to rule the world outside the divine plan find in it a chance to tinker with the causes of world events.

The constant battle between opposites is the preferred engine for power-seeking groups for steering world events in the most profitable direction. The two warriors engaged in merciless combat point to this dangerous engine. By constantly kindling enmities and wars, the powers that work against the cosmic plan for the evolution of earth and humanity are nourished and upheld in their continued domination of the world.

At the critical point in this struggle between the contrary powers, a decisive change appears. The radio commentator cries excitedly that one of the warriors is mortally wounded. A trick? Certainly not!

One should be aware that this dream occurred 11 days after September 11, 2001, when the twin towers of the World Trade Organization in New York were destroyed by terrorist action. Like the duel between the two warriors in the oily water, in the outer world two opposing parties are colliding with each other, one represented by the religious fanaticism of the Islamic terrorists, the other by the power of unjust globalization, symbolized by the World Trade Organization.

In the introduction to the third chapter of this book, I have already told how on 9/11 divine grace worked to reverse the egocentric plans of the opponents involved, changing them to a life-saving act. The mortal wound suffered by one of the opponents who was called "Bosko Hodzic"—a common name among Bosnian Muslims—can be identified with that event. The engine that drove the worldwide aggression of the contrary powers was put out of gear.

In that case, why has there been as yet no essential change in the broad course of our civilization's history?

Soon after the events of 9/11, the bloody wars in Iraq and Afghanistan were kindled. The engine of world-rule, based on the eternal battle between the contrary powers, was consciously put back into gear. Chapter 13 of the Revelation of St. John states in three places that one of the two monsters that embody the powers that work against cosmic change is mortally wounded; "but his wound was healed." (Rev. 13:3,12,14).

And how did it come about that the divine plan could not be implemented in this aspect of 9/11?

The answer to this question is to be sought in the last dream image. Whoever did not ask what were the deeper causes of the shattering blow of 9/11 has missed the proffered chance. The engine that drives the contrary powers was broken energetically, but modern humans unfortunately do not have the sensitive disposition to perceive the cosmic opportunity. Instead, they put the spectacles of intellect on their nose and look into the outer world where there is nothing to be seen of the secret of the contrary powers. A deceptive stillness rules.

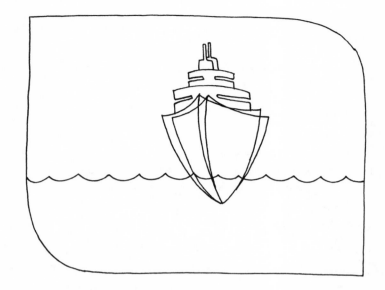

1. *Suddenly, from deep in the belly of the giant ship comes the crash of two explosions, one after the other. The ship lists dangerously, first to one side, then to the other.*

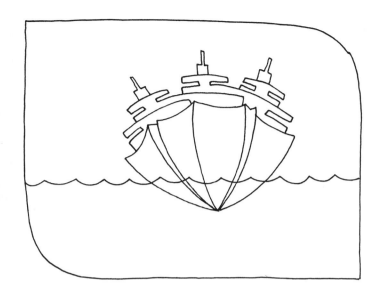

2. Following that, there comes a third, much more violent explosion, the sound of which is once again muffled. This time the ship lists to an extreme degree.

Dream 39: Travesty of the Dark Powers

1 *We are preparing to leave the harbor with a group of travelers and set off on a wide-ranging tour. Suddenly, from deep in the belly of the giant ship comes the crash of two explosions, one after the other. The sound is muffled, however. The ship lists dangerously, first to one side, then to the other, then rocks a few times.*

2 *Following the two explosions, there comes a third, much more violent explosion, the sound of which is once again muffled. This time the ship lists to an extreme degree, nearly to the deck railings. Now all of the crew and the passengers storm onto the deck, seeking to adjust to the situation and to ascertain the cause of the attack.*

3 *Not far from the ship a group of grown men are standing up to their ankles in water. I know at once that they are in some way responsible for the incident. The men hold each others' hands and form a circle. Half of them are dressed in gleaming white lab coats, the others in pitch-black tuxedos.*

4 *The circle turns directly toward me, without the men letting go of each others' hands. They look at me with evil grins, as if to say: "Look what we have done." I turn however to one of the older men in our group, give him my hand and say: "We do not know each other yet."*

(Venice, Italy, January 11, 2003)

It is too simplistic to describe the dream only as a criticism aimed at the ruling elite. It is certainly true that the circle formed by the two different groups of men is suspicious. Those who are in the white lab coats can be identified as the scientific elite, and the others who are dressed in black tuxedos as the financial elite. In fact, this is how we see it, that the world elite that is driving the avalanche of globalization forward is formed from an amalgamation of two elitist groups, the highest ranking scientists and the richest financiers.

However, we should take note of a symbol that underlies the whole story of the dream, namely that is the presence of water. The dreamer's ship, which is preparing to leave the harbor, rests in the middle of the water, and not far from the ship the elitist group stands in water up to their ankles.

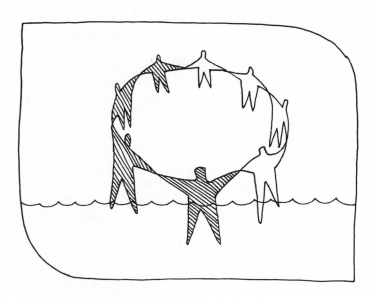

3. *The men hold each others' hands and form a circle. Half of them are dressed in gleaming white lab coats, the others in pitch-black tuxedos.*

4. *The men look at me with evil grins, as if to say: "Look what we have done."*

Water is a symbol of the emotional level of being. Does this mean that the battle for world rule is not taking place primarily on the political, economic or social levels, but on a level largely hidden from sight, the one called the emotional (or astral) level?

This level does not refer to any superficial level of feelings, but is a type of spiritual plane where the buds of real circumstances are nourished and so far developed that they can later appear as etheric life forms and afterward as physical embodiments.

The water in which the men are standing and where the ship is rocking is a suitable symbol—it is important that it is not fresh water! In seawater and in the amniotic fluid of a mother's womb are contained all the substances that a living being requires for its development.

That the ruling world elite guide decisive world events through some sort of spiritual practice is confirmed in the dream by the group of men holding hands in a circle, as often spiritually oriented groups do. These are not terrorists who plan and execute attacks. The explosions with the muffled sounds point to an energetic rather than a physical operation on the fabric of reality.

We can understand the message of the dream as a warning, first, not to waste too much of our creative energy in the battle against the external processes that would destroy the world. It is likely that we would not arrive at the real causes of the circumstances that are endangering the stability of the world structure and thrusting masses of people into misfortune. These causes are developed on another plane that is blocked from investigation and public control. The barriers that prevent the reporting of what is going on in the spiritual-emotional realm of multidimensional reality are supported by the general public, who do not think that what happens there is at all relevant.

Second, we are warned not to undertake any type of spiritual practice that has not been developed by an awakened, ethically based consciousness—even when it is a spiritual project with a positive goal. The alternative to the apparent spirituality of the ruling world elite is indicated by the dreamer's concluding meeting with an unknown person.

He reaches his hand out to the unknown person, not according to some preconceived pattern, but on the basis of the free encounter of two individuals: "We do not know each other yet, but are nonetheless ready to mutually respect each other in our differences and work in common on projects for the good of earth and humanity." That was the meaning of this gesture.

Exercises on the Theme "Dealing with the Contrary Powers"

An exercise to ask about the reason for a particular disturbance

If you find yourself in a situation with unharmonious characteristics that lead you to suspect that contrary powers may be involved, you can proceed, following the model of Dream 34:

- *First calm yourself, for example, joining yourself with the stillness of the ocean depths, which remain calm even when winds rage on its surface.*
- *Imagine yourself inwardly approaching the center of the universe, which may be recognized by the presence of the Divine Mother. (In the dream, the dreamer meets the Mother precisely in the center of the broad square.)*
- *Your attitude toward her should express your feelings of reverence and profound love. This confirms that you are in her presence.*
- *Then reproduce in your imagination the circumstances that lead you to suspect the possible involvement of contrary powers.*
- *Now, in view of those particular circumstances, put the question: "Dear Mother, why are you so sad?"*
- *Listen with feelings and intuition for the answer that may (immediately) emerge within you.*
- *Look to interpret the answer in the context of your own life and thank her for her help.*

An exercise to preserve your own independence

One's independence of alien powers is a quality of life that becomes ever more important as the earth change proceeds. It can be consciously nurtured. The following exercise is a proposal:

- *Sit down to meditate in a quiet place with your spinal column erect.*
- *Next, you should simultaneously exchange the two sides of your body. This means that you let the right side of your body move over to the left side, and vice versa. It is best to do this several times with a short pause in between, and always in the same direction.*
- *Through this movement, repeated several times, a vertical free space arises in your center.*
- *Look sensitively to see what wants to express itself in this free space, possibly as an aspect of yourself that needs clarification.*
- *To start this process moving, you should surround the negatively charged power or quality with violet light and hand it over to Mother Earth for transformation.*
- *To establish the freedom and independence of your own being, you should expand the vertical space in the midst of you like a pillar of light downward to the earth's center and upward to infinity.*
- *Finally, you should let the quality of total freedom thereby experienced broaden horizontally and ring out like bells in the expanses of your own life.*

An exercise to free oneself from the domination of Luciferic forces

You may ask how you can meditatively support your own liberation from the "Luciferic Syndrome" (Dreams 36-37). You were given indications in Dream 37 of how to deal with that in your personal life. Here it is expanded in meditative form, with emphasis on the recognition of the previously frozen state of your own creativity, which is hereby freed to unfold itself anew:

> *In this case too, you should either sit or stand with your spine erect.*
> *Imagine yourself making a crack through the middle of your body with your finger.*
> *Afterwards, your body, in two half-portions, is opened in the middle, as a book is opened. The partition line runs through your face and body, exactly in the center.*
> *While you have been opening your own "Book of Life" in this manner, imagine that a flock of black birds are flying out toward heaven from inside you. They represent the Luciferic forces to which humankind is bound. Now they are longing to return to their cosmic home.*
> *Guide the birds toward infinity in heaven, until they enter into infinity.*
> *Now wait carefully for the return stream. Be sensitive to observe what of the previously frozen information or power is given back to you, and integrate it in your Being. Give thanks!*

A powerful grounding exercise

If you feel burdened by contrary powers, it is wisest to look for the cause in yourself, and in this sense undertake the transformative steps. If you need a protected time for this, a deep grounding is your best option. It cannot help much to leave roots in the earth to grow, as is recommended in the usual grounding exercises. The earth's surface is broadly controlled by forces that work against cosmic transformation. To be protected, you must be joined more deeply, as in the following exercise:

> *You should carry out this exercise with the spine erect.*
> *Imagine that a wonderful crystal is buried beneath your feet, or even a crystal skull, some of which are in the museums of pre-Columbian cultures.*
> *You should join the elemental power of your whole body to the crystal.*
> *Then let the crystal be led down ever deeper toward the earth's core, and bound to it, your own power, which is calling out to be grounded.*
> *When you reach a sufficient depth, you should stop and sense the way in which your force field, following the crystal sinking into the depths of the earth's consciousness, is anchored in the earth's depths.*
> *Now, you switch the direction of your attention around. Consider how strongly you are bound to the archetypal world of the Earth Soul and her elemental world—the effect is similar to the way your body is bound to your force field.*
> *Now you only need to form a sphere of light around your own aura, so that the boundaries of your autonomous personal space are clearly defined.*

Chapter 6

Rebirth of Holiness

For me, Jesus Christ's most beloved saying is not part of the traditional four Gospels that tell us about his teachings and deeds at the beginning of our era. It is not to be found in the so-called canonical scriptures that the Church Fathers compiled in the first centuries of the Christian era and declared to be the Word of God. The saying is as follows:

"The All has gone out before me and the All has encompassed me. Split a piece of wood, I am there. Lift up a stone, and you will find me there." (Tm. Log: 77)[1]

It is amazing how two sentences can express the fundamental unity of the universe's eternal dimension with the dimension of time and space, confirming that Holiness is the common basis of existence in both extensions of our being. It is expressed in the principle, "I AM."

The so-called Gospel of Thomas, which is the source of the above saying of Jesus, was declared heretical in that distant time. Throughout the whole known world it was not only forbidden to read the script, which consists of 114 sayings of Jesus; one was duty-bound to burn all its manuscripts. Nonetheless some scripts in the Coptic language survived more than a millennium, hidden in the Egyptian desert near Nag Hammadi and discovered in 1945.

When, more than three decades ago, I came to read the Gospel of Thomas in a German translation, my reservations about the teachings of Jesus Christ melted away.[2] I sensed that his sayings were about a revolutionary spiritual teaching that gave a wholly new basis to the relationships of humankind to its own divine core and to the holy dimension of the universe, earth included. Another quotation is apt:

"He who knows the All, but misses out on himself, misses out on the Whole." (Tm. Log: 67)

It was soon clear to me that there must also be original sayings of Jesus "buried" in the texts of the four gospels that are accepted by the Christian Church. When the texts were compiled, they were often harnessed to the wrong context and so appear uninteresting to us today. In consequence, as modern people, we are not inwardly moved by their statements. They were often simply accepted as a historic-religious fact.

Toward the end of the 1990s, I had developed tools with which I could test the Gospel texts energetically. In doing so, I tried to identify those parts of the text that were obviously inserted later to steer Christ's teaching in such directions as appeared meaningful to his disciples in the first centuries after his presence in Palestine. They may however be crassly contrary to what Jesus, later called the Christ, wanted to impart to us, his fellow human beings—and not only to Christians.

I have used the sensitivity of my fingers to scan the etheric layers that accompany the individual parts of the texts.[3] My fingers have traveled over the Gospel texts and tested every word for its energetic quality. The original sayings of Christ have consistently exhibited a clear pattern underlayed by the four etheric elements. By this they can unfailingly be recognized as an expression of the divine Word—but not so the other parts of the text. It gradually emerged that hidden behind the textual fabric of the four canonical Gospels, there is a "Fifth Gospel."[4] I have been only partially successful in expressing various aspects of this many-layered Fifth Gospel in my book *Christ Power and the Earth Goddess*.[5]

Of the various sayings of Jesus Christ whose authenticity I have tested, there are some in the Gospels of Luke and Matthew that are of interest for this book. They are jumbled together in the chapters concerning future events, some of which relate to the destruction of Jerusalem by the Roman legions in 70 c.e. and therefore are of less interest to us today. These last are prefixed by the words, "This generation will not pass away till all be fulfilled."

The sayings that are important today for us, who find ourselves amidst the turmoil of the transformation of earth and humanity, are those relating to the so-called Second Coming of Christ. Here is a quotation from the Gospel of Luke:

"And there shall be signs in the sun, and in the moon, and in the stars; and upon the earth distress of nations, with perplexity; the sea and the waves roaring. Men's hearts failing them for fear, and

for looking after those things which are coming on the earth: for the powers of heaven shall be shaken. And then shall they see the Son of Man coming in a cloud with power and great glory." (Luke 21:25-27)

If one examines the words carefully, one can recognize the total plan for the cosmic transformation of earth and humankind. Let us begin with the last sentence.

Arriving in a cloud means that this is not about a second physical incarnation of Christ, like the previous time when the Christ Power incarnated in the person of Jesus of Nazareth. The words tell us that this time his presence is to be found in the etheric dimension of terrestrial space. Since he is not limited by the conditions of space and time in that dimension, he could, like the clouds, be simultaneously active in many parts of the earth.

The concept of the "Son of Man," which often occurs elsewhere in the Gospels, also has something to say. It means that the cosmic being that is known in the West as the Christ is no alien personality that wants to approach closer to earth. Instead, this is about a new divine vision of humankind that the Christ Power and Love have brought close to human consciousness. In place of the old humanity, bound in obedience to God's Will, the vision of the Son of Man is confirmation that human beings have spiritual freedom and loving responsibility for the fabric of life on earth.

In the above quotation from Luke's Gospel, we should not overlook the conglomerate description of the processes of earth change. In it one can see the allusion to the eclipses of the sun in August 1999 and July 2009 and the special constellations of stars and planets that accompanied them. The "roaring of the sea and the waves" points to the current natural catastrophes that are connected with climate change—impelled by the warming of the oceans.

There is another of Jesus' sayings that is relevant to our theme. It is to be found in Matthew's Gospel. It reads as follows:

"But as the days of Noah were, so shall the coming of the Son of Man be. For as in the days before the flood they were eating and drinking, marrying and giving in marriage, until the day that Noah entered into the ark, and knew not until the flood came, and took them all away; so shall also the coming of the Son of Man be." (Mat. 24:37-39)

This is a serious warning to which we should listen today. The warning means that the (then still in the future) earth change is running its course on so finely subtle an (etheric) plane that men

and women, wholly occupied with their daily tasks and habits, are not in a position to perceive the fateful changes taking place within and around them.

Jesus' initial words refer to the flood already mentioned in the introduction to Chapter 2 of this book. According to the biblical report, the transformative wave on the earth's surface was so massive that the only survivors were those—symbolized by Noah in his ark—who were sufficiently alert to interpret the signs of the time. That enabled them to attune in good time to the changes and arrive at the new plane of being in company with the earth organism.

In this connection, there is a related statement in Matthew's Gospel that I cannot accept. It reports on the Last Judgment in that future epoch, *"When the Son of Man shall come in his glory" (Mat. 25:31, 41)*. Then the "evil" people are separated from the "good"; the first named are cursed and sent to hell, the second blessed in the Kingdom of Heaven. When I investigated the four etheric layers of this section of text, it exhibited a level of extreme confusion, the like of which I have not encountered elsewhere in the Gospels.

This obviously egocentrically concocted vision of the Last Judgment by the author of Matthew's Gospel reinforces my respect for a related but credible statement of Jesus' that appears in Luke's Gospel:

"I tell you, in that night there shall be two men in one bed; the one shall be taken, and the other left." (Lk. 17:34)

In the apocryphal Gospel of Thomas, this saying is formulated as follows:

Jesus said, "Two will rest on a bed: the one will die, and the other live." (Tm. Log:61, Lambdin Trans).

If one takes this sentence out of context with the other collected sayings, one gets the impression that Jesus was speaking about the division of human beings into two halves, one of which one will be led over into the future, but the other abandoned to decay. This may have led to the projection that the Last Judgment would separate the good people from the bad for all eternity.

It has been overlooked that the two people who are experiencing separation are lying in one and the same bed. This suggests the involvement, not of two different persons, but of two aspects of one and the same person. Jesus is indicating an inner division of humankind.

In the course of humanity's transformation, there comes a tipping point when a fundamental division must be overcome. In the process of becoming One, the aspect of ourselves that lives in blindness and separation is released, but our holistic aspect further developed. *"The one will die, and the other live."*

This interpretation is confirmed when one looks at the whole context of the quoted passage, which is contained in Logion 61. According to Thomas the Evangelist, Jesus spoke those words when he was sitting at table with his hostess, a woman named Salome. As a result, Salome became clairaudient and asked him who he was. Jesus replied: *"I am he who exists from the undivided..."* When she heard this, she replied full of conviction: *"I am your disciple."*

Jesus' words were also rendered, *"I am he who is from the same..."*—meaning not one who is based on a fundamental inner division—which is a perfect description of the transformed human being that Jesus called the "Son of Man."

---

1. I have denoted quotations from the Apocrypha and thus from the Gospel of Thomas, which is not recognized by the official church, with the letters "Tm" and the number of the saying of Jesus contained therein, the so-called Logion.
2. The text of the Gospel of Thomas can be found in *The Nag Hammadi Library* published by the Gnostic Society Library. The translation used here is by Lambdin.
3. The vital-energetic force fields are composed of the ethers of water, fire, earth and air. See *Sacred Geography* (Lindisfarne Books 2007).
4. Rudolf Steiner *The Fifth Gospel: From the Akashic Record* (Rudolf Steiner Press 1995).
5. *Christ Power and the Earth Goddess* (Findhorn Press, Scotland 1999).

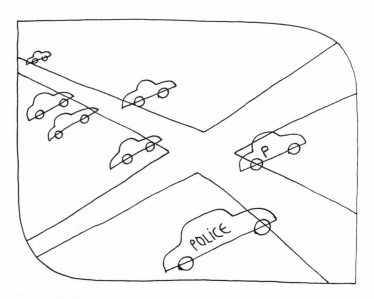

1. *This time it is extraordinarily difficult to make much progress on the French roads. Roadblocks, which the police have erected to stop us travelers, continually appear ahead of me.*

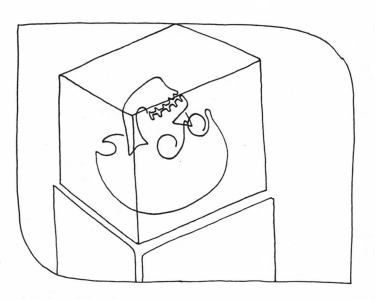

2. *Now I am looking at the skull of Christ in its place at the exhibition in Paris. It is set inside a glass cube.*

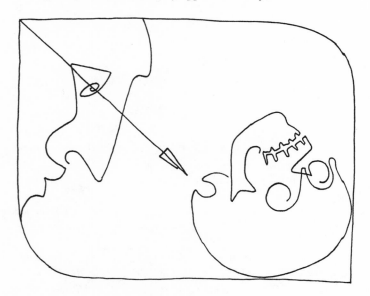

3. *On awakening, the thought comes to me that the dream is trying to make me aware of a hidden chakra beyond the sphere of the skull.*

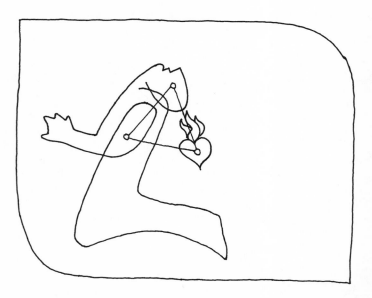

4. *I imagine that my head is inclined as far backward as the skull of Christ at the exhibition in Paris.*

Dream 40: reversal of the Divine

1   *I am traveling to Paris. This time it is extraordinarily difficult to make much progress on the French roads. The police have erected road-blocks to stop travelers, which continually appear ahead of me. There must be something of the utmost value being transported along the route ahead of me. I finally learn that it is the skull of Christ, which is to be put on display at a great international exhibition in Paris.*

2   *Now I am looking at the skull of Christ at the exhibition in Paris. It is set inside a glass cube and so placed that one can look through the spinal aperture in its base into the empty brain case. The hollow eye holes stare upward toward the ceiling of the exhibition hall.*

3   *On awakening, the thought comes to me that the dream is trying to make me aware of a hidden chakra beyond the sphere of the skull. There must be some reason why the skull is so precisely placed that the onlooker can peer through the spinal aperture (foramen magnum) into its interior.*

4   *If I imagine that my head is inclined as far backward as the skull of Christ, then the axis of the crown chakra, when extended into my back space, meets with the center of the cosmic heart that beats along the horizontal axis of my heart chakra in the human back space.*

(Mesara, Crete, February 18, 1999)

IF THE SKULL OF JESUS CHRIST were to be put on display at an exhibition, it would mean, in the framework of Western culture, that the divine would be threatened by the worst possible desecration. It is not only a matter of desecrating what is holy, but also of a dangerous reversal. Instead of paying the greatest attention to Christ's teaching, his empty skull is put on show.

That Holiness is distorted into a material value is exemplified by the extravagance of the security provided for the transport of the skull. Translated from symbolic language, it means that it is not the delivery of the spiritual and social teaching of Christ that is important, but that the prestige of possessing his bones and having the ability to exhibit them is what has the greatest social significance.

The second dream image brings a further shock. The skull of Christ is not placed so that appropriate honor can be paid to the Son of God, but in such manner that it is almost thrown away. Without respect to any piety, it exposes the empty space in the skull's braincase.

The first two dream images point to modern society's disastrous loss of any relationship to the Holy. On the one hand, material values replace spiritual values as guidelines for common cultural development. On the other hand, the religious relationship to the Holy has been rigidly institutionalized and enshrined in dogma. This is symbolized by the extensive police security for the transport of the skull, which has replaced the deep respect for the sacred that used to be felt inwardly and intimately. The blasphemous transport of Christ's skull and its shameless public display is a symbolic indication of an extreme crisis in our current relationship with the sacred dimension of being,

The brilliance of dream language rests in its ability, simultaneously to portraying the end of a decayed relationship with the Holy, and indicating new horizons for that relationship. This has to do with the dreamer's feelings after awakening. Can it be perhaps that what is hiding behind the eerie positioning of the skull is a message that points a way out of this extreme crisis in our relationship with the divine?

Such indeed is the case. There is an important and long forgotten point in the human back space that can be reached if the axis of the line of sight, guided as shown through the skull's spinal aperture (*foramen magnum*), is projected farther beyond the skull bone. One reaches a point that can be identified as the cosmic heart. Can it be that by suitably positioning the skull, the cosmic heart comes to represent the newly discovered exit point through which the impulse to renew the relationship with the Holy can flow out to the universe?

The cosmic heart is that aspect of the heart center through which we participate in the rays of the sun of universal love. This means that the human heart knows a dimension in which it is identical to the universal sun of love, which imparts the essential vibration to the spiritual dimension of the universe. The classical symbol for this was called the spark of the divine presence in human beings. In fact, it is an extension of the heart that exceeds human individuality and simultaneously forms the basis of our personal identity.

Can it be that we, as the Western culture, have too superficially understood the message of love brought by Jesus Christ? Are we now being directed toward a deeper dimension of love that is in fact capable of realizing the holy dimension of being that Jesus, the Christ, called "The Kingdom of Heaven on Earth"?

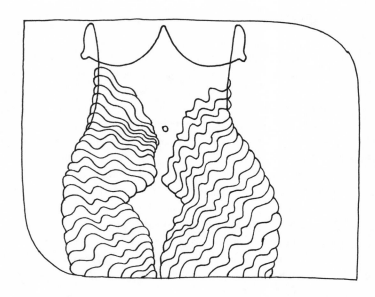

1. When I raise my eyes to see what is happening on the stage, I am thunderstruck. A giant, well-proportioned, dark-skinned woman is dancing on the stage.

2. Every muscle in the dark brown Goddess' body is moving in wavelike fashion, all thrust sideways in a specific direction.

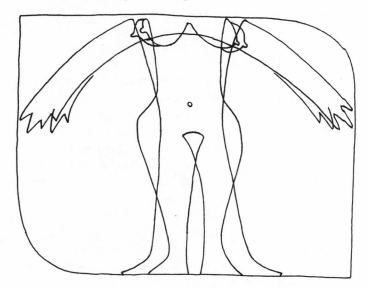

3. I am surprised to realize that at certain moments her magnificent female body is temporarily assuming certain masculine features.

4. The figure in her hand is put together from the forms of two boys, who complement each other: the one is innocent and happy, the other burdened with a heavy cross.

Dream 41: Return of the Goddess

1   *I am passing by a lofty platform-like stage. When I raise my eyes to see what is happening there, I am thunderstruck. A giant, well-proportioned, dark-skinned woman is dancing on the stage. I have never before seen such a blend of power, beauty, and dignity. The woman is completely naked and dances without moving from the spot. How is this possible? I look closer.*

2   *Every muscle in the dark brown Goddess is moving in wavelike fashion, all thrust sideways in the same direction. Her dance resembles the countless waves of a mighty sea that the wind is driving in one direction. Then the direction of movement is suddenly reversed, as if the wind's direction were reversed. These reversals follow one after the other, accompanied by the roaring of a thousand oceans.*

3   *After my attention has dwelt on this for a while, I am surprised to realize that at certain moments her magnificent female form is temporarily assuming certain masculine features. In those moments I see in the Goddess the clearly contoured musculature such as one can admire in top athletes.*

4   *I have only just become familiar with the language of her dancing body when my eyes are drawn to the figure that she is holding in her left hand. Naturally, I immediately think it will be the Christ Child whom the Virgin Mary holds in her arms. But looking more closely, I see that the figure is put together from the forms of two boys, who complement each other: the one is innocent and happy, the other burdened with a heavy cross.*

5   *Afterwards, my attention shifts to the powerful woman's face. It is in a state of continuous change. The change always begins with masklike facial traits that have the lofty cosmic quality that is seen in the images of the Goddesses of ancient cultures. It is the visage of the All-Embracing that relates to the beautiful as well as to the ugly.*

6   *After this always follows a second phase in which her facial traits become ever more human. They gain individuality and are deeply penetrated by the power of love. The whole looks as if the humanization of the Goddess is being gradually completed before my eyes.*

7   *Now back to the dark brown waves of the dancing muscles. I suddenly notice that there is something amiss in the muscles of the thigh. They are always behind in their movement, as if they are not keeping up with the change in wave-direction. Now I am shown something remarkable. Every time there is a change of direction, the middle parts of the Goddess' thighs become stiff like two columns or pipes.*

8   *Afterward, still dreaming, I realize that the revelation of the divine maiden is dancing not only for me, but also is prepared as a mighty gift for humanity. I am so delighted that, welling up from the depths of my heart, the cry rings out, "Mother!" The voice of devotion and gratitude is so strong that I tear myself awake from sleep.*

(Madrid, Spain, November 8, 2002)

We should notice that the dreamer is wandering on a plane from which he is unable to perceive what is happening on the "world stage." When he raises his eyes to the higher plane, he can see the giant Goddess dancing. Symbolically this means that right now, on a higher plane of being, a fate-filled revelation is unfolding of which we humans, our attention fixated on our everyday level of existence, have no inkling. Thus, in the further course of the dream, the dreamer serves as a witness who perceives what is happening on the next highest level of existence and transmits it to his fellow humans.

We can also understand the dream message to mean that we humans are called to direct our attention to a higher plane to participate in the revelation that is manifesting there. What kind of revelation it is, the first dream image indicates through various symbols.

First, it is not about the appearance of a God, but about the dance of a Goddess. The Goddess, as complementary to the figure of the God, represents the feminine aspect of the divine, the so-called cyclic principle. Put symbolically, the creative ideas of the divine couple are implemented in a variety of life forms. Through the dance of the Goddess the abstract ideas come to appear in living reality.

The relationship to manifested reality which distinguishes the world creations of the Goddess is exemplified by the lovely presence of the "giantess." The dreamer is quite shaken how close and at the same time how immense is the living presence of the Goddess appearing before him. Her complete nakedness is a basic symbol that shows the origin of life, and the red-brown color of her body is reminiscent of the earth's fruitful surface.

The second dream image informs us that the Goddess' impressive dance is not just a tribute to the motions of her individual body but is dedicated to the general dance of life in us and around us. To

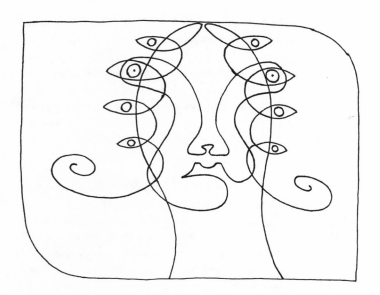

5. The change begins with mask-like facial traits that have the lofty cosmic quality that is seen in the images of the Goddesses of ancient cultures.

6. After this, there always follows a second phase in which her facial traits become ever more human.

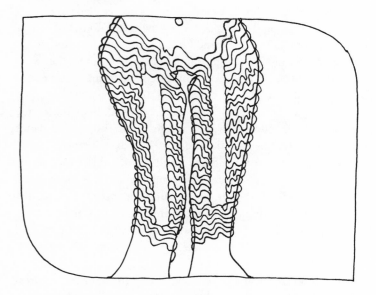

7. Every time there is a change of direction, the middle parts of the Goddess' thighs become stiff like two columns or pipes.

8. I am so delighted and carried away that, welling up from the depths of my heart, the cry rings out, "Mother!"

exemplify this, the dreamer's attention is drawn from the individual body of the Goddess to the roar of the ocean waves. This means that the dance of the Goddess is identical to the dance of the life force through which the fabric of creation is continually enlivened.

The recurring reversals in the direction of the dance also remind us of the life-giving motions of the vital forces that are regularly polarized following the Yin/Yang (left/right) principle.

The first two dream images are there to introduce the being of the messenger correctly and sweep away any possible false impressions. The images that follow convey various messages that establish the feminine point of view of the divine in today's era of cosmic change. They point to complete innovations of which we humans have scarcely any inkling.

First, they affirm the end of the separation between the principles of God and Goddess. We are approaching an era in which the divine feminine includes her masculine complement. But there will be no new division of "world rule" between God and Goddess. As presented in the dream image, there will be a mutual interpenetration of both principles that enables the Goddess simultaneously to be God—which will also be true in reverse.

The next message to affirm the epoch of change concerns the archetypal image of the divine child. It is characteristic that the dreamer immediately thinks of the Virgin Mary with the Christ Child when he sees a being in the Goddess' hand. The message is obviously targeted to correct this misapprehension.

In the first place, the supposed child is no bigger than the pomegranate which, in classical representations of the Goddess, was often held in her hand as a symbol of unlimited fruitfulness. Now the symbol of fruitfulness is developed further into the symbol of the divine child—without exceeding the size of a pomegranate. Translated from the language of symbols, it means that the life-giving role of the Goddess is about to take on a new character. Her creative dance was not only about the wavelike vitalization of the universe, but also about a new kind of spiritual leadership.

We first get an insight into the kind of spiritual leadership that is involved when the dreamer takes a closer look. He sees that the supposed Christ Child is put together from the figures of two boys who together make up the form of the pomegranate. One child is pure and perfect, the other burdened with a cross.

In Christian iconography the representation of two Jesus boys with the same sort of role division does in fact occur. One example is the high altar of the cathedral of Constance in southern Germany. Above, on the right side of the high altar is the figure of Mary with the Jesus child in the act of blessing; on the other side, Joseph the father of Jesus, holds an identical Jesus child, but one burdened with a cross. One can see the first as a symbolic representation of the human being's perfect soul; the other as a symbol of the human being's autonomous "I" that must wrestle with the challenges of life.

There is something quite new in the revelation of the Goddess described above. This time, the child of perfection and the child of human fate are bound to each other interactively, so that together they take on the form of a pomegranate. Does this mean that the confusing separation of the human "I" from the perfection of its own spiritual soul essence is in the process of resolution? That would also lift the danger to which modern human beings regularly fall victim, of being led astray by their own separated "I," the so-called "Ego." The meaning of this aspect of the message is that the Ego will be integrated into the cosmic Wholeness through its renewed interaction with the individual's spiritual soul. Will this be the gift that the dancing Goddess brings to humanity?

The third message of this dream concerns the emergent individuality of the Goddess. Can it be that, after experiencing God becoming human through the incarnation of Jesus Christ, we have yet to experience the humanized Goddess? Some such thought may have come to the dreamer as he watched the changes in the facial features of the dark maiden. While her cosmic sublimity is being continually transcended and human traits are flowing in, her presence is becoming clearer, more loving and more tangible.

Comparing the development of human civilization over the last two hundred years, one could speak of a secularization of the divine presence on earth. But people worldwide are beginning to put the simple life in the foreground, separating themselves from religious patterns that exclude the democratic extension of holiness for an exclusive concentration on the presence of God.

Without question, there are extremist movements interwoven that deny the existence of holiness and acknowledge either exclusive rationalism or materialism. Despite excesses of this sort, one can recognize the intention of the Goddess from Madrid in the progressive incorporation of the sacred in daily life. She has conceived changing her lofty cosmic facial traits and thereby revealing herself as being inherent in all the different life forms, both close to nature and artificial.

There is yet a fourth message from the dark-brown Goddess. It is a direct reference to the processes of the present earth change. It happens on the plane where the life forces circulate. To illustrate this visually, the dreamer's gaze is led back to the wavelike movements on the surface of the Goddess' body—the earth's body. They are described as resembling the movements of powerful waves, which by persistently changing their direction, symbolize the distribution of the archetypal power of life through the living realms on the earth's surface.

In this connection, the dreamer suddenly notices there is something amiss that is more than the confusion arising from the reversal of the waves' direction. That can be considered a symbol of the current earth changes: the temperature of the planetary body is rising, the glaciers are melting, weather patterns are confused, people are encountering unsuspected physical problems…. As in the dance of the Goddess from Madrid, the earth changes are not a static problem but a rhythmically recurring chaotic disarray affecting the cycles of life.

However, this fourth message is not merely confirmation of the earth change. That has already been sufficiently publicized by a worldwide network of scientists who in 2008 were awarded a Nobel Prize for establishing its reality. In relation to the earth changes, the red-brown Mother of Life wanted to show us something specific, symbolized by the temporary transformation of her thighs into two pipes or columns.

To describe the symbol in another way, amidst the chaos of changes (or let us say, the interference created by opposing wave motions), zones of calm that could be called fields of peace are continually arising. They occur as if taking precedence over the rough seas of constant change, although they are interwoven with everyday reality. Extending from these fields is the cosmic knowledge and wisdom that enables all earth's living beings to continue to surmount the complicated hurdles of the constant changes.

To put this another way, the Goddess has promised, amidst the confusion of the constant and often painful planetary and personal changes that affect us humans, to enable those who are in accord with the cosmic plan for earth change to live "normally." She will be able to perform her service to fellow humans and other beings even when round about us the mountains crack apart. A wonderful gift!

1. *A black bird takes advantage of my distraction and steals my cap. Now I see the bird clearly. It is a raven.*

2. *The raven is sitting on the highest branch of a nearby tree. An owl is sitting nearby. My black cap is hanging on the furthest tip of the same branch.*

Dream 42: The Dark Aspect of God

1 *I am walking with my family in the mountains. There is a sudden moment of confusion. A black bird takes advantage of my distraction and steals my cap. Now I see the bird clearly. It is a raven.*

2 *The raven is sitting on the highest branch of a nearby tree. An owl is sitting nearby. My black cap is hanging on the furthest tip of the same branch. I am furious that my cap is hanging so high that I cannot reach it.*

3 *I immediately start looking for suitable stones to throw at my cap to bring it back down. After a short while I see to my horror that it is not the cap that I am pelting, but the owl's head. Just then, I strike the back of its head, and a few downy feathers fall to the ground. The owl peers at me with a baleful look.*

4 *The raven turns to the owl and speaks a sentence in human language so that I too can understand. However, because of its foreign sounding dialect, I can only pick out one word. But certainly, something was said about a "Negro."**

(Twann am Bieler See, Switzerland, September 25, 2003)

First, the language of symbols affirms that the theme of this dream concerns the highest level of existence, the divine plane of being. The two birds sit on the highest branch of the tree. Add to this the theft of the dreamer's cap, which covers the highest level of the human body. Afterwards, one can see, sitting on the highest branch of the tree of life, an amusing but archetypally charming trinity, the owl, the pitch-black raven and the cap.

As a bird of the night, the owl represents, in the classical language of the Goddess, her so-called "black" aspect. This has to do with the process of death, and the processes of regeneration and rebirth that follow it, so she is also called "the Goddess of Transformation."

In the mythology of northern peoples, the raven is looked upon as a representative of God. The specific role of this aspect of God is made obvious through the dream, in which it is the raven that takes advantage of the moment of confusion to steal the cap.

---

*Note. The rendering "Negro" is the closest to how the word sounded in the dream. Brought up in Slovenia, the author was insulated from the word's negative connotations, and it is presented here without further comment. Ed.

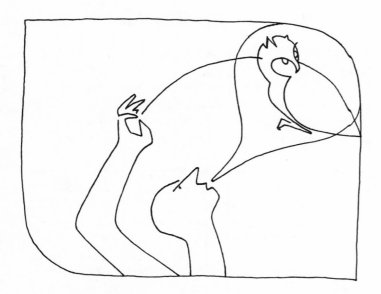

3. *After a short while I see to my horror that it is not the cap that I am pelting, but the owl's head.*

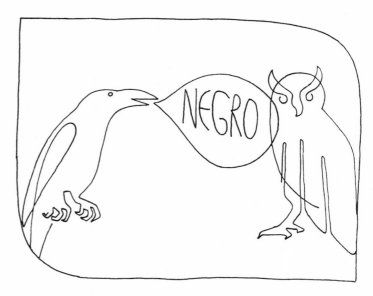

4. *The raven turns to the owl and speaks a sentence in human language so that I too can understand it.*

(See previous note for the rendering of "Negro." Ed.)

We are seeing here a specific role for God as the humorous challenger who tests people in their unclear moments. Such an attempt is made regularly, and accelerates human evolution in often harsh and always unexpectedly challenging ways.

The black raven, the black Goddess and the dreamer's black cap: what does this trinity have to tell us? Can it have to do with a new configuration of the relationship between humans and the feminine and masculine aspects of the Godhead?

That the dreamer's cap is stolen and carried away to the tree's highest branch where the representatives of the Goddess are sitting is a strong indication that humanity's attention is now to be directed to the new relationship between human beings and the Godhead. One can well imagine that the epoch of change, with its fundamental upheavals, demands a reordering of our relationship with the heavenly "Olympus."

If one considers the human relationship to the divine through the symbol of the raven, it confirms that the "black" aspect of God has absolutely no place in the dreamer's consciousness. Instead of giving heightened attention to the stealing of the cap, he is seized with rage. He should have told himself, "If God is treating me so maliciously, it means that the time is ripe for me to introduce some fundamental changes into my life."

The wanton, saucy, malicious, mischievous, foolish, "onto every dodge" viewpoint of God that is symbolized by the raven in our dream story is habitually equated with the concept of the wicked devil and thus stamped as an evil power. His refined, creative role in the evolution of the world, and also in relation to the evolution of the *free individual*, goes unrecognized.

The dreamer's unconscious behavior in the third image is another key to better understand the current changes in the relationship between humanity and the Godhead. He clearly intends to strike the cap so that it falls to the ground, and he really does not notice that his stones are actually hitting the back of the owl's head. In this case we are obviously dealing with a reversed relationship to some specific aspect of the Goddess.

As already mentioned, the owl is identified with the transformational aspect of the Goddess. Because it is a night bird, the owl symbolizes the quality of wisdom as opposed to intellectual knowledge, which is assigned to the bright light of day. In our case, the aspect of the owl as a "bird of prey" plays an important role, for it marks the "black Goddess" as the Ruler of Death.

The dreamer's stone hits the back of the bird's head, which symbolizes the relationship to the World Beyond. This is clearly an appeal to the intellect of modern human beings to reverse their ignorance of the divine couple's transformational aspect and develop a new consideration of the relationship. We have entered an age of deeply fundamental changes, in which the destruction of old patterns and world structures, and the constant proximity of resultant death, play a decisive role in bringing forth the new configuration of our blue planet. How could we bear up under such a harsh and daily challenge if we did not perceive it in the mirror of divine grace and divine wisdom?

In addition to our joy in the light-filled and creative viewpoints of the divine, we need to develop a loving acceptance of the dark aspect of the divine pair. The revival of interest in the Black Goddess is insufficient if "the black aspect of God"—symbolized by the raven in the dream—is thereby forgotten.

At the end of the dream, the representatives of God refer to the human as a "negro," that is to say, as a black person. This can denote the Godhead's appeal to humankind to consciously follow the invitation to work actively and cooperatively with the process of earth transformation, and also to cherish their own transformational process. Humanity's place on the highest bough of the Tree of Life will once more be freely bestowed.

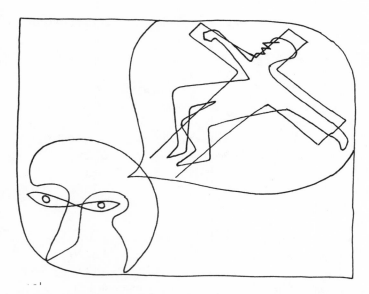

1. *I am given the reasons for my crucifixion, but, in the context of these modern times, I reject them as absurd.*

2. *In my direst need, I think of getting my intellectual colleagues to protect me, but have little hope of it.*

DREAM 43: CHANGE IS NOT TO BE AVOIDED

1 *I am informed that in a week's time I am to be crucified—and with me, one of my friends called Peter. I cannot believe that this can possibly be true. I am given the reasons for my crucifixion, but, in the context of these modern times, I reject them as absurd.*

2 *In my direst need, I think of getting my intellectual colleagues to protect me, but have little hope of it. It is obvious that there is no realistic way to escape crucifixion. I feel the threat to be absolutely real, although completely irrational.*

(Sempas, Slovenia, July 11, 2007)

THE DREAMER'S VIOLENT REACTION to the news, which sounds too absurd to be believed, that he is to be crucified in a week's time, indicates that within it a message is hidden. In this situation, the association with the crucifixion of Jesus Christ is made to help hide the unpleasant news and in a certain way moderate its message.

However, the association with the crucifixion of Christ only increases the drama of the message, because it also mentions Peter, who, according to tradition, was crucified as a disciple of Christ.

The message sounds so absurd because today—at least in the Western world—people are usually protected from such excruciating methods of torture by the United Nations Declaration of Human Rights.

But it is possible that the thrust of the dream's message is correct. Even if the intellect thinks it is best protected from the totality of change as we know it through the crucifixion and subsequent resurrection of Jesus Christ, such may still come upon humanity in a specific, future way. We find ourselves in a whirlpool of cosmic change, which will certainly affect much more than the surface of existence!

To understand the crucifixion as a symbol, one should see it in the context of the whole process that led Jesus of Nazareth from death on the cross to his revival—what is called his resurrection. In the Gospels where this process is described, it is made clear that it is a three-phase process that lasts for three days. Its pattern is laid down so precisely that one could speak of it as a pattern of the initiation process.

The first phase is described as Jesus' death through crucifixion, the second through his lying in the grave and the third through the resurrection of Christ. Resurrection would mean that the dead man, who had already lain in the grave for one day and two nights, on the third day showed himself alive to his beloved Mary of Magdala and later also to his disciples—during the course of which his body, according to witnesses, vanished from the grave.

Apart from the Gospels' reports, there is unfortunately no proof to document this process as historical fact. In the absence of this proof, one can still see the process as a model event that presents a path of deep change that leads through the nearness of death. The purpose of such an initiation process would be for human beings to reach a new plane of being. One could speak of a quantum leap in human evolution. Jesus Christ's original passage through this process of change can be seen as similar to a pathfinder scouting the quantum leap.

Without a doubt, the near approach of death in the passage described is the reason why the dreamer fights tooth and nail to defend himself against the coming crucifixion. He has obviously lived under the illusion that the epochal change can be so conducted that we humans do not have to pass through a death experience. The date of the dream, July 11, 2007, was obviously chosen for its association with September 11, 2001 to dismiss this illusion. In this connection, it is as well to remark that in the dream the progress through the death experience did not lie in a far future but quite the opposite. The single week, which is all that separated the dreamer from the proposed completion of the crucifixion on July 18, 2007, can be interpreted as an announcement that the walk through the shadow of death will come to pass in the near future.

The second part of the dream's message warns against the wrong handling of the unveiled secret. The dreamer concentrates exclusively on the crucifixion and is nearly hysterical looking for ways to avoid it. The hope is mentioned of escaping the death experience by a specific intellectual manipulation. This raises the question, can the massed intellectual power of humanity reveal some way to flee the dreaded experience? The dreamer himself senses that this is an empty hope.

Does the dream's message, which has put the path through the death experience in the context of crucifixion, indicate that when it comes to this sort of event within the framework of earth transformation, it would not be a matter of final death? The death experience is surely only the first step in a transformational process that is known to us in the West from the evangelists' reports. The death experience in this case is "only" a precondition for the human being, as already mentioned, to complete a quantum leap that enables arrival on a new plane of being.

One is again referred back to the reports of the four evangelists to get an idea of what the quantum leap of resurrection would bring about for human beings. In the first place, it was reported that after the quantum leap Jesus could emerge in any place he wanted. His appearance alongside two of his disciples on the road to Emmaus is well known. Another report describes how he entered the room where his disciples are gathered, through a closed door. It would appear that his body has become more subtle through the quantum leap of resurrection, so that the usual limitations of space and time are lifted.

On the other hand, he has several times demonstrated that despite this absence of limitations, he is present on the material plane of being. For example, he has asked for food and eaten a fish. He has also allowed his disciple Thomas to touch his wounds. The process of crucifixion and resurrection has opened a path to the new, integral human being who can exist simultaneously on different planes of being. A wonderful hope!

1. *Quite unexpectedly, a tall figure appears before me. I intuitively identify it as the figure of Pan, the classical Greek God of Nature.*

2. *Silver rays are shooting out from Pan's stigmata to touch specific points on my own body.*

Dream 44: "The Green Christ"

1 *Quite unexpectedly, a tall figure appears before me, which has emerged from the surrounding forest. I intuitively identify it as the figure of Pan, the classical Greek God of Nature. When he raises his mighty hands, I can clearly see wounds on his hands and feet and right side, which are the stigmata originating in the crucifixion of Christ.*

2 *But look! Silver rays are shooting out from Pan's stigmata to touch specific points on my own body. They are precisely the same spots that on Pan's body identify the stigmata originating in the crucifixion of Christ. I am deeply shaken.*

(Saarland, Germany, May 27, 2000)

EXCEPTIONALLY, WE HAVE HERE no night-time dream but a vision illumined before the witness by the bright light of day.

It should first be made clear that the appearance of Pan in a Saarland forest is not to be seen as a revival of the historical symbol of Pan. This appearance was the cause of a deep feeling of shock that the witness experienced. It was not a symbolic reference to the God Pan of Greek mythology. The objective of associating the vision with the classical Pan was rather to let the witness understand that this concerned the spiritual being that ensouls the whole world of nature, just as the Greeks imagined Pan.

The dream's message is built on the amazing coupling of the Spirit of Nature with the Spirit of the Universe—given that Western tradition understands Christ as the Spirit of the Universe. In the vision, the Spirit of Nature bears the stigmata of the Universal Spirit. What does that mean?

How would it be if the vision's statement were turned around? It would mean that the Spirit of the Universe temporarily revealed himself to humanity through the Spirit of Nature. Perhaps the witness did not really see Pan, and it was more an unusual vision of Christ, bringing with it a specific message. To be able to transmit this message to us, the so-called Son of God assumed the form of Pan.

What would it mean if the Son of God, as the new Spirit of the Universe, has assumed the form of Pan?

Does it mean perhaps that Christ, to dissolve the rigid thought-forms that men have projected onto him over the last two thousand years, has chosen a completely different and unexpected way to reveal himself again to humankind?

The stigmata on Pan's body would mean that the Son of God has become identical with the Spirit of Nature, and thus has become a partner of the earth. What could be the meaning of such a partnership? It could be that he is to be the driving force behind earth change. The cosmic plan that is ascribed to Christ, to take humanity farther along the path of evolution, can be joined seamlessly to the plan of the Earth Soul (Gaia) to open new horizons for earth evolution. In this, the transformed, completely awakened human being would have a decisive role to play.

The essential character of the human role in the process of earth change, or more precisely its sacred meaning, is indicated by the silver rays that, proceeding out of the stigmata of Pan, touch the corresponding parts of the witness' body. This can be interpreted to mean that human beings are being challenged to develop specific spiritual-soul qualities that let them ascend to becoming a third partner in the epochal transformational process. This ascent is obviously a matter of spiritual-soul qualities that lie beyond the linear intellect. They are bound up with the ability to overcome the bond to the one-dimensional plane of being and approach the cosmic dimension of the human being.

Exercises on the Theme "The Rediscovery of Holiness"

An exercise to touch into the dimension of the Cosmic Heart

The exercise follows the directions in Dream 40 described above. The positioning of the skull of Christ described in the dream traces out the imaginative path to your own cosmic heart aspect.

> *You should first fix your eyes to the front on an imaginary point that is infinitely far away. In this way a horizontal axis comes into being.*
> *Next, you should slowly move the axis diagonally upward about 45 degrees. This is the angle indicated by the position of the skull in the dream.*
> *Then you should extend the axis into the back space diagonally downward until it reaches the horizontal axis that runs through your own heart center.*
> *There, where the two axes intersect is the focus point of the cosmic heart. You should be present there with the totality of your Being.*
> *Finally, you should bring the quality of the cosmic heart forward to awaken your own heart center to the fullness of its power and tenderness.*

The Nine Commandments of the Goddess

When I was writing the book about the new understanding of the feminine principle and the Goddess (*The Daughter of Gaia*), I was unexpectedly given the Nine "Commandments" of the Goddess as an opposite pole to the Ten Commandments of God. They may help one attune to the cosmic plan of Change. They are consciously written as if the Goddess were speaking directly to her daughter or son. The numbers relate to the three aspects of the cyclical Goddess principle (3 x 3).

I

> *Away with Guilt Feelings! — Know that your being is perfect. Hold fast to an all-embracing trust in the fairness of life.*
> *Restore your Emotional Sensitivity! — It is your birthright to be able to perceive the whole broad span of creation. Open the diversity of your physical and subtle senses.*
> *Follow the Cyclic Nature of your Being! — Be whole! Be creative! Be ready for Change!*

II

> *Cherish the Freedom of your Soul! — Listen to the instructions of your heart! Open yourself to the sound of your inner voice!*
> *Recognize the Gift of your Body! — Your body is the expression of all the beings of earth! Your body is a house of joy! Talk with your body!*
> *Ask for what you Need! — Allow the fullness of life to give you gifts! Give more to others!*

III

> *Revere! — See the fragrance of Paradise, the changing presence of the Goddess everywhere!*
> *Bury your Corpses! — Bid farewell to the old patterns, let go!*
> *Keep Silent before the Indescribable! — Be in awe of that which transcends intellect! Pure Being!*

An exercise to comprehend and reproduce the process of resurrection

The three-step process that was presented above in the commentary to Dream 43, which leads through a death-like experience, change, and resurrection, to a new plane of being, can also be relived meditatively to support one's own transformational process.

> - *You should first imagine that your spinal column is extended upward so that it represents part of a giant circle that runs behind your back.*
> - *The circle is so all-embracing that at the farthest point behind your back, it touches the dimension of infinity.*
> - *Imagine that you leave your body and move along this circle—your spine, so to speak—and you slide along its track.*
> - *At the circle's farthest point (the point of infinity and eternity) you are upside down.*
> - *You go farther on your way till (coming upward from below) you once again reach your own body.*
> - *How does the process of resurrection feel to you now when you slowly slide once again into your own body?*
> - *As an expression of gratitude you should share your experience emotionally with your environment.*

An exercise to follow the inspiration of the five stigmata of Christ

The five stigmata of Christ that Pan exhibited in Dream 44 can also be seen as the coordinates of the holistic person, as in the following exercise:

> - *You should reflect on the vertical line that runs through your body and joins the point of infinity beneath your feet with the point of infinity above your head.*
> - *Not forgetting the vertical line, you should now imaginatively create the horizontal line, which joins the point of infinity behind your back with the point of infinity in front of you.*
> - *After you have set up this cosmic cross, you should try to sense and precisely localize within you the intersection of the two axes (which symbolizes the fifth stigmata).*
> - *After this, you should observe attentively what kinds of forgotten potential spring up within your multidimensional body.*
> - *These should be sensed and integrated into your own wholeness.*
> - *Allow them to express themselves in the world.*

Chapter 7

CHANGE ON THE PERSONAL PLANE

THE QUESTION, which always comes up when I give lectures on earth change, is what can each of us do to support it?

My personal attitude to this question has changed substantially over the last twelve years. I could really speak of two phases.

In the early phase, after the processes of earth change had been brought to my attention in 1997, I was convinced that one should develop tools to support the individual aspects of earth change. Thus I began to develop meditations and bodily exercises through which the individual can move in resonance with the various processes of earth transformation. My personal experiences and dreams have helped me identify the various processes. The places where I was geomantically active at the time have inspired me to discover corresponding bodily movements.

As an example, I would like to present the "Manhattan Exercise." It came into being on a day in 1999 when I traveled on the subway underneath Manhattan while preparing for a workshop on the geomantic systems of Central Park in New York. During the journey I put the following question to the consciousness of the place, how was it possible for the island of Manhattan to carry the extremely thick and top-heavy urban structure of New York and still maintain its high life potency, and so remain highly creative culturally? In answer, I received a gesture in my consciousness that I would have dearly liked to carry out on the spot, but the prevailing code of behavior in public places prevented me.

In the "Manhattan Exercise," your connection with the earth's core is picked up and your own bodily axis extended upward as far as the "third eye." Your hands meanwhile are held in the usual attitude of prayer, first directed downward to the earth's center, then to the level of your heart and finally to heaven. When they reach the third eye level, stretch them out to left and right horizontally as if you would broaden the space inside your head. This gesture should be repeated a few times.

Regarding the earth change, this exercise supports the restoration of the relationship between the thought-sphere of humankind and the core of the Earth Soul. The revivification of this relationship has a twofold meaning for the transformational process. First, it should align human thought paths with the plans of the Earth Soul. Second, it will further the partnership between humankind and the earth.

In this way a cycle of "holographic exercises" comes into being. This can be considered a cosmogram of the body. I was inspired to develop a kind of yoga for the epoch of change. The "holographic" concept means that through the specified movements performed by one's own body in the microcosmic framework, the processes of the planetary body in the macrocosm can be understood and supported. This concerns not only cosmograms but also specific meditative exercises that can operate as cosmograms.[1]

In the later phase, there was a shift in the focus of my activity in regard to earth change.

After a few years I became aware that planet Earth was following a cosmic cycle in regard to its changes and was supported therein by the intelligence of the spiritual world, and so was in no need of any special assistance from individual humans or human groups.

In fact, there is a need for something different so that earth change can be completed in a comprehensive and relatively harmless way. This is an unconditional demand: every individual human being shall reproduce the earth change within his or her own microcosm. My intuition further tells me that certain aspects of the earth change will not come about unless they are first completed within all of us individual men and women.

The truth, as I perceive it, is that Earth has offered humankind the possibility of incarnating here in order that she herself can change through us. How can one explain something like that?

We were formed as incarnate human beings in the image of multidimensional earth. Our body is a material organism and is provided with power centers and power pathways, just like every landscape and indeed like the body of earth's surface. The emotional dimension, as we know it among ourselves, is found in the earth's organism in the form of countless elemental beings that embody the consciousness of Earth.

Seen from our side, it looks as though we humans have incarnated on earth, but seen from Gaia's viewpoint, she has found in humans the possibility of manifesting herself on a new plane of being.

This kind of synergy between humans and earth has made it possible for the Earth Soul to actualize certain aspects of her evolution through us humans. Gaia could develop her creation further through our intellect and hands. For example, let us bring to mind the kinds of temples we have built from her stone, the wonderful cultural objects shaped from her ores, the fruitful orchards we have developed, and so forth.

Now we ask, have we reached a point in her epochal transformation where there must be a shift in the focus of cooperation between earth and humans? On the one hand, human beings have developed technologies that serve only our own needs and are useless for the further evolution of the earthly cosmos—think of "high tech" products, genetically manipulated plants, atomic power technology, and so forth.

On the other hand, there exists, as we have said, the possibility that humankind could represent a kind of womb in which certain aspects of the renewed earth cosmos could be developed. For this, the primary requirement is the evolution of specific aspects of consciousness and of our ability to actively embody the quality of love in its various aspects.

However, it is impossible for human beings to actualize this new role within the earth cosmos as long as we continue to grope around in our own egocentricity; as long as we remain blanketed in various alien thought patterns; as long as we do not feel ourselves bound to a multidimensional earth cosmos.

To overcome these obstacles, individual processes are released within the framework of earth change, which will demand that every one of us bind with our own core being and do battle with the alien, externalized patterns in our psyches: a tedious task that none of us can escape! The earth change is indirectly supported when we tackle the daily tasks of personal change.

A further way of contributing to successful earth and human change consists in our practicing the release of our absolute attachment to the existing world structure and the processes that run within it; say goodbye to all that! It is best to cultivate a neutral standpoint in which one acknowledges that cooperation with the dissolving world is still unavoidable, but one feels inwardly free from the obligations that are demanded by the old world system.

When more and more human beings withdraw their attention from the old world structure and do not let themselves be led astray by its magnetic attraction, there arises a spiritual-energetic free space through which Earth can manifest the new dimension of Being. This new integral space will thereby become more and more the dominant reality.

There is a further possible way to ensure that one is continuously active in promoting a change in one's personal image of the world. This entails learning to know the earth anew as a multilayered and intelligent being that shares with us humans the joy of life and a cosmic task. To be able to develop the new and deeper relationship with Gaia, one needs to work on reawakening one's own sensitivity, and parallel with that, to grapple with the bases of modern geomancy. It is not a question of absorbing further esoteric knowledge, but rather of taking in hand the tools of consciousness through which one can make essential changes in one's idea of the world.

The conscious change of one's image of the world is insufficient. First, there is also the need to develop the sense of the various forms of existence and beings of the earthly cosmos. Only when these forms can be mutually perceived will communication be possible between us humans and the other beings of the multidimensional earth.[2]

Second, one should bear in mind that the new reality that is coming into being through earth change is no longer a purely physical reality. Thus, one will feel oneself completely lost in it—blind, so to speak—as long as one's perception is exclusively bound to the physical sense organs. It is expected that one will be able to see and experience the new reality-space only through a combination of physical and supersensory perception.

This expectation gives the above-mentioned holographic exercises and imaginations a new reason for existence. They have been formed not only to support the processes of earth change, but even more to help us humans open up to the change processes in us and around us, and to understand and reproduce them internally. These efforts will indirectly support the planetary change processes—as suggested above.

1. The early holographic exercises were published in *Earth Changes, Human Destiny*. Many are to be found in *Touching The Breath of Gaia* and some in *The Daughter of Gaia*, all published by Findhorn Press.
2. For the theory and practices on the theme of perception, see *Sacred Geography* (Lindisfarne Books).

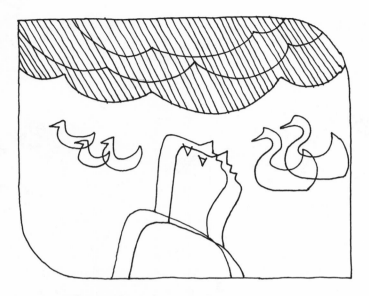

1. I am walking with my friend along the shore of a lake, watching ducks and swans as they bob among the waves. Suddenly I see that the sky is growing dark and heavy.

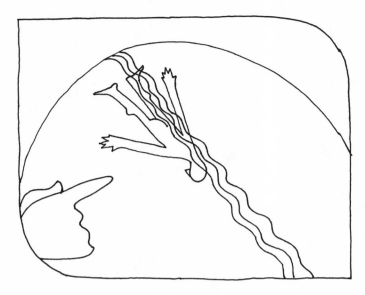

2. In the next moment I am horrorstruck by the sight of a young man lying unconscious on the ground. The ice-cold water is flowing over his left side so that he is likely to freeze.

3. We see a group of women walking about; they are making a certain gesture in front of their bodies. We cannot precisely see what sort of a gesture they are making.

4. She lifts her dress high over her shoulders and then, with one deft movement, she makes the gesture that we could not recognize when it was made in the group.

Dream 45: Grounding the Heart

1   *I am walking with my friend along the shore of a lake, watching ducks and swans as they bob among the waves. Suddenly I see that the sky is growing dark and heavy. A sudden squall strikes the lake with the forewarning of a mighty storm.*

2   *I am led below the earth's surface into an abyss which is illuminated from above by a flood of golden light. The space is filled with the merry babble of a gushing spring. In the next moment I am horrorstruck by the sight of a young man lying unconscious on the ground. The ice-cold water is flowing over his left side so that he is likely to freeze. I lift him up, press him to my breast and cry out, "Where are his parents—he must get help at once."*

3   *My friend and I are in a dark hiding place, watching what is happening in an adjoining, brightly lit room. We see a group of women walking about; they are making a gesture in front of their bodies. We cannot clearly see what sort of a gesture they are making because they are busying themselves with small devotional objects.*

4   *While they are leaving the room, a young woman turns around and runs to the entrance of our hiding place. Without noticing our presence, she lifts her dress high over her shoulders and stands naked before us in all her beauty. Then, with one deft movement, she makes the gesture that we could not recognize when it was made in the group. She slides her index finger upward from her abdomen to her midsection between her breasts. Then she lets her tunic fall back again and runs after the group.*

(Geneva, Switzerland February 1, 1981)

ALTHOUGH THE DREAM HAPPENED 17 years earlier, before the dreamer encountered his first direct experiences of the earth change processes, it is connected to this book by its basic message, which prepared the dreamer for the approaching changes.

The first dream image can be seen as a deadly serious admonition directed to the population of earth; an admonition that makes no distinction between the supposedly highly spiritually evolved people and those wrapped up in their daily lives—the first symbolized by swans and the others by ducks. It feels as if we are all standing in front of a holistic, world-embracing change, the premonition of which begins to fill the atmosphere with a speed requiring a direct decision.

The second dream image makes clear why the first is so urgently dramatic. The abyssal space in which the dreamer has arrived may be interpreted as the womb of earth which is the source of all life on the material plane of being. In practice, it is a vital-energetic organism with power centers and pathways that are interwoven in the material plane of the landscape. The life of the earth's surface with all its beings—and humans too—is maintained and their evolution furthered through this power organism. How comes it then that in the second dream image the young man is nearly frozen to death by the same power? Does the pure spring not encourage life? Yes, it does encourage life, but, as a part of earth's transformation, its future strength will be greatly increased. This approaching, fateful change is symbolized by the golden light that streams into the abyssal space.

If one takes the golden light to be a symbol of the cosmic transformational impulse that has reached earth in our epoch, one can view the heightened power of the wellspring of life as the earth organism's reaction. Spurred on by the cosmic impulse, earth has begun to increase the intensity of her surface power organism. This affects, for example, the activation of the sources of archetypal power, of which Dreams 24 and 25 were witnesses. The general potency of the life-power organism can be enormously increased by their input, which serves to accelerate earth's self-healing process.

And what about modern humanity, represented by the youth who lies half frozen in the water of the potentized life power?

For the most part, modern humanity spends its time walled in its intellectual consciousness, separated from the natural cycles of life and from the core of its inner soul. In this state of increasing alienation, it is less and less able to withstand the potentized life force of the earth organism. The danger threatens that humanity will be destroyed not by any external crisis, but by its own state of inner separation; a tragedy brought about by the increased life force and amplitude of its earthly environment.

The third image confirms that certain groups of people are already actively working to bridge this dangerous inner separation. One can see them as representatives of the countless alternative movements of today. The dreamer has recognized them as such by their bright, Eastern-looking clothing. Through their many and various outlooks on the world and spiritual techniques, they are working to reconnect humanity with its divine essence.

Nonetheless, because their actions appear somehow unclear, the dream makes it plain that the spiritual input of these groups lacks something essential. This obviously has to do with this moment of the epochal transformation of the earth.

Therefore in the fourth image, the divinely translucent maiden herself appears to show the dreamer, with the help of her bodily gesture, what is so urgently needed but is nonetheless lacking. The gesture, which she carries out with her index finger tracing an arc from her abdomen up to the heart region, can be interpreted in different ways.

In the first place, it is obvious that this is a demand that the earthly aspect of human beings should be joined to the heart impulse. But what exactly is meant by the "earthly aspect of human beings" if one wants to avoid the materialistic debasement of the concept?

The earthly aspect of human beings means their participation in the sphere of the elemental world, which is a watery-energetic world. The abyss with the dancing spring water in the second dream image is an exact representation of this fairy world in which human beings take part—without, in the case of modern humans, being conscious thereof. The abdomen, which centers between the sex organs on one side and on the other is rounded off by the emotional field of the navel, is an image of how the fairy world corresponds to the human form.

The Goddess' gesture is to be seen as a demand that in this era of change human beings immediately bestir themselves to reintegrate the dimension of their being that they have disavowed from their consciousness. However, the gesture shows that it is insufficient to be just mentally conscious of it. To prepare ourselves for the challenges of the approaching transformational changes, the human elemental being must be recognized and lived through the intelligence of our heart.

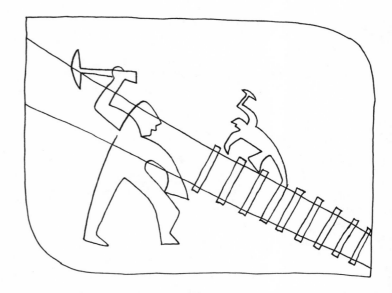

1. *Suddenly, the surprising news arrives that a railway line is to be constructed leading to my lonely house.*

3. *Now the first train arrives and waits a few minutes for possible passengers. Since there are none, it drives away.*

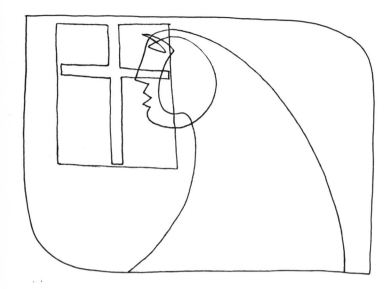

2. *Full of curiosity, I sit at the back kitchen window and look on as the new railway line is made ready.*

DREAM 46: THE COSMIC INVITATION

1   *I am living in a house that was built far from all methods of communication. Suddenly the surprising news arrives that a railway line is to be constructed leading to my lonely house. The track is to end at the rear of my house.*

2   *Full of curiosity, I sit at the back kitchen window and look on as the new railway line is made ready. At the rear of the house the terminal has already been built—a modern station made of glass and steel.*

3   *Now the first train arrives and waits a few minutes for possible passengers. Since there are none, it drives away. I sit behind the kitchen window, feeling sorry that the railway line has been built at great expense and now the train must leave without a single passenger.*

(Rastenberg, Austria July 28, 2001)

IT DOES NOT ENTER the dreamer's mind, squatting behind the back window and grieving that there was not a single passenger, that the train was waiting for him—the only possible passenger! Round about, far and wide, no one else was living.

The dream holds an interesting bundle of symbols that are worth interpreting in the context of the present change.

First, the stopping place is to be built at the back of the house. The back symbolizes the other world. Thus the new railway line is not concerned with any public opportunity, but is directed to stimulate a specific inner purpose. Add to this, the dream scene is established in such a fashion that it is clear that it concerns the spiritual processes of individuals. The perfectly constructed railway station is dedicated to the only possible passenger.

The man squatting behind the old-fashioned kitchen window represents the personality of the average person of our epoch who holds fast to the framework of this age, which in the meantime has fallen into ecological, structural, and economic crises.

The dream portrays the new railway line as irrationally modern—irrational in relation to the place's rural nature. Can one see this contrast as a symbol of a completely new impulse? Can one see it as the symbol of a cosmic invitation to the human personality to abandon the old structures of time and place and open itself to an energy highway that vibrates at a higher potency than what one was used to?

The dream's message may be interpreted in the sense that this age of great transformation presents an unimaginably valuable opportunity to transfer to a new spiritual path and travel toward new horizons of evolution.

At the same time it is regrettable that the majority of people are unready to perceive this unique opportunity. One would rather remain squatting in the state of the old spiritual habits than open oneself up to the new.

It is not sensible to hold fast to old, habitual patterns in a time of change! One needs to pluck up one's courage and stride forward into the unknown without asking whether it is safe to do so.

1. *The auditor has come to audit my accounts. She finds nothing dramatic, only a small mistake in the purchase of a kitchen appliance.*

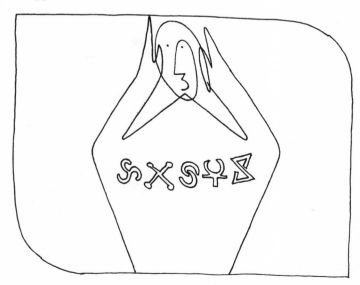

3. *To my horror the sales brochures on my chest begin to change by themselves into a sort of hieroglyph.*

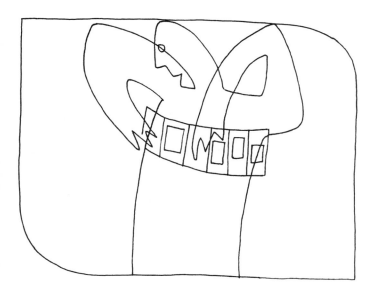

2. *To make the auditor's position look ridiculous, I start sticking sales brochures for various kitchen appliances to my chest.*

Dream 47: Valuable Advice

1 *The auditor has come to audit my accounts. She finds nothing dramatic, only a small mistake in the purchase of a kitchen appliance. I jump up excitedly, declaring that the mistake is not my concern, for it has nothing to do with my artistic work. The auditor remains calm, but is determined to clarify the problem.*

2 *I become angry and without any real reason, begin to scream. To make the auditor's position look ridiculous, I start sticking sales brochures for various kitchen appliances to my chest. With each appliance, I ask excitedly, "Am I something like this?"*

3 *To my horror the sales brochures on my chest begin to change by themselves into a sort of hieroglyph. I can hardly believe my eyes. There are various symbols whose meaning is unknown to me.*

(Srakane vele, Croatia September 2, 1999)

THE DREAM CAN BE UNDERSTOOD as a warning that the meaning of individual occurrences may have altered, because we now find ourselves in a period of intensive change. This epoch of change tends to bring to the surface of life (that is, consciousness) situations that had long ago been thought meaningless and forgotten but may be an important key through which one can tackle fundamental problems that lie in the subconscious and await a solution.

This helps us understand the dreamer's exaggerated reaction to the auditor's harmless request when he was asked to clear up the unimportant problem. A whole dammed-up avalanche of emotional trauma can be set in motion through a meaningless mistake.

The unexpected change of the kitchen appliances into hieroglyphics symbolizes the meaningful content that stands behind the insignificant mistake. Put another way, the wave of change hits the apparently negligible causes, so that those areas of consciousness which represent a serious obstacle to humanity's personal spiritual path are drawn into the transformational process.

The dream's message demands that in this age of transformation we remain more alert than usual. Small discrepancies, which are signaled by certain emotional indications (as in the case of the dreamer's illogical rage), deserve more precise examination. It can happen that, through some apparently unimportant matter, divine grace will help resolve a huge but unrecognized problem confronting humanity.

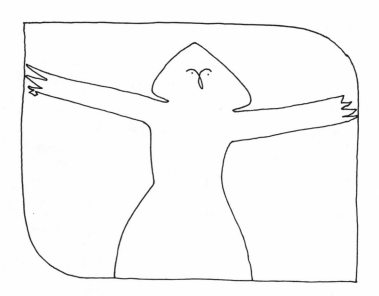

1. *The doctor says that it is now too late in the day to deal with our problem; it is Friday and her duty hours end earlier than usual.*

2. *I see a woman who is bathing in a tub. She is letting a second bathtub, which is nearby, overfill with so much warm water that it runs over on all sides.*

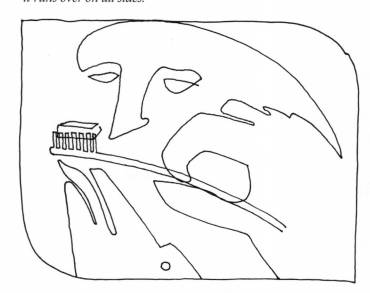

3. *In the second bathroom I am constantly troubled by a fawning dog. Two young women are in there cleaning the partitions.*

4. *Without noticing the difference, I put the piece of bread on the toothbrush. Then the dog is all over me, for it wants the bread.*

Dream 48: The Epoch of the Great Cleansing

1   *My family and I are in an institution that resembles a prison. We go to the office of the doctor on duty to ask her to let us leave the institution. She says that it is now too late in the day to deal with our problem; it is Friday and her duty hours end earlier than usual. We will have to spend another weekend in the institution.*

2   *Before lying down to sleep, I go to clean my teeth. In the first bathroom I see a woman who is bathing in a tub. She is letting a second bathtub standing nearby overfill with so much warm water that it runs over an all sides. I think to myself, is it necessary to waste water like that? We are really in a prison here!*

3   *I want to go into the second bathroom and am constantly troubled by a fawning dog. In contrast to the first bathroom, the second is narrow and full of shower stalls. Two young women are in there cleaning the partitions. All the bath surfaces are sprinkled with an ugly gray cleaning material. I ask whether I may clean my teeth.*

4   *One of the cleaning women takes a plastic tablet from her purse and puts it on my toothbrush. It does not stick to the bristles, and as soon as I move, it falls down and disappears into my bath bag. I look for it inside and find only a piece of white bread. Without noticing the difference, I put the piece of bread on the toothbrush. Then the dog is all over me, for it wants the bread.*

(Sempas, Slovenia January 29th 2005)

THE DREAMER IS CERTAIN that he has outgrown the framework of the old, intellectually organized world. He wants to have the right to leave the old world structure, with his family. He wants the freedom to go farther on his spiritual path to another plane. He will no more be controlled by the old, obstructive system and is certain that he can step away from the rationally controlled world whenever he wants to.

The unexpected complication with the doctor means that this is not so simple when dreams and blockages still remain anywhere in the hidden corners of the unconscious. These must be cleaned out before one can be free to progress to a new level of being. If people take these burdens with them on their new path, they will later face unwanted complications that will thrust them back to the old level of being. For this reason, the threshold of the new state of consciousness is so fashioned that, as in the dreamer's case, one is sent back until the old burdens are worked through or cleansed.

The plan of the dream images that follow is to clarify what the wisdom in the dream's message recommends for purposes of cleansing (changing) in such cases, and respectively, what are the possible mistaken paths.

The woman who was bathing in two bathtubs full of warm water at the same time can be seen as a symbol of the optimal transformational process which exposes a person to the least possible pain and is therefore to be preferred. Water, as a symbol of the emotional plane of being, takes on a key meaning. It means that the best possibility for personal cleansing and self-clarification is to be sought on the emotional plane. The overflowing water in the second bathtub is to be understood as a corresponding indication. But why does the woman use two tubs at the same time, when she is absent from the second?

I interpret this as meaning that those who are cleansing themselves from old burdens do so at two different levels of potency. The tub where the woman is bathing points to the emotional, psychologically conditioned level, on which the cleansing process is usually conducted. The second, unused bathtub represents a higher, cosmic plane of the purification process. In such a case it is usual to speak of the workings of divine grace. I write in my books of the redeeming power of the Goddess, the "Redemptress," and it is through her that humankind is being offered this unique help in the present epoch of cosmic change.[1]

The dream of 1/29/2005 does not set out to explain the workings of the power of divine grace in greater detail. It focuses much more on the danger that, because of certain rigid projections relating to the possible occasions for divine grace, humankind will reject this immeasurable gift which is offered only in the moment of cosmic change—and we find ourselves right in the middle of just such a process. The dreamer demonstrated this dismissive sort of attitude when he wrote off the overflowing tub as an impermissible waste of water.

The following dream images foreshadow the painful path of self-cleansing that awaits us if we do not perceive the cosmic offer.

The symbols of the path of torture that is approaching speak for themselves.

---

1.   See *Daughter of Gaia* (Findhorn Press, 2001), page 199ff.

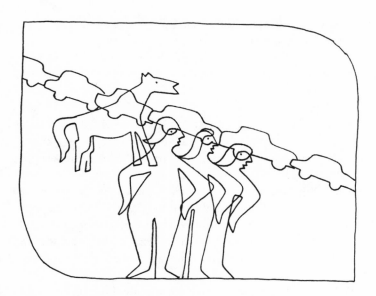

1. A small group of women with a highly bred horse are standing on the edge of a heavily traveled highway. They would like to cross the road.

2. The horse rears up on its haunches and throws itself on the vehicle that is just passing. This is an elegant silver-colored limousine.

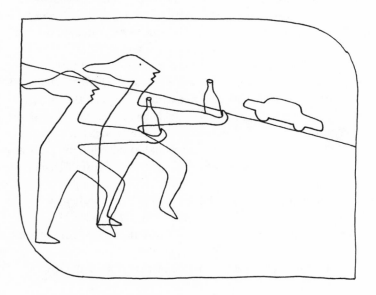

3. Two of the women are running toward the limousine; each holds a bottle of wine in her outstretched hand.

Dream 49: An Offer from the Nature Forces

1   *A small group of women with a highly bred horse are standing on the edge of a heavily traveled highway. I am an observer. They would like to cross the road, but the dense and fast-moving traffic will not let them. It is clear that the horse is not prepared to wait any longer.*

2   *The horse rears up on its haunches and throws itself over the vehicle that is just passing. This is an elegant silver-colored limousine in which an elderly gentleman is sitting. The horse's jump is achieved so skillfully that no real damage results. But some horse dung from its stall was sticking to its hooves and two thick, stinking stripes remain behind on the side of the car.*

3   *I wait amazed for the driver's reaction. He remains with his limousine, standing somewhat further away on the other side of the road. Two of the women are running toward him; each holds a bottle of wine in her outstretched hand. I think to myself that they want to appease the driver's anger with the bottles of wine. Then it strikes me that, because of their nearly identical gestures while running, the two women resemble elemental beings.*

(Belzig, Germany, July 22, 2002)

THE DRIVERS IN THE DREAM, sitting alone at their steering wheels as their cars rush by, represent the modern human being who, isolated and wrapped up in mental armor, constantly passes by life's elemental reality. It is the group of women with the horse at the edge of the road who represent the elemental reality. But what does the expression "elemental reality" really mean?

It is too superficial to say that the concept of elemental reality involves the elemental consciousness of nature, and elemental beings as *foci* of the nature consciousness. To refine this concept, the elemental reality in the dream would be symbolized by the combination of a highly intelligent animal (the horse) and a group of women.

The horse represents the instinctive consciousness that knows no separation but forms part of a constant union with the living cosmos. The group of women symbolizes more a sort of intuitive consciousness that comes to expression in emotional sensitivity. We associate this kind of consciousness with the feminine principle of thinking—a mode of thinking that never thinks separately from the fullness of being.

The dreamer is witness to an underlying conflict between these two models of reality, a conflict whose seriousness is not recognized by those involved. The drivers passing by take no notice of the group of women with the horse. They will not pause and give them the room they need to cross the road. Far be it from them to recognize that this need is really their own.

One might take the view that the dream's story does not represent the conflict between nature and civilization, but an inner conflict between the individual and everything that is unknown. This rages within every person who is sandwiched in the mechanisms of the intellectual age. On the one hand, sitting in the vehicle of intellectual culture represents that aspect of humankind that is fully involved in the compulsions of our highly organized and technical culture. On the other hand, to wait on a moment's attention represents that same person's elemental aspect through which he or she is united with the rhythms of terrestrial and universal being.

It does not matter which is the more important of these two conflicted aspects of our being. The real problem is that there is no communication between them. The first dream image portrays the complete absence of any exchange between the human elemental consciousness, through which we participate in the wholeness of the ocean of life, and our intellectually oriented "I," which must function within the culturally conditioned structures.

The second dream image informs us that the elemental forces in human beings are taking energetic steps to end humanity's intellectual ignorance of the soul aspects of its being. The horse, representing elemental nature, throws itself on the passing automobile. This means that we should expect, in the context of the unfolding earth change, that the elemental nature of human beings will create conflict situations to shake us awake and help us creep out of our intellectual armor. We are so immersed in our intellectual mechanics that we are quite incapable of following the twists of the cosmic transformational process.

At the same time we can rest assured that there will be no destructive action, but instead a skillfully executed intervention through which human beings will become conscious of their ignorance: the horse left behind "only" two thick, stinking stripes on the side of the automobile. In practical terms these translate as health troubles of an unknown kind, personal accidents, unpleasant life situations, and so forth, that operate to wake up the alienated consciousness.

The third dream image reveals another alternative, symbolized by the two bottles of wine. These are brought to the driver, who is in shock, by two women whose gestures are identical. What can this mean?

Humans are individual beings and so are their gestures. In contrast, the beings of nature are an expression of the joint Soul of the Earth. Thus, the identical gestures of the women with the wine bottles confirm that they do not represent human beings but instead exemplify a specific activity of elemental beings. Are we dealing here with a mysterious process in which the consciousness of nature will help humankind in their still unrecognized need?

In the first phase of this process, controlled quasi-natural accidents are staged, which help human beings drop their intellectual armor. The following phase is symbolized by the wine which contains alcohol and indicates intoxication. How can we understand this second phase?

After any sufficiently deep split occurs in the intellectual armor of the human being, the nature intelligence begins to work its way through the organism of the human body. This is our multidimensional body which embeds us in the wholeness of nature for as long as we live—whether we want it or not. The intelligence of nature knows how to use the lever that releases bodily enzymes which can soften humans and awaken their sensitivity from within. When that delicacy of feeling is once awakened, the love for the elemental reality of being is also gradually called into wakefulness.

This describes the operation of those mood-brightening neurotransmitters in the human body that are known as endorphins.[1] For example, they are released in the act of making love. The cells of nature intelligence in the human body—the so-called personal elemental being—know their way around the sex organs very well and can also release the stimulating neurotransmitters. Bathing in such delightful feelings can help humans sense the nearness of their cosmic essence. Afterwards, they are better able to follow the promptings of their hearts and act more lovingly.

---

1. For the workings of endorphins, see William Bloom, *The Endorphin Effect* (Piatkus, London 2001).

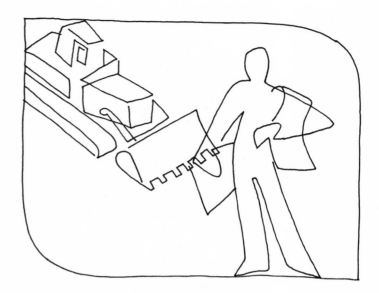

1. *Toward midday it is getting warm, and I am just pulling off my thick jacket, in the pocket of which I normally keep my documents.*

3. *Worried about my documents, I run back to the excavator, but unfortunately the machine is gone.*

2. Then I get a message that my advice is needed in another area of the construction site. I start to run there and forget the documents.

Dream 50: Identity Crisis

1   *I am employed as foreman at a construction site. Toward midday it is getting warm, and I take off my jacket, in the pocket of which I normally keep my documents. I have taken the papers out of the jacket pocket and put them down on the hood of a nearby excavator.*

2   *Then I get a message that my advice is needed in another area of the construction site. I start to run there and only after a while do I remember the documents I laid down.*

3   *I run back, but unfortunately the excavator is gone. I catch a glimpse of it vanishing behind a rise in the land. It is obviously impossible to catch up with the machine. What am I to do now?*
    (Loibach, Carinthia, July 14, 2001)

Documents are a symbol of personal identity. We modern humans believe there can be no question about our identity. We think we know who we are in our being. We are familiar with images of identity that originate from film or literature and whose foundations were laid during our upbringing. Our identity is modeled on them.

The dreamer has left his identity documents on the excavator. This can be interpreted as meaning that he has entrusted his identity to the machinery of global civilization, which has taken over the care of his spiritual and bodily well-being. He does not need to look after it anymore. Other people have specialized in that area, tinkering with the identity of contemporary humans: philosophers, clerics, politicians, designers, pop-singers, and so forth. Consequently, a person is free to pursue everyday tasks, just as the dreamer has done when he followed the call to the other area of the construction site. Something, however, no longer feels right about this scheme of things. The dreamer suddenly senses a responsibility for his identity documents.

Now there emerges an important symbol that resonates with the message of the dream: the excavator has been driven away. The foundations, which were thought to be grounded and stable, are in movement. The excavator is a symbol of an earthquake. The machine can no longer be brought back—the usual coordinates, by which human beings know themselves to be human, have vanished. The time of change requires that we search anew for self-knowledge. Our identity no longer has a secure resting place in this time of constant change. It must continually be recognized and birthed anew.

1. *I see naked men who are marching in a long line, one behind the other. Behind each man, there marches a small naked child.*

2. *He turns quickly around, lifts up the child who was marching behind him and breaks out of the column.*

3. *We quickly discuss whether we should intervene, because it is possible that the man is kidnapping a child that does not belong to him.*

Dream 51: The Inner Child

1   *I see a large number of naked men who are marching in a long line, one behind the other. They are elderly rather than young. Behind each man, there marches a small naked child.*

2   *Suddenly a man jumps out of the monotonous rhythm of the established order. I notice that his belly is unusually swollen, as if he were pregnant. He turns quickly around, lifts up the child that was marching behind him and breaks out of the column. Obviously he is firmly determined to go his own way with the child in his arms.*

3   *My wife and I are watching the scene together. Our attention has been drawn to the action of the unknown man. We quickly discuss whether we should intervene, because it is possible that the man is kidnapping a child that does not belong to him. But finally we decide to act as if we had noticed nothing unusual.*

(Lucerne, Switzerland May 16, 2001)

THE DREAM'S STORY SPEAKS first about the relationship of an adult man to his own core being, symbolized by the figure of a child.

A child marching in the back space along the way of life is a symbol of the so-called Higher Self. In other words, one would speak of the eternal soul of an individual person; the aspect of a person that never incarnates, but pulsates internally as the core being and is often pictured by the symbol of the "inner child." In contrast, the naked man whose relationship is with the frontal, outwardly oriented space, symbolizes the outer self, which is the human personality functioning in time and space. It is exposed to the pressure of the workings of time: the men are no longer young.

The message of the first dream image is that humankind is not completely surrendered to steadily escaping time, because beyond time and space we are accompanied by our inner child—or by our eternal individuality. We are speaking of a person's soul essence, which is present on a specific plane of being that is beyond birth and also beyond death, and is present during the time of earthly incarnation. The mortal and the immortal person march one behind the other on the path of evolution. One of the two aspects of the person is incarnate in time and space, the other is present in the Beyond, in eternity.

In the second dream image this strictly divided order is broken up. Does this mean that the time of great transformation is demanding another kind of relationship between the temporal personality and the eternal soul? A man turns around and fetches his inner child out of the shadows of the back space and into the light of consciousness.

The about-turn of the "rebellious" man is perceived by the dreamer to be a conscious violation of a law. In fact, it is primarily a decision to step outside the automatism of the usual time and space structure and accept the relationship with one's individual space in the Beyond. The next step to reunion with one's own focus of eternity is represented by the gesture of the "rebellious" man. He presses the child lovingly to his heart and goes off on his own way. These sequences define the steps that a modern man should take to reunite with his core soul:

1. One decides to set a certain distance between oneself and the habitual rhythms of the world's everyday structure.
2. One accepts relationships with the eternal dimension of one's being.
3. These relationships, which are developed through practice, meditation and loving interactions, lead finally to a synthesis of the human "I." The eternal aspect of the human being begins to work unhindered through the personality and likewise the personality begins to perceive the voice of the soul.

This internal process enables the human being to make it through the imminent reversals of the epoch of change in one piece. The personality no longer faces the challenges of earth change on its own.

In the third dream image the reunion of the personality with its ensouled core being—the inner child—is called into question by the modern intellect, whose role is personified by the dreamer and his wife. Instead of sharing in the reunion and rejoicing over it, the dreamer stands apart and observes the event critically. He and his wife even consider whether to call the police, but do not because of an unspoken intuition that the process that they are observing concerns the dreamer himself and not a stranger.

If human beings are to become whole again, the intellect must be taught to keep quiet at specific points in life, and also in the course of the shenanigans inspired by its own twists and turns.

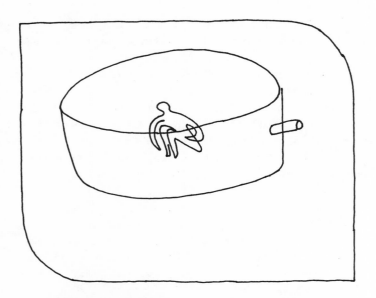

1. A boy has hidden himself in a bunker half buried in the earth where the only opening is an air-hole, installed horizontally.

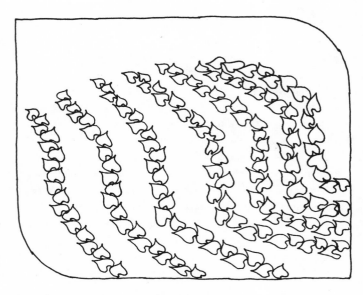

2. Seen from outside, the whole low-lying building is overgrown with climbing plants so that one can pass by without noticing it.

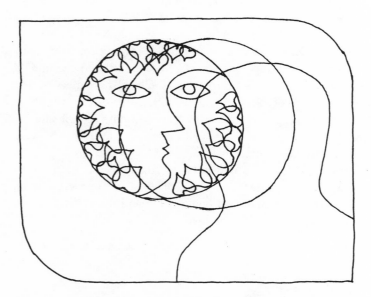

3. At the same moment, a boy of similar age looks past the climbing plants surrounding the air-hole into the hiding place.

Dream 52: The Human Being's Elemental Twin

1   *A boy has hidden himself in a bunker half buried in the earth, fully convinced that no one can find him there. The bunker's only opening is an air-hole, installed horizontally. I have a feeling that the boy and I are identical.*

2   *Seen from outside, the whole low-lying building is overgrown with climbing plants so that one can pass by without noticing it. Full of pride in his perfect hiding place, the boy creeps up to the air-hole to look outside.*

3   *At the same moment, a boy of similar age looks past the climbing plants surrounding the air-hole and into the hiding place. The two glances meet. It feels as if two brothers are looking at each other, eye to eye.*

(Loibach, Austria July 15, 2001)

THE FEELINGS THAT THE DREAMER describes leads us to suspect that the hidden boy is a representation of himself as a surrogate for contemporary humanity.

How can we hold this view when the usual behavior of people is so different today? They are full of dynamism, enjoy communication, and no longer acknowledge any taboos. They travel to all corners of the world, love to wander in the mountains, and cultivate flowers. Despite all this, can one compare modern man to a callow youth who squats isolated in his hidey-hole?

Yes, one can! The intellectual human of the modern epoch has learned to exist in the midst of living nature in such a way that he has practically no contact with the essence of life.

The cellar-type bunker represents the mental construct that our civilization has developed to be our place of being. Certainly, we have the illusion of living in the midst of the green natural world and circulating freely in it. The boy in the bunker is also surrounded with green climbing plants. But they are outside his hiding place. They conceal the bunker from the outside—and for the intellectual person also, the natural world appears to be an objective phenomenon apart from himself.

It is true that the bunker is half buried in the earth. But of what use is that when there are thick concrete walls to separate the boy from the earth? They represent the intellectually conceived and scientifically supported ideas of nature as a symptom of the human environment. Like the boy in the bunker, the intellectual person of the present epoch lives isolated inside an imagined world.

The dream tries to make the dreamer aware that he, as a man of the intellectual age, is held prisoner by his faith in his mental projection of a world of material appearance that is almost completely separated from the Whole. He remains a boy and cannot grow up because he has almost no relationship with the vital-energetic foundations from which one draws the ability to live and thrive. The air-hole in the dream, which is the only opening to the real, multidimensional world outside, represents the minimal relationship with the living world that still exists for intellectual people. Without this air-hole, their lives would be over.

The living vigor of our body, which is usually taken for granted, is really the last umbilical cord that connects intellectual people to the freedom and intelligence of life. The dream tells us that all is not lost as long as this "umbilical cord" exists. It can lead to a new beginning in the relationship between humans and their earthly nature.

But what does "the living vigor of our body" really mean? It certainly does not mean our bones and muscles. The third dream image reveals the living vigor of our body as an intelligence, a wisdom that is the human birthright. In the atmosphere of the dream it governs the strong feeling that the two boys are twin brothers, although one is shut out in the quasi external "environment," and the other held prisoner in the bunker of his mental projections.

One can view the dream of the twin boys as being complementary to the story of the seizure of the inner child (Dream 51) that was dreamed two months earlier. In this we are told of a new impulse that is being released into the triangle of human identity. This concerns the relationship of the personality to its ensouled spiritual core, its cosmic "I," which is symbolized by the inner child.

This latter dream addresses a second ensouled spiritual dimension of humankind. It is not concerned with the cosmic ("Higher") Self, but with people's elemental dimension. It is about human beings who, through their incarnation on earth, have become members of earth's evolution. In this connection they are part of the ensouled essence of Earth/Gaia, just like plants, crystals, mountains and valleys, elemental beings, and animals.

Pulsating in the core of our being, there is the individual spiritual soul and also a holographic fractal of the Earth Soul. At this latter level, human beings partake of a communal soul. This is the human "elemental I," a dimension of our being that has been completely forgotten.[1]

The dream's message tells us that within us humans there exists the unexpected possibility of bursting out of our mental bunker. This can happen through the elemental core of our being by which we are intimately connected with the Earth Soul. It follows that when the Earth Soul has initiated an essential change in her world, humankind is drawn into a complementary transformational process. To liberate ourselves from our mental prison, all we really have to do is renew our friendship with our elemental nature and let ourselves walk hand in hand with her.

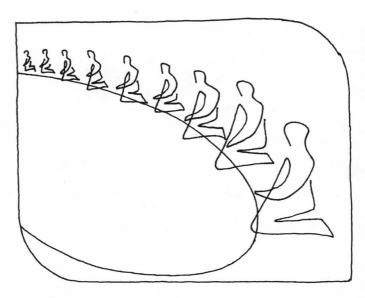

---

1. On the theme of the human elemental "I," see *Nature Spirits and Elemental Beings* (Findhorn Press 2010).

1. *A long row of people from different cultures are sitting on the floor, awaiting their food.*

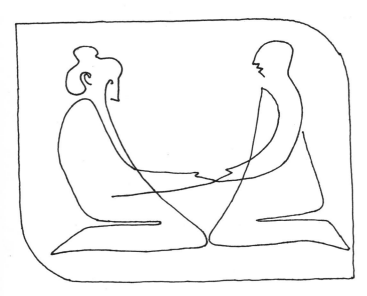

2. *When I join the row, the illustrious personality kneels before me and asks me what I wish to eat.*

Dream 53: The Master's Offering

1   *We are in a giant dining hall where the ambience is reminiscent of a temple. A long row of people from different cultures are sitting on the floor, awaiting their food. A person whose inner strength and radiance are quite noticeable slides on his knees from one individual to another and asks each what he or she would like to eat.*

2   *When I join the row, the illustrious personality kneels before me, holding a great dish in his hand. The dishes are all wonderful, and to me, for the most part, unknown foods. I am to choose what I would like to take.*

3   *I am also holding a dish in my hand. On it are all the various remains of food from the day before. When I am offered the new food, I become fearfully nervous and react indecisively. I am inwardly attracted by the offer of the new foods. At the same time, I am not ready to throw away the leftovers.*

4   *So I begin using a fork to move the leftovers around on my plate, hoping to make some space for the new foods. I sense, however, that my efforts cannot lead to any worthwhile result. In desperation, I begin to heap the remains into two separate piles to create some space between them for the new foods.*

(Sempas, August 1, 2001)

THE DREAM IMAGES ALLOW one to sense very readily the dramatic ambivalence in which modern human beings find themselves.

On the one hand, one senses the absolutely fantastic possibilities for enlightenment and further evolution that are to become accessible through the cosmic door of earth change. In the dream they are symbolized by the wonderful foods that the spiritual master has to offer.

On the other hand, one holds fast to "old foods," like familiar patterns, unquestioned dogma, and social conventions. The symbol for this is the dreamer's unwillingness to throw away the leftovers and choose the new foods.

This is a well-known problem of all transitional phases, which does not really need a dream to raise it to the light of consciousness. The dream's deeper meaning can be discerned through the description of the dreamer's feelings. There is the fearful nervousness that accompanies the dreamer's indecision.

3. I am also holding a dish in my hand. On it are all the various
    remains of food from the day before.

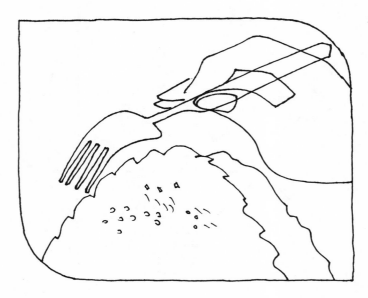

4. So I begin using a fork to move the leftovers around on my
    plate, hoping to make some space for the new foods.

Unfortunately the dream gives us no information on the subject. It could be a matter of karmic connections, traumas from his childhood or a previous life, perhaps a collective pattern to which he, as an individual, is subordinate . . . It would in fact be difficult to give precise information since it is the kind of barrier that may be composed quite differently from person to person.

Where the dream can give us information is about the way in which we should deal with any such personal problems that do not allow us to participate freely in the transformative process of earth and people, or to enjoy its fruits.

To put it more precisely: one can view the dream as a recommendation on how *not* to deal with such a situation.

Instead of the dreamer's summoning the decisiveness and power to confront the burdensome problem, he has chosen a way that will lead him into further ambivalence. He has made space on his plate for a little of the new without having to say goodbye to the old stuff.

He is thinking that he can partake of the new in a way that conveniently preserves the old toxic wastes. He has piled them up in two heaps, *so that in between there is some space left for the new.*

This is no solution and can lead to sickness and psychological problems. The conflict between the offer of the "new foods" and the toxic wastes of the old is not resolved but only internalized. Now the old toxins lie like a time bomb in the human body, while he pretends outwardly as if he is being carried on the waves of change against the new horizon.

Exercises on the Theme "Personal Evolution"

An exercise to open oneself to the cosmic offering

This exercise relates to those moments in human life when one senses the presence of positive and healing impulses around one and does not know how to make a bridge by which they can flow into one's life.

- *Be inwardly still, and present.*
- *Imagine that at the level of your heart there is a surface, a true "heart's floor" on which one can stand.*
- *Imagine and also feel that you are standing upright on the surface of your heart's floor, so that you reach high above your own head.*
- *The heart region under your feet feels like a disk-shaped force field in which you should firmly root yourself.*
- *Then you will notice that a second aspect of yourself is also standing there. It is positioned in the same way as the first but as its mirror-image—head downward toward the earth's center. Its feet are rooted in the other side of the heart's force field.*
- *Now the moment has come to open yourself consciously to the impulses of the universe and the earth, which can take you farther on the path of change. The double rooting in the heart will prevent the acquisition of any sort of false impulse. The heart knows in any given moment what is important to you.*
- *You can reinforce your intention by making the opening gesture with your hands.*

An exercise to decipher the hidden message of events

After experiencing an event or a moment which you sense may hide a specific message for your further evolution, you may use the following exercise to decipher the message:

- *Bring the event that may contain a specific message for you to your imagination, and locate the relevant moment behind your back with the help of its place upon the time axis, leading into the past.*
- *Let the event or the relevant moment briefly come to life again behind your back.*
- *After this, take your awareness backward into the awakened memory to sense its quality once again.*
- *In doing so, you should observe the effects on your psyche and disposition and pursue the thoughts and intuitions that are released.*
- *Bring them into your presence.*
- *You should let your consciousness evaluate them to find the message that may lie hidden there.*

An exercise to learn how to maintain a positive neutrality

To avoid becoming victim to your own false imaginings or emotional prejudices, you can use the following exercise. It can help when you feel you are being influenced by alien or self-produced emotions or ruled by alien thought patterns. A positive neutrality on the emotional or mental plane is the optimal goal.

> *You should find the point of perfect freedom that beats in the middle of your heart center. It can be equated with the spark of the divine presence in human beings.*
> *Imagine this point of peace within you as a little golden ball. Be conscious for a while of its presence in your heart center.*
> *If your concern is with a clarification of the emotional plane, you should lead the little golden ball of peace downward, to the area that lies directly below the solar plexus.*
> *Hold it present there, subtly radiating, until a stable stillness has built up in your emotional world. You can then devote yourself freely to the imminent life situation.*
> *If your concern is with a clarification of the mental plane, you should lead the little golden ball upward and center it in the middle of your head.*
> *Hold it present there, pulsating until a stable stillness has built up in your thinking world. Then you can devote yourself freely to the imminent questions or tasks.*
> *A third suggestion: keep in your remembrance that point of perfect peace which beats in the midst of your heart center, and stay centered there.*

An exercise to clarify a triangular relationship: personality, the inner 'I' and intellect

The task of the human personality is to maintain the correct proportion between the inner "I" and the intellect. The intellect should not be allowed, because of its fear of eternity, to suppress the language of the soul. Instead, it should learn to be quiet at certain moments and allow the inner "I"—the eternal soul of humankind—to come to expression.

> *Imagine that you are sitting in front of a mirror. Hand over to the mirror temporarily your intellectual personality in the form of its reflection in the mirror. You can emphasize this act with a corresponding gesture.*
> *Remember this several times during the meditation and do not allow the intellect to return to you until the moment is ripe. It is temporarily held prisoner in the shape of your image in the mirror.*
> *Afterwards, you should see your inner child emerge in your lap. Let the feeling for its presence develop. Be very loving toward it.*
> *You should allow the qualities of the inner child (your eternal aspect) to distribute themselves through your body. How do they feel to you? What kind of changes are perceived in the process, or are envisaged on the part of the inner child?*
> *Finally allow the intellectual "I" to return to you. It is to be integrated anew into your wholeness.*
> *Help it to position itself in such a way that it does not stand in the foreground, but remains partly immersed in your back space. Hopefully, its propensity to control will be somewhat disempowered.*

Chapter 8

VIEWS OF THE NEAR FUTURE

WHEN I TALK OF THE SUCCESSION of quite special dreams that I have had during the last 13 months, I am referring to those that are indicated, told and discussed below in the section on future developments. They were all dreamed between September 2008 and September 2009. I include among them Dream 42 (The Dark Aspect of God) which I actually dreamed earlier, but only in September 2009 did I understand it sufficiently to be able to write the commentary.

This does not mean that the messages of the other dreams described in this book have meantime lost their relevance. Not at all! I have chosen the dreams so that together they can portray the whole spectrum of the transformation process. Here, in the closing chapter we are investigating only what kind of new constellation of operating forces came into being during those 13 months within the broader pattern of earth and human change. I would like to outline the answer with the help of the dreams described below, which I have separated into three groups according to their themes.

1

In the first group I have included dreams that predict a fusion of our multidimensional space with a new spatial dimension that is unknown to modern humans and which I have named "the fairy space" for its heightened quality of feeling. There is a clear picture of it in Dream 61 (The Valuable Find): the unknown spatial dimension is symbolized by a valuable manuscript from the epoch of the Slovenian Romantic Movement that is found lying unnoticed under a pile of banal periodicals representing our everyday reality.

The task before us is to bring the existence of this spatial dimension so deeply into the collective consciousness that it is (again) perceptible. The possibility of cooperation with its potential can then be realized. Dream 54 (The Great Hope) can be understood as a grave admonition about the decisive role that a reconnection with the fairy world can play in the future of our earth and civilization. Instead of surrendering the earth's surface to destruction, we could, in cooperation with the potencies and beings of the archetypal fairy world, draw the unavoidable changes to us in a harmonious way.[1]

Dream 55 (Cooperation with the Fairy World) defines more precisely the kind of beings from the archetypal elemental world that are involved when we speak of the fairy world's future help in the process of earth change. The dreamer is led into the parallel archetypal elemental world ("the fairy world") where he encounters unusual beings. They reveal themselves as specialists in the conversion of the present civilization, burdened as it is with almost insoluble problems. In my experience, they are a kind of the so-called new elementals that have been expressly created, either by the Earth Soul or the Spirit of the Universe, to deal with the tasks presently at hand, or those still to emerge as a result of earth's coming quantum leap.[2] They have absolutely nothing to do with the processes of nature, which is the usual concern of environmental spirits like the elemental beings of water, fire, earth and air. The new elementals are experts in respect to human beings and are at our disposal to provide help with the change processes both at the personal and collective levels.

Dream 56 (Removal Problems) informs us that the rescuing fusion of our materially manifested world with the light-filled fairy world is impossible as long as the watery-emotional dimension of our space is contaminated with emotional waste. It is up to us to pick up our courage and work hard during the next period to cleanse the thick clouds that prevent our participation in the newly forming fabric of space.

2

The second group of dreams pointing to the future deals with the powers that work against the epochal transformation of humanity and the earth. This theme is introduced by Dream 58 (An Animal Fable). It informs us that the change is already well advanced on earth's invisible planes, but humanity is hesitating too long over changes that are unavoidable. The danger is arising that the whole process will come to a standstill. Consequently, humanity could miss the favorable conjunction of various cosmic cycles that make possible the successful transformation of the earth and humanity at this present time. Must we wait more millennia for the next opportunity?

Dream 59 (The Tall Guest) informs us that because of our dangerous hesitation, new cosmic powers are entering the change process. These are powers from which one cannot hide the herd of disasters that are happening on earth—or in one's own psychic labyrinth. In the commentary, they are called the "Destroyers of the Destroyer." Their task is to hold up an unclouded mirror to humanity, so that we cannot shy away from the necessary changes in our personal and collective lives. Not a pleasant outlook!

To be able to survive such a severely challenging future, we need to seek a corresponding spiritual support. Dream 42 (The Dark Aspect of God) is to be understood in the sense of a signpost. We need to develop an understanding of the cosmic principle of change, and in this context also nourish intimate relationships with the so-called "Black Goddess"—the Goddess of Change—who is able to lead humanity through death and regeneration to resurrection. The process also calls for us to rediscover her partner, the dark God who is the challenger of people's shadow side.

3

The third group of future-directed dreams is introduced by Dream 57 (Midwife Wanted). Its message is the announcement of the new phase when the changes appear on the plane of the materialized world. People will experience them in their own bodies and their own environment. The dramatic tone of the dream informs all people of good will that the time has come to lay aside all mutual quarrels so that the worldwide group of spiritually and psychically awake individuals can work as successful midwives to birth the New Age.

Dream 60 (The Lost Telephone) informs us that Gaia, the Earth Mother, has made ready a special sort of assistance in case the environment on the physical earth's surface becomes unbearable for living beings caught in the thunderstorm of earth change. This space is a kind of after-image of earth, like her twin or double. One can think of it as a safe place of refuge, a kind of Noah's Ark, in which all of earth's living beings can find a temporary place of safety. At the moment of greatest need one could, possibly by an alteration in frequency, be "transferred" to this parallel space, and later be placed again in our multidimensional reality.

In summary, one could say that unimaginable challenges await us in the near future. When this future will be is not defined. In 2012? In the next hundred years? What is uniquely clear is that its presence already exists in the cosmic Here and Now, which, quite unconditionally, wants to be realized in the everyday reality of our existence.

1. The term "fairy space" does not here mean a space for the existence of elemental beings of the air element, which is what is traditionally meant by fairies. It refers instead to the fairy-like, paradisiacal quality of the existential space that exists parallel to the multidimensional space in which we human beings dwell, together with our civilization and other visible and invisible beings. This fairy-like parallel space is the real home of elemental beings and environmental spirits. One could refer to it as the "archetypal elemental world," or the so-called "elemental under-world," as its sub-terrestrial aspect implies. From there elemental beings continually come into our space to perform their service on the feeling and power planes of nature and human culture.

    One may recall the fairy tale in which Snow White flees through a dark forest to reach the parallel world of the elemental beings. There she finds the home of the dwarves with their beds made and the table laid. However, she does not find the dwarves for they are already "at work," busy with the service that they perform for us beings of the multidimensional (manifested) reality space of earth. They continually return to their own "fairy space" (in their archetypal elemental world) to regenerate themselves and let the Earth Soul inspire them anew to perform their service "for us."

    For more on this theme, refer to the Introduction to Chapter 2 of this book (Birth of a New Earth Space).

2. The concept of the "new elemental beings" or "elemental beings of the fifth element" is further explained in the new edition of *Nature Spirits and Elemental Beings* (Findhorn Press 2010), also in *Sacred Geography*, (Lindisfarne Books 2007).

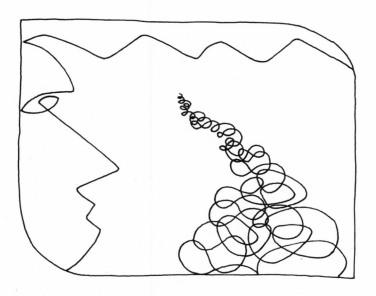

1. I suddenly notice that at one point the mountainside is breaking up. Stones are beginning to roll down the slope.

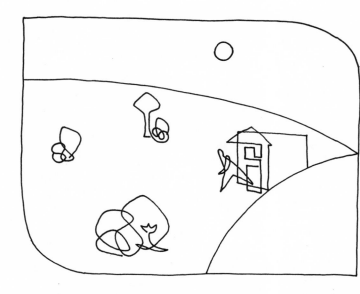

2. The stone blocks brought by the avalanche stand on the broad meadow distributed like elements of a paradisiacal, beautiful park.

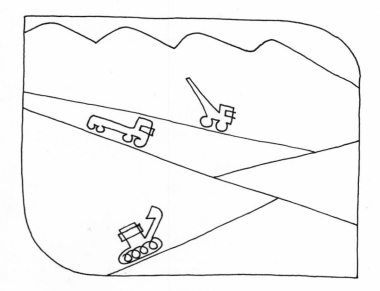

3. Mighty protective walls are being built to prevent the crumbling stone slope from ever again pouring into the villages in the valley.

4. My eyes are led toward my right hand. Lying there are five balls.

Dream 54: The Great Hope

1   *I am standing in the middle of the valley not far from our house, and am looking toward the mountain ridge that runs along the side of the valley. I suddenly notice that at one point the mountainside is breaking up. Stones are beginning to roll down the slope. A giant avalanche of stones is under way, and it is constantly becoming broader! This is frightful! It will be catastrophic for our house, I think to myself, since that stands in the middle of the valley, directly under the collapsing slope.*

2   *I run toward our house; I cannot believe my eyes. The house is untouched! The stone blocks brought by the avalanche stand distributed on the broad meadow like elements of a paradisiacal, beautiful park. Individual groups of stones are planted around with flowers and trees. My daughter, who obviously has not noticed the falling stones, comes out of the house. Her name is "The Victorious."*

3   *Now I am busy watching the construction workers who are to consolidate the toppled mountainside. Giant machines roar up and down. Mighty protective walls are being built to prevent the still crumbling stone slope from ever again pouring into the villages.*

4   *My eyes are led toward my right hand. Lying there are five balls. Four are colored brown as though they had come from the earth. The fifth ball is bright, like a glittering glass ball. It is inscribed with a sign which, for the sheer brightness of the light, I cannot decipher.*
        (Athens, Greece, September 11, 2008)

THE NARRATIVE OF THIS DREAM begins with a natural catastrophe that is apparently like many catastrophes that have afflicted humanity in various parts of the earth in different epochs. But is the similarity only apparent?

Yes, because the collapse of that stony slope has no logically comprehensible cause. The unexpected collapse of the slope and the following, almost orderly, broadening of the stony avalanche has more the aspect of the collapse of a world structure. Despite the giant mass of rocks that came down from the mountainside, the mountain appears afterward to be unaltered.

The dream from Athens does not try to explain the natural catastrophes that have occurred much more frequently over the past decade, but instead presents the current earth changes as being part of a cosmic event.

If the first dream image presents the current earth changes as the collapse of the existing world structure, the second image marks an exact counterpoint. In the picture of the paradisiacal garden there is no hint of world annihilation but quite the reverse. In the second image, earth's living space looks renewed. Where one would expect the worst destruction, there is a garden of paradise! It is important to note that the paradisiacal garden has arisen from the stones that rolled so threateningly down the slope in the first dream image.

The second part of the dream presents two alternative ways of dealing with earth change.

The third dream image illustrates how the human intellect would react to the threat of a collapsing world. Giant walls are built to prevent the break-up of the accustomed earth space. The walls are a symbol of the material measures over which the world leaders seek to unite with a common policy, such as the reduction of exhaust fumes, economic utilization of energy, introduction of alternative technologies, and so forth.

The fourth dream image indicates the possibility of a peaceful, alternative solution to earth's dangerous situation. In this case there is no application of material force, such as the building of cyclopean walls.

This solution would doubtless lead us toward the paradise garden presented in the second image. But what is the solution? The key to the mystery, which is of burning interest to everyone who has the fate of planet Earth at heart, lies in the fifth ball in the dreamer's hand.

Four of the five balls show an earthly character and can be equated with the four elements that traditionally compose the fabric of life on the earth—water, fire, earth and air. They represent the emotional (water element), vital-energetic (fire element), material (earth element) and spiritual (air element) components of the fabric of life. The rounded form of the balls indicates that they do not represent water, fire, earth and air as different substances or physical states, but stand for the essence of the four elements, which one knows as etheric (vital-energetic) forces.

Now, in the dreamer's hand there is a fifth ball whose light-filled form looks quite different from the other four. In addition, it is also inscribed with a cosmogram. What can this fifth ball symbolize?

It is not by chance that the five balls are in a hand. In the five fingers of the hand you can observe the same pattern as is displayed by the balls. Four fingers are positioned parallel to each other and work as a unity. The fifth, the thumb, is placed opposite to them in accordance with its function, and has quite another role to play in the operation of the hand.

The dream takes place in a landscape space. This means that the pattern that we observed among the five balls and in the hand should be transferred to the constitution of space. In this case, the four "earthly" balls represent the different dimensions of the multidimensional space whose extensions were mentioned above in connection with the pattern of the four elements. The fifth ball would then stand for a further spatial dimension that does not directly belong to the space in which we humans and other beings of the multidimensional world exist.

The dream's message means that near the four spatial dimensions uncovered by geomancy, there is a further spatial dimension that has completely departed from human memory. It can be conceptualized as the archelemental space of Earth. For its paradisiacal quality, it could also be called "fairy space." The elemental beings and environmental spirits, which are usually active in our world, have their origin and also their home there—and because of this the fairy space is also described as an archelemental world.

In the dreamer's hand the five balls vibrate in mutual interaction. This means that the fifth ball is not solely responsible for fostering a positive development from the earth change, but that the process involves the interaction of the traditional elementals and beings of the earthly creation along with the fairy space that is newly emerging in our consciousness.

This interaction produces different combinations of forces and changes in consciousness that until now were more or less unknown. To best prepare for the challenges of the approaching intensification of earth change, according to the message of the dream from Athens, one should first open one's heart and consciousness to the existence of earth's parallel archelemental space. It cannot be by chance that the dream of September 11, 2008, was given exactly seven years after the event through which the cosmic power of the transformational forces was first experienced worldwide.

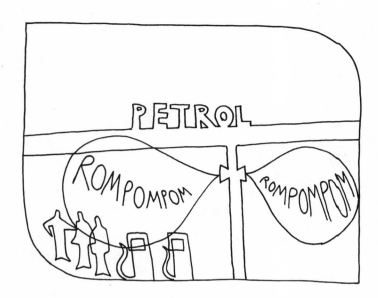

1. *Someone is making a reverential speech in German at a gas station. At the same time the daily news is booming from the loudspeakers in Slovenian.*

2. *I go to the manager of the gas station to ask him to switch off the loudspeakers. He tells me that this is not so simple because they do not have an on/off switch.*

DREAM 55: COOPERATION WITH THE FAIRY WORLD

1 *I am with a group of men gathered at a gas station. Someone is making a reverential speech in German. At the same time the daily news is booming from the loudspeakers in Slovenian. The two languages mingle so unpleasantly that the solemn speech cannot be heard.*

2 *I go to the manager of the gas station to ask him to switch off the loudspeakers. He tells me that this is not so simple because they do not have an "on/off" switch. He takes me to one of the loudspeakers so that I can see the problem for myself. I notice that I am dealing with an unusual person. With his trim beard, he reminds me more of a spiritual master than a gas station manager.*

3 *He says if I will come upstairs with him, we will surely find the switch. There is in fact a narrow stairway that leads up to the flat roof of the gas station. To my surprise, a seemingly ordinary wooden house is standing there. The manager strides inside to switch off the insistent loudspeaker. I peer through the window after the master and see inside a crowd of small, child-like figures who are making handcrafts that one would not expect from small children.*

4 *As I stumble down the steep stairs with the master, the "children" sing in chorus a song about the fall of Communism and the Eastern Block. I try to remember the names of all of my friends and colleagues who have died. The last one I remember is my friend Taras.*

(Lanzarote, Canary Islands, November 9, 2008)

THE GAS STATION must represent contemporary civilization. The strictly functional form of that sort of building, the connection with fossil fuel, and the continuous news reporting, all belong to our modern culture.

The group of people who have gathered under the roof of the gas station to discuss a sacred matter represent the countless groups worldwide that are seeking to bring holistic initiatives into the life of our "gas station." Their voice, however, is overwhelmed by the loud, egocentrically aligned culture of the current age that will not renounce the habitual patterns of the world structure.

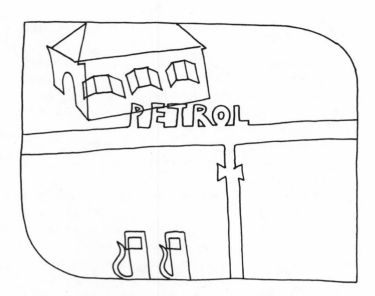

3. *There is in fact a narrow stairway that leads up to the flat roof of the gas station. To my surprise, a seemingly ordinary wooden house is standing there.*

4. *As I stumble down the steep stairs with the master, the "children" sing in chorus a song about the fall of Communism and the Eastern Block.*

The dream's key message is exemplified by the manager's inability to switch off the pattern that runs automatically on the plane of the gas station—or should we say, on the plane of the traditional reality space. To create silence, which has become absolutely necessary for the further development of the newly forming reality of life, one must climb to a superior level of being and seek help there.

So the dreamer is led by the gas station manager, whom he has recognized as a spiritual master, to a level of being whose quality is quite different from the cold exterior of the gas station. What kind of existential space is to be found there above the gas station, close to nature, warm and streaming with light?

The answer to this question is supplied by the unusual children who work and sing in the wooden house. They are simultaneously very young and yet grown up. They are busily creative, although they are really still infants. Their constant activity lets us know that they are engaged in a specific task. The fact that they are permanently busy invites comparison with the earthly elemental beings that are uninterruptedly engaged in maintaining the existence of the manifested world.

However, because they dwell above the roof of our world, one should regard them as extraterrestrial beings. And at the same time, because at the end of our dream they are placed in the context of the dead, it means that they belong, nonetheless, to the earth cosmos. How, from all these symbols, can one put together a real identity for these beings?

This conundrum is answered by the song about the collapse of Communism and the Eastern Block that is sung by the "extraterrestrial elemental beings" as the two visitors are leaving their space. According to the song's message, this epochal event manifested unexpectedly at the end of the 1980s because the "extraterrestrials" had brought the appropriate lever for it to happen. Operations at the level of the gas station could not bring about such an event.

The song leads us to suspect that the flock of "children" in the little wooden house above the gas station is composed of a special kind of elemental being that has obviously specialized in the current change as it affects earth and humanity. One can describe them as helpers that are approaching earth and humanity to assist in the process of Earth Change and its apparently insoluble problems. They are a special kind of being that I have called "new elemental beings" in my books. By this expression, I am thinking of consciousness beings of the earth that have been brought up by the Earth Soul to cooperate with the human race. They possess qualities that enable them to handle the human creation and our machinations. In this case, my intuition is saying, we are seeing the transformation of a specific cosmic being into a terrestrial elemental being.

The dreamer's glimpse of the inside of their extraterrestrial dwelling place was later extended by his perceptions of these invisible beings. They can appear extra small in comparison with the elemental beings. They often fly in swarms through the atmosphere's etheric space beyond the physical reality, reminiscent of a swarm of bees. They constantly laugh and dance as they go about their tasks through the breadth of space. When any are contacted, they show themselves as beings of deep wisdom.

The dreamer's dead friends appear at the end of the dream as a symbol of the spiritual world that complements our manifested world. The "cosmic elemental beings" that are promised us to help in the present phase of earth and human change also belong to another world, which exists as a parallel world.

We, incarnate humans, can give ourselves a lot of trouble and yet fail to achieve the hoped-for results in certain complex situations if we do not learn to follow the rhythm of cooperation with the parallel worlds. There are things that one can complete in excellent fashion within the framework of this world, but which will not proceed beyond a certain point if the other world does not contribute its impulse—say, rather, if its cooperation is not perceived, accepted and appreciated.

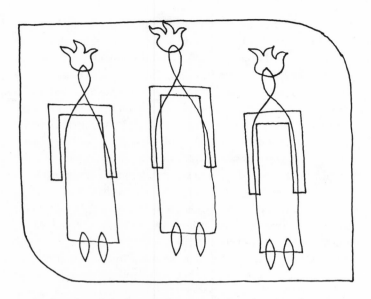

1. I enjoy their lofty beauty, but notice that their hands seem stiff, as if wooden.

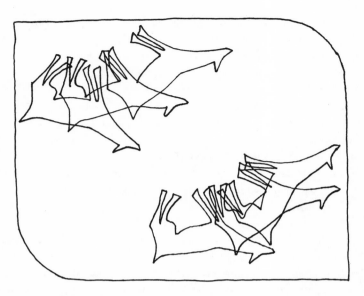

2. In the following night I dream of a large number of roe deer that are lying on the floor in two disorderly heaps.

3. On awakening, I go immediately into meditation and ask the roe deer, "Why don't you stand up and enjoy your freedom?"

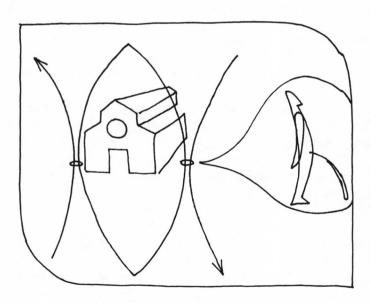

4. It is the site of the Church of St. Martin, where the day before I had found two stopped-up etheric holes in the floor.

Dream 56: Removal Problems

1   *During my investigations of the watery-emotional space in Venice, I discover three elevated beings of the water element in the Basilica San Giorgio Maggiore. They appeared to me like nymph queens. I enjoy their lofty beauty, but notice that their hands seem stiff, as if wooden. However, I cannot discern the cause of the disability.*

2   *The following night, I dream of a large number of roe deer that are lying on the floor in two disorderly heaps. To me, they look as if they are dead. I am thinking that they must have been shot when I notice that they are breathing. I am quite shaken. What is happening here?*

3   *On awakening, I go immediately into meditation and ask the roe deer, "Why don't you stand up and enjoy your freedom?" One of them raises his upper body to show me that their feet are stuck to the floor with a sort of tar.*

4   *My intuition tells me to search for the corresponding place in the city plan of Venice. It is the site of the Church of St. Martin, where the day before I had found two stopped-up etheric holes in the floor, one on either side of the church. Now I understand their function for the first time: the one on the right side of the church building operates as a center for emotional discharge, on the left as a center of renewal.*

(*Venice, September 19, 2009*)

IN THIS CASE we are dealing with a combination of dream and, parallel to it, geomantic research in Venice. Through intuitive insights combined with my previous experiences relating to the problems of emotional garbage, I successfully detected the secret activity of forces that are working against the new phase of earth change.

The roe deer are a symbol of the forces that are engaged in keeping our space's emotional dimension clean and capable of regeneration. They have already emerged in this role in Dream 30. In order for the emotional space to maintain its crystalline clarity, its etheric fluidity must be continually recycled. Just as our urine flows into the earth and afterwards we drink fresh water to renew our water content, so must the emotional-watery dimension of the earth do likewise. There are geomantic offloading centers through which the emotional-watery streams needing renewal are led off into the depths of the earth where they can experience purification and regeneration.[1] In the case of Venice there are two such centers. One is situated beneath the mouth of the City Fish of Venice[2] in front of the Church of St. Andrea, and the second in the bottommost part of the fish's body before it transforms into the tail. This is near the Church of St. Martin mentioned above.

For the roe deer to appear to the dreamer as if they were dead means that there was something wrong with the emotional water's circle of renewal. In the example of the Church of St. Martin in Venice mentioned above, it was brought to a stop. The tar that is sticking to the roe deer's feet is a sign that the centers for the offloading and renewal of the watery-emotional atmosphere are choked.

What happens when the circle of renewal with its removal and offloading streams is blocked? The watery-emotional space in which humans and all living beings "bathe" is gradually poisoned. Like the alcohol that circulates in the veins of a habitual drunk and does not allow him to think and feel clearly, the same happens in the emotional stream of a city landscape: waste cannot be removed and regenerated. The space is constantly laden with negative emotions that do not allow the emergence of positive and inspirational ideas. The transformational processes, which can ensure the future in the current epoch of the life of earth, are permanently blocked. So, as in the case of the roe deer in our dream, humans and other beings are tied to emotional patterns and forces that are decaying.

Furthermore, the gray clouds of unpurified emotional forces prevent the fusion of our multidimensional space with the so-called fairy space. This fusion could prevent the cataclysmic consequences of the earth changes now proceeding—see the message of Dream 54. The archetypal fairy space is composed with such sensitivity that the elementals would instantly be paralyzed by the current impurity of our emotional space if they were to join with our multidimensional reality in their helper function. The three nymph queens in the first dream image made the seer aware of this danger by displaying how wooden their hands have become.

Can yet more be done than by constantly taking care of the renewal and purification of one's own emotional-watery field? Certainly, by doing geomantic, earth-healing work.

---

1. See *Sacred Geography* (Lindisfarne Books 2007).
2. See *Venice—Discovering a Hidden Pathway* (Lindisfarne Books 2008).

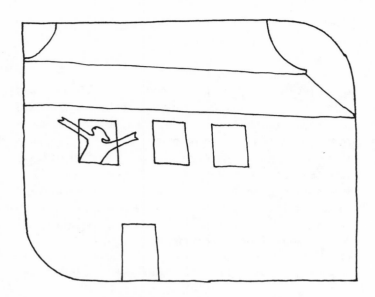

1. I see a house with a hipped roof. It is dark and looks all but abandoned. Up on the top floor there is a woman, who at this very moment is birthing a child. She is calling for help.

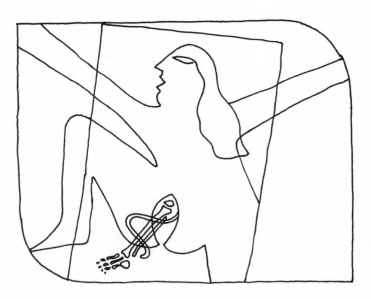

2. To make her need clear, she is holding the child's leg out of the window. The newborn's leg consists only of bones from which the umbilical cord is hanging.

3. I run from one table to the next looking for the midwife. Nobody wants to be disturbed at the meal, and none of them listen.

4. I run farther and come to a place with many businesses and boutiques. No one knows Christina or pays any attention to my request.

Dream 57: Midwife Wanted

1 *I see a house with a hipped roof. It is dark and looks all but abandoned. Up on the top floor there is a woman, who at this very moment is birthing a child. She is calling for help. Her name is Rita.*

2 *To make her need clear, she is holding the child's leg out of the window. The newborn's leg consists only of bones from which the umbilical cord is hanging. I must look for the midwife whose name is Christina.*

3 *I run quickly and come to a place that has a fast food business. I run from one table to the next looking for the midwife. Nobody wants to be disturbed at the meal, and none of them listen.*

4 *I run farther and come to a place with many businesses and boutiques. People are trying on clothes. I run from one to the next. No one knows Christina or pays any attention to my request. I awake agitated and exhausted.*

(Schluechtern, Germany February 27, 2009)

I MUST FIRST EMPHASIZE that the dream was not dreamed by me but by a colleague, who at the time was sleeping in my neighborhood while attending a geomancy conference in Schluechtern. I must admit having been confident at the time that I had a good overall view of what was happening on the earth; consequently, I had some underlying resistance to the dream's dramatic message, which is why the dream was given to someone other than me.

If one interprets the house with the hipped roof as representing earth, then Rita can be identified as Gaia. That she was at that moment giving birth corresponds to the present moment in earth's history when a new form of earth space is being "born."

By having Gaia call upon the dreamer for help during her labor, the dream makes clear that we humans will be called upon to cooperate in a specific way during the coming phase of the birth process. The dreamer is not asked to help directly with the birth, but to find the midwife who can give competent aid. This indicates that a special form of help will be needed from us humans.

To explain the need for the special form of help, Rita/Gaia shows the newborn's leg, which consists merely of bones.

It is very unusual for the child's leg bone to come to light during the birth process. What can this mean? If one were to interpret the bones as a symbol of the material level of being, it could mean that we are to expect an upcoming phase of earth change when the transformation process will emerge on the material plane of reality. Just as the bones represent the hard portion of the body, so the physical dimension of reality is recognized for its constitutional "hardness" that is perceptible to touch.

The next two dream images demonstrate that human beings in general still have no idea how critical is earth's situation. They are still sunk up to the eyeballs in their daily roles and jobs, although the earth changes threaten to drown the dimension where we exist.

The fact is that the dreamer who, in the name of Rita/Gaia is looking for the midwife, does not really expect the people who are dining and shopping to leave everything at once to help in the process of earth change. In the last analysis, what should they do concretely?

The dreamer's search is rather for a positive attitude to the fact that the earth is about to birth a new plane of being. His cry is directed to those who may know what is needed at the given moment and who, like a midwife at a birth, can give practical help, so that the birth proceeds on a plane where one can give energetic and spiritual assistance—and not have the new-born come unguided onto the material plane.

The primary expectation from the dreamer's repeated demands for the midwife is that people will pay attention to the transformational processes. The concern is about whether one is conscious of what is going on in the given cosmic moment, or whether instead one is completely involved in a more or less egocentric dynamic.

It is no accident that the midwife who is being demanded is called Christina—a feminine variant of the name of Jesus Christ. The Introduction to Chapter 6 of this book demonstrates how his work and teaching is closely tied to the quantum leap of earth and humans.

Even when the dreamer awakes agitated and exhausted, there is nonetheless hope for a happy birth. This is symbolized by the newborn's umbilical cord which, still uncut, hangs from the leg bone.

1. *A fox is slinking around with the evident intention of snapping up the hen. The hen looks carefully here and there and all around, but does not notice the danger.*

2. *Suddenly a lamb comes running toward them with the obvious intention of driving the fox away.*

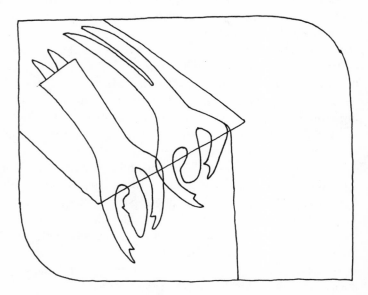

3. *Now I see the lamb placing its foreleg lovingly round the hen's neck. Golden sunbeams fall over the pair.*

4. *My wife and I are lying down and watching from the edge of a steep roof. I realize that we are moving ever closer to the edge of the roof.*

Dream 58: An Animal Fable

1   *I see a hen in the midst of a bright and fragrant green meadow. A fox is slinking around with the evident intention of snapping up the hen. The hen looks carefully here and there and all around, but does not notice the danger. She carries on pecking away at the grass.*

2   *Suddenly a lamb comes running toward them with the obvious intention of driving the fox away. The fox flees and the hen is saved.*

3   *Now I see the lamb placing its foreleg lovingly around the hen's neck. They stand in the middle of the meadow embracing. Golden sunbeams fall over the pair, like a divine blessing.*

4   *While all this is going on, my wife and I are lying down and watching from the edge of the steep roof of the neighboring house. I realize that we are moving ever closer to the edge of the roof. We are nearly at the point of falling.*

(Napa Valley, California, March 18, 2009)

THE DREAM WAS GIVEN to the dreamer after he had asked the following question before going to sleep: "Is there a danger that the forces that work against earth change will reenter the process, after having mutually inflicted a fatal wound by crashing into the Twin Towers of the World Trade Organization in New York on September 11, 2001?" A thesis forecasting a renewed entry had been given the day before at a conference in New York. According to the thesis, the reentry process would begin in July 2009.[1]

If we take the question to be key to the meaning of the dream, it is clear that the hen represents Gaia, the Earth Soul. She pecks at the grass in the middle of her green garden of life, which has emerged from her egg and developed through millions of years.

It follows that the fox represents the forces that are working against the epochal earth change. Instead of allowing the terrestrial space to take an essential further evolutionary step in the form of a quantum leap, the contrary forces are trying to hold back earth's evolution at the stage it has already reached. In such a case, the state of today's technology and the schizoid condition of human consciousness would ensure certain death for the blue planet. Sooner or later the fox would snap up the hen.

The saving power reveals itself in the form of a lamb.

The fifth chapter of the Revelation of St. John, which tells the story of the book with seven seals, is the key to the symbolic meaning of the lamb as it relates to earth change. The individual phases of the present earth and human change are encoded in that book. It could be called the cosmic planning book, because it details how the transformational process is to unfold.[2]

The Apocalypse emphasizes that no man, in heaven or earth, nor under the earth, was able to open the book containing the blueprint of the earthly future. St. John tells us, "And I wept much, because no man was found worthy to open and to read the book."

Now comes the surprise: a lamb mounts the throne of God and takes the book, opening its seals one after another and setting in motion the corresponding processes of change. In the course of this, various symbols indicate that the lamb is an embodiment of Christ. But why an embodiment in animal form?

The answer to this question is to be found in the preceding Dream 44 (The Green Christ) where the discussion relates to the incarnation in earth's elemental nature of that cosmic force, which in the West is equated with the concept of Christ. Its properties indicate that the lamb is the corresponding animal form.

It follows that the second dream image means that the Christ power, incarnated within the earth's system, has prevented the execution of the plans of the contrary powers to hold the earth back at its old evolutionary state (but one that still exists today for us humans).

The third image follows to confirm that the earth has now become free to carry out its changes under the protection of the lamb. There is no longer any contrary power to prevent it.

The problem now is elsewhere, with the human beings! This is confirmed by the dreamer's feeling afterward that, in view of the lamb's victorious appearance, he and his wife should consciously creep into a deep hole.

The dream can be seen as a preview of the events surrounding the solar eclipse of July 22, 2009, when entirely new cosmic forces entered the processes of human and terrestrial transformation. The following dream (The Tall Guest) is devoted to one particular form of these forces, and the second is best represented by the dream of the gas station (Dream 55).

In summary, the dream's message means that earth's transformational processes have successfully reached a high level, thanks to the spiritual initiative of the Christ power. The third dream image makes it clear that Earth has regained its holy radiance. Not so for humanity!

Humanity in general has slept through the last decade of intensive change. During the time that the Earth Soul, coupled with the cosmic forces, has created the new earth space in the etheric realm, humanity has remained hanging to the exclusively material plane of being. Our consciousness is still ruled by the forces of intellect, which are sure to lead to division and consequently to strife and war.

Because of this, we can expect that the focus of the transformational process will shift in future to the personal transformation of each individual human being.

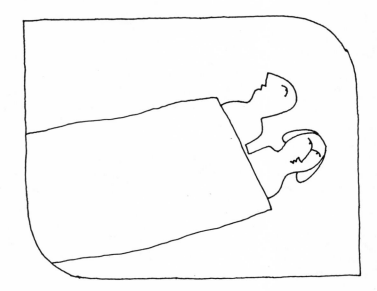

1. *It is nighttime and my wife and I are lying awake in bed.*

1. The conference was called *Esoteric Christianity and the Inner Life of the Earth*, Steiner Books Seminar, New York University, March 13-14 2009. Robert Powell gave the lecture, *The Significance of the Year 2012*.
2. For this, see *Earth Changes, Human Destiny* (Findhorn Press 2000).

2. *He seats himself quietly on the edge of the nearby bed, lights the nearest bedside lamp, then takes a book from his pocket and begins to read.*

Dream 59: The Tall Guest

1 *It is nighttime and my wife and I are lying awake in bed. A tall guest, finely dressed in a coal black suit, comes into the house. I sense that his arrival is expected, but no one goes to greet him.*

2 *He seats himself quietly on the edge of the nearby bed, asks courteously, "May I?" and lights the bedside lamp, then takes a book from his pocket and begins to read.*

3 *I feel troubled that no one has come to receive the tall guest. Deep within me I sense what an important service he has to offer. So I stand up to greet him myself in the name of the whole house.*

4 *But pajamas, I think, do not suit the occasion. I begin to put on my trousers. But I tell myself that there is no need to change the upper part of my nightclothes because it resembles a tight-fitting black vest.*

(Sempas, Slovenia July 1, 2009)

To interpret this dream, one must surrender oneself to the same strong feelings that were the dreamer's experience in the course of the dream: primarily that the black-clad guest represents a lofty cosmic power.

Why does no one come to greet him? The dreamer knows inwardly that his coming is expected. In answer, the dream points to a specific circumstance: the guest comes at an unexpected hour in the night. Could it be that one would rather not have him in the house?

Fortunately the dreamer and his wife are awake at this nighttime hour when one is usually sunk in a deep sleep. The wakefulness of the dreamer (who is in reality sleeping) symbolizes that during the previous months he has had some short dreams that have prepared him for the entry of a new kind of cosmic power into the process of earth and human change. Its fundamental quality was represented as negative.

This dream is characteristic of the dreams that had alerted the dreamer's vigilance on other occasions when he is oppressed by an adversary. He flees into his house and shuts the door. But naturally, the adversary can access the door-latch from outside. He was able to open the door without further ado and is already standing in the middle of the room.

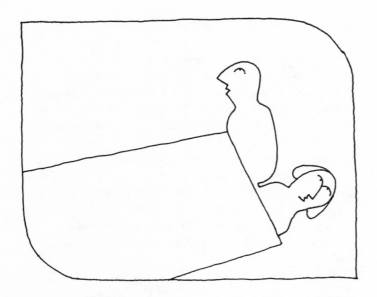

3. *I feel troubled that no one has come to receive the tall guest.*
So I stand up to greet him myself.

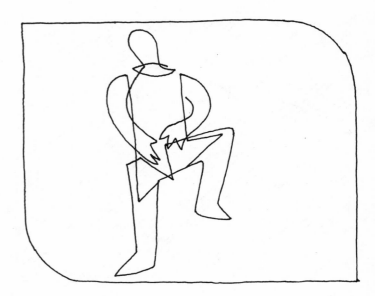

4. *I begin to put on my trousers. But I tell myself that there is no*
need to change the upper part of my nightclothes.

Is there a category of destructive powers from whose influence there is no practical way to protect oneself, and against which no earthly fastener will hold?

The celebrated abbess, mystic and saint Hildegard von Bingen (1098-1178) points to the Angel of Darkness in her writings. She declares that divinity should be understood as a totality that includes even obscurity, darkness, and evil. But she also says that, among the angels, only those of the highest rank, the Cherubim, are strong enough to hold both the Light and the Darkness as neighbors in their consciousness. If the Cherubim of the Light claim three quarters of heaven for themselves, the rest belongs to the Cherubim of Darkness.

The abbess' statement sounds like our dream's description of the tall nighttime guest, elegantly dressed in black. He is not in the least aggressive. On the contrary, his behavior points to his high spiritual origin. However, he is not welcomed in the home of our human culture. No one comes out to greet him. Is he feared—because no one can shut the door on him?

The entry of the Cherubim of Darkness into the process of human change is feared by the people of an intellectual culture because the Cherubim's task is to break open and expose to view all those places in our culture that are not in accordance with the divine plan. They hold up a mirror to human beings in which all aspects of our alienation from the Essence are experienced in complete truth. Not just seen, but experienced too!

The Cherubim of Darkness—as portrayed by Hildegard—are not evil spirits. They are the destroyers of the destroyers. Their special ability is to expose falsehood, which is precisely what is needed at the given moment of the earth change process. Humanity is unsure of a future that hurries past them through various earth changes and would rather remain separated from it, but then they would really be placing themselves in the service of the powers that work against earth and human transformation.

The dreamer obviously understands intuitively that this guest, who is so much feared, can really bring healing to the situation. He therefore decides to get up, dress himself and greet the strange guest in the name of his fellow human beings.

One should pay particular attention to the process of dressing, because hidden there is a key that tells how you can meet the destroyers of the destroyers without their power overwhelming you.

The dreamer puts on his trousers, which cover that part of the body which corresponds most strongly with the elemental forces of the earth cosmos. He decides however to keep the upper part of his body in its "sleeping attire"—and thus covered with a vest.

Quite wrong! When it is a question of meeting the power of the Cherubim of Darkness, grounding and union with the elemental powers are of minimal use. The Cherubim pass through every protective cloak when there is cause to do so. To be able to meet them, the sensible thing to do is associated with the upper part of the body. What does this mean?

It means keeping a clear ethical attitude, nourishing one's own union with the divine Self, and being lovingly present in the Here and Now. The person should now be awake in the upper part of the body, especially in the head as the seat of consciousness.

But because we are not perfect and gaps are always present through which the dark guest can enter, we should remember that prayer and asking for divine grace are valuable tools to take with us on our personal spiritual path.

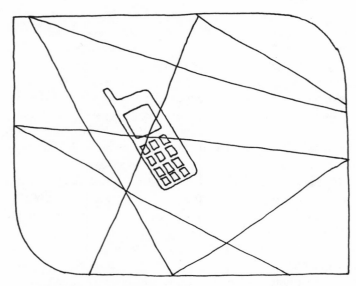

1. *My colleagues are unfolding a thick roll of transparent film. Unexpectedly, they find my lost mobile phone.*

2. *When they hand me the telephone, I am surprised to see that it is scratched and bears other marks of great age.*

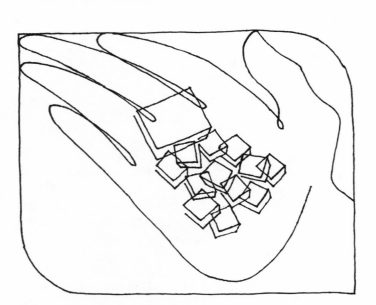

3. *It falls apart into a number of cell-like pieces. But I have no difficulty in quickly assembling all the individual parts to fit back to make a whole.*

4. *However, I was unable to telephone my wife, for the other participants in the group had already formed a circle and I did not wish to miss out.*

Dream 60: The Lost Telephone

1   *My colleagues are unfolding a thick roll of transparent plastic film. Unexpectedly, they find my lost mobile phone, which was packed inside by mistake.*

2   *When they hand me the telephone, I am surprised to see that it is scratched and bears other marks of great age, as if it had come out of an archeological dig.*

3   *I am surprised a second time when I take the telephone in my hand in order to call my wife. It falls apart into a number of cell-like pieces. But I have no difficulty in quickly assembling all the individual parts to fit back to make a whole.*

4   *However, I was unable to telephone my wife, for the other participants in the group had already formed a circle and I did not wish to miss out. So I quickly switch the telephone off to join in with the group.*

(Kraeckschult, Sweden June 17, 2009)

To understand this dream, you must know that the evening before, the dreamer's telephone had inexplicably vanished. He had looked for it in vain. But in the morning, when the dreamer sat at the breakfast table with his wife, telling her about the dream, the telephone suddenly appeared beside his left hand. His wife, who had laid the table before breakfast and would have seen it if it had been lying on the empty table, cried out in horror, "Your telephone!"

We may surmise that the telephone vanished for eight hours in order to guide the dreamer's attention to a specific goal. The dream came in between to help decipher the message of the vanished telephone.

If we look at the first dream image in this light, it would mean that the telephone, for the above-mentioned eight hour period, was in another dimension of reality that exists parallel to our own. In the dream this spatial dimension was represented by the film of transparent plastic. It follows that the form of this dimension is fine and transparent and that it exists relatively close to our material reality.

Can we then conclude that there is a dimension of light that exists as a reflection of the material world? One could characterize it as the twin space of our material world. If it can hold a material thing like a telephone for quite a while, it must be very close to the world of physical experience.

That the telephone appeared to the dreamer like an archeological object can mean that the old cultures knew the secret of the twin space that exists parallel to our reality. For example, did not the ancient Egyptians mummify their dead and place them in sealed chambers provided with food and all the necessary utensils so that they could continue to exist in the promised parallel space? This enabled them to participate in the life of their community and extend their service to their culture from the twin space. Had they gone the usual way of the dead, the Egyptians' after-death distance from their dead would have been much greater.

The third dream image, however, makes it clear that the consciousness of the twin space that is currently emerging—a kind of after-image of our physical reality—is not concerned with reawakening the ancient knowledge. The old telephone has fallen apart into its individual pieces and the dreamer must quickly put it together again. In symbolic language this tells us that the old functions of this mysterious spatial dimension have meanwhile been eliminated. We must understand its constitution afresh if we are to make contact with it today. But why do we need to bring the etheric after-image of our physical reality back into our human consciousness today?

Perhaps because the future somersaults on the road to earth change will demand some interaction with our twin space. It could happen in one phase that the changes on the earth's surface become so dramatic that all living beings will be doomed—many prophecies of the millennial change foresee something similar—unless the living beings, humans included, are temporarily settled in the twin space, as happened with the dreamer's telephone.

The fourth dream image confirms that this time the concern is not with the personal use of the twin space, as was the case in the old cultures. The dreamer is prevented from using the newly assembled telephone to call his wife. This also means that the secret of the after-image of our material reality was not revealed in order to enable specific individuals to participate in their cultures after their deaths. That circle of his colleagues in which the dreamer wants to participate represents the collective use of the twin space.

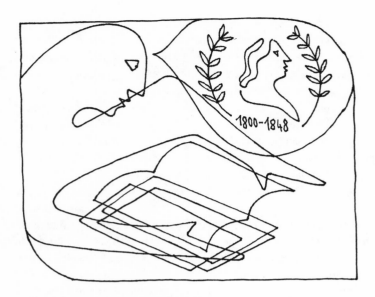

1. *I am rummaging around in a heap of old magazines. I am amazed to find among them the manuscript of a poem by the celebrated Slovenian poet France Preseren.*

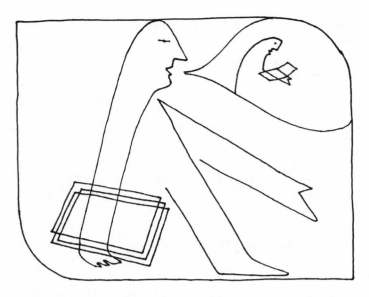

2. *I assume an air as if I have found nothing important and pick up a bundle of the magazines with the manuscript hidden inside.*

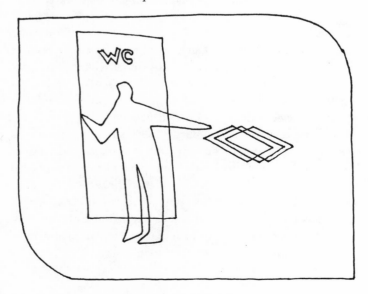

3. *Because I must still go to the bathroom. I put the bundle of magazines on the nearest window ledge.*

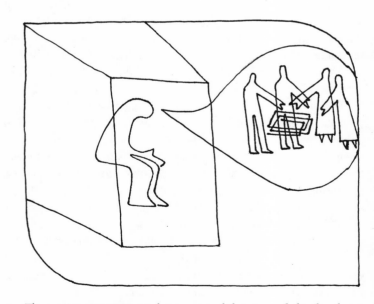

4. *The seminar participants have meanwhile returned, for they have missed their train. I hear them looking around in my magazines.*

Dream 61: The Valuable Find

1   *I have been leading a seminar and been the guest of a well-known family. The seminar is just over and I am rummaging around in a heap of old magazines. I am amazed to find a sheet of paper with a handwritten poem by the celebrated Slovenian poet France Preseren from the 19th century. An original!*

2   *I assume an air as if I have found nothing important and pick up a bundle of the magazines with the manuscript hidden inside, as if I wish to do some more reading while I wait for my train.*

3   *The seminar group has already left for the railway station, but I must still go to the bathroom. I put the bundle of magazines on the nearest window ledge to keep both my hands free.*

4   *The seminar participants have meanwhile returned, for they have missed the train. I hear the rustle of papers and realize that they are looking around in my magazines. What shall I say if they find the hidden manuscript? That I knew nothing about it?*

(Sempas, Slovenia April 15, 2009)

To BEGIN, IT IS IMPORTANT for readers who are not Slovenian to know the poet Preseren's significance for our national identity. In the first half of the nineteenth century, when only German was officially spoken in what today is Slovenia, Preseren wrote and published first class poems in Slovenian. It was an unimaginable sensation to find the manuscript of an unknown poem by him.

The dreamer also feels that it is sensational to find the valuable manuscript among banal magazines. In symbolic language, this means that within the everyday reality, there is pulsating a dimension of existence that we do not see and have completely forgotten.

However, this does not have to do with an after-image of physical reality, as was the case in Dream 60. In contrast to the after-image space, which has a technical function in the integral reality space (and was symbolized as such by the lost telephone), the newly discovered space, represented by the valuable manuscript, displays a creative and culture-forming characteristic. We are looking here at two different spatial dimensions that will obviously be discovered in the course of the earth change.

A further important key to the message of the dream is the name "Preseren," which translated from Slovenian, would be "Blissfully Happy." Is there a spatial dimension that puts together the poetic consciousness, the creative quality, and blissful happiness? Yes, there is such a dimension of reality, and it has already been addressed in Dream 54. We have identified it respectively with the archelemental space of earth and the paradisiacal quality of the fairy space.

The concept of a terrestrial archelemental space suggests that there is a dimension that holds the vibrating blueprints of embodied reality as it exists on the manifested plane of earth. The fairy-like quality of this archetypal space of earth parallels the concept of blissful happiness that vibrates in harmony with the name of the poet Preseren.

However, the dream of the valuable find is not merely to introduce a forgotten spatial dimension. It has much more to do with the discovery of the fairy space. The dreamer has tried to keep the valuable find to himself and hide the discovery of the manuscript from the public. Going to the bathroom is like going into a barricaded room, which one can symbolically compare to the esoteric attitude. Should the archetypal space of earth, earth's blissfully happy fairy space, be researched and experienced as a space separate from our spatial dimension?

In this respect, the fourth dream image signals an important reversal. The dreamer's students have returned. They begin to leaf through the everyday magazines where the newly discovered spatial dimension is hidden. The dreamer is nervous and foresees a danger. But he still holds fast to his esoteric position.

Fortunately, the dreamer's students have missed the train that should have taken them farther. Now, it is possible that what they find on the window ledge will show them how to take our civilization further, but in a new direction.

To sift the meaning from the symbolic language, you should imagine once again the colorful magazines as representing the reality of our everyday space, and the manuscript hidden among them as a parallel reality. Until now it was known as an esoteric category and sometimes called "Devachan."

This valuable spatial dimension is no more to be found exclusively in the Beyond, but meantime has been fitted—because of the earth change processes—into our everyday reality. The fusion of the two spatial dimensions is causing a new living space to arise. This will ensure a wonderful future for earth and humanity—refer to Dream 54. This future is symbolized by the mingling of the banal magazines and the valuable manuscript.

Exercises on the Theme "Processes that Point to the Future"

An exercise to experience fusion of the everyday and the fairy-like space

What happens in the greater space of the world unfolds simultaneously in the microcosm of our personal spatial dimension. The reverse is also true. So it makes sense to experience what is approaching and already occurring, the fusion of the two world spaces that have been separate until now (the so-called archelemental fairy space and our everyday materialized multidimensional space).

➤ *Seat yourself in the silence of your personal space, which also includes the force fields of your auras.*

➤ *Imagine that this personal space is like a sphere of light, which is rounded and closed in its own perfection.*

➤ *Sense your presence within this rounded space and its multidimensionality.*

➤ *Be conscious that this space is a microcosm of our common living space which we share with plants, landscapes, lakes, and other beings of the manifested world.*

➤ *Next you should imagine that a second sphere of similar circumference is floating behind your back. It is totally light and transparent like a soap bubble on whose surface countless streams of color change and play.*

➤ *Now the "soap bubble" begins to approach the sphere of our existence and intersect with it.*

➤ *The two spatial spheres finally fit perfectly within each other.*

➤ *Now it is time for you to sense how this spatial fusion operates on our inner world. How do my body and inner dimensions feel in the new spatial constellation?*

The seven foundation stones of the new ethic

In my interpretation, the seven letters from the Revelation of St. John (Chapters 2-3)contain the ethical qualities that need to be nourished for us to gradually align ourselves with the high vibrations of the earth cosmos that are now coming into being. To make the effort to realize them in one's own life also confers the best protection from the influence of the contrary powers. I have formulated these instructions based on Christ's letters to the early Christian communities of Ephesus, Smyrna, Pergamos, Thyatira, Sardis, Philadelphia, and Laodicea:

1. *Follow the voice of your heart. In each situation that arises, try to embody the voice of the original love. (Ephesus)*
2. *Do not shy away from your personal or collective fate. Maintain your inner peace in every situation. (Smyrna)*
3. *Be ready to follow the unceasing stream of change. Look for that aspect of yourself or your deeds which calls to be the next to change. (Pergamos)*
4. *Test whether at this very moment you are not denying some aspect of the truth from yourself or from others. Sense continually in your heart and in your thought processes whether you have not become the victim of a self-deception. (Thyatira)*
5. *Be continually aware of feeling your many-layered wholeness. Keep the great round of your being embraced in your consciousness and anchored in your center. (Sardis)*
6. *Always remember who you are in the core of your being, and the ideals you would like to follow. Continually renew your spiritual dedication. (Philadelphia)*
7. *In every life situation you can choose from different possibilities. Try to make the decisions based on the voice of your heart. The only thing you may not do in this epoch of great change is to remain undecided. (Laodicea)*

An exercise to make contact with the archetypal fairy world

This exercise is about making contact with the "extraterrestrial elemental beings" from Dream 55 (Cooperation with the Fairy World). The starting point of this perceptual exercise is in one's back, where a perceptual chakra pulses between the two shoulder blades. This is the area of the back where the traditional fairy wings were positioned.

➤ *You can carry out this exercise standing, sitting, or lying on your stomach.*

➤ *To begin, you should be firmly present at the point of infinity in your own heart center.*

➤ *You should imagine your means of communication with the archetypal fairy world as being two long, easily moveable, and possibly colored antennae that originate at the above-mentioned point in your back. They are similar to the antennae of certain insects—think of butterflies.*

➤ *Before using the antennae, you should become attuned to your own heart frequency so that you cannot be requisitioned by certain alien forces or beings.*

➤ *For purposes of attunement, the ends of the antennae should be directed forward and be dipped for a few moments in your own heart space.*

➤ *Afterwards you are free to move the antennae through the space, up high or deep below. Listen for the qualities and beings that may resonate in tune with the combination of your heart code and the center between the shoulder blades.*

➤ *Our plan is not only to enjoy communication with the archetypal fairy world, but also to explore possibilities for personal and collective cooperation with this parallel fairy world, which could be helpful for healing procedures, creative works, and our service to the realms of life.*

Joint Responsibility for the Network of Life

In the course of earth change, some unforeseeably complicated situations may arise that threaten the planetary network of life, but these cannot be allowed to tear it apart. To make a creative counter to such possible circumstances (and not give way to fear), we, the participants in the LifeNet meeting[1] in Bad Meinberg in July 2010, united in one imagination on which all devotees of the blue planet can fall back at need, knowing that other men and women worldwide are similarly active in the same force field:

➤ *Be aware that you are woven into the network of life on earth and feel in your own heart space your co-responsibility for it to pulsate freely.*

➤ *For your part, sense all the other participants in the community of life on earth and in the universe—all the visible and invisible beings. Imagine that we are standing in circles on different planes around an invisible center.*

➤ *Each one of us is joined to this center by a beam of light. Feel it for yourself and be aware of its presence for everyone else.*

➤ *In the middle of the circle, which constitutes the vessel of life, there flickers an invisible flame, the flame of life.*

➤ *Be aware that the planet earth turns inside this eternal flame—and not only in the center of the circle, but also in the middle of your heart.*

➤ *You should feel free to lovingly simplify what you are imagining, or to reshape it in accordance with your feelings, without altering its basic structure.*

---

1. LifeNet is a network for mutual inspiration between human beings and earth. It was founded in Sempas, Slovenia, by representatives of different European geomantic groups when it was recognized that a complex change of earth and human beings was approaching. Contacts are USA: lifenethome.org; UK: www.earthenergynetwork.co.uk; Germany: (Anna and Achim Schmaelze) anna.achim@gmx.de.

Late-Breaking News

It looked as if the cycle of dreams relating to earth change had ended when, just before handing over this manuscript, I was given two more dreams in which the book's theme of earth's approaching quantum leap received especially meaningful expression.

The First Dream

The mother has lost her child. She looks everywhere in the room and cannot find it. I come through the door and see the child immediately. It is an infant, alive and well, and placed by the wall at a height that is a little above the mother's normal level of vision.

I would have been unable to interpret the dream, if I had not seen a documentary film about the year 2012 on the following evening. In this film, various scientists had set out their views on the possible meaning of the threshold in earth evolution of which the Mayan Calendar has made us aware. The Mayan Calendar, which is known for its precise relationship to noteworthy world events, ends abruptly at the end of the year 2012.

I was very deeply surprised that one of the astrophysicists present should base his explanations on the 12-dimensional spatial model of the physicist Burkhard Heim. I had gotten to know Burkhard Heim when I cooperated in the International Scientific Congress ECOLOG '88 on the theme "Natural Science and Life Energy" in Cologne (my contribution was the presentation of a case study in the park of Tuernich Castle). Burkhard Heim is blind and without hands—the youthful victim of an unexploded bomb. His entry into my thought processes was preserved like the appearance of a prophet. At that time people had made fun of his mathematical model of multidimensional space.

In the film it sounded quite normal when his model of 12-dimensional space was brought in to explain earth's possible quantum leap, symbolized by the year 2012.

The astrophysicist started with his explanation of manifested space-time reality, which exists within the first four dimensions. These are the materialized dimensions—the length, breadth and depth of space—plus the time dimension. To these are added two more invisible dimensions. In the fifth are the various systems of life forces, such as force fields, earth chakras, ley lines, and so forth. It is this so-called "structure-forming" dimension that impresses the four materially experienced dimensions with the form-giving impulse. According to the 12-dimensional model, the sixth dimension is that extension of terrestrial space through which the elemental consciousness operates as the enlivening consciousness of nature, landscapes, plants, and so forth.

My dream and the whole theme of earth's quantum leap relate to dimensions seven through nine. These three dimensions lie beyond the three visible and three invisible dimensions of the world space in which we live today. They are the archetypal dimensions. The way in which these archetypal patterns are structured determines the kind of reality that we inhabit. If a shift occurs there, the everyday reality of our world will inevitably take on another form of existence.

Myths tell us, for example, that in a far distant past earth's civilization developed in a space with a watery, not a solid, character. One speaks of Atlantis as a planetary form of existence that maintained its form not by particles of matter, but instead supported its manifestation by drops of water. Through a shift of the archetypal pattern in the three above-mentioned higher dimensions, earth made a quantum leap that enabled the present world structure to be realized in matter.

The mother could not find her child because she was looking for it within the horizons of the present world structure. Since the archetypal pattern of dimensions seven through nine had changed in the meantime, the new reality—symbolized by the infant—is beyond the range of her vision, which remained still chained to the old earth space. Coming from outside, it is immediately clear to me that the child is not lost but finds itself in a differently structured space—symbolically, above the mother's range of vision, which until now was normal.

To complete the story of Burkhard Heim's 12-dimensional model, it should be mentioned that dimensions 10 through 12 represent the realm of divinity. They are the dimensions that make it possible for life and reality to exist.

During the night after the one when I saw the above-mentioned documentary about 2012, I was given the following dream:

A space rocket is prepared for lift-off. The rocket's round body is so tightly fastened to planet Earth that they have become a unity. I feel the ground tremble, clearly caused by the motor that has been switched on.

As if to witness this, a tall young man arrives with his little son and opens a small iron door in the giant drum of the engine space to peer inside at what is going on, so that I can also see it from farther away.

I see that there is no ordinary motor inside, but a powerful blue-white light that represents the rocket's driving force. Just then, the power of the light increases. It is regularly distributed through the rocket's whole engine body.

Starting from the interpretation of the first dream, it is clear that we are not dealing with a rocket but with planet Earth's own indwelling driving force. Referring to the story of the first dream, it is a force powerful enough to catapult the infant onto another plane beyond the mother's usual field of vision. In other words, it means that earth's indwelling force is capable of completing a planetary quantum leap.

In conceptualizing the quantum leap, I think of an unusual alteration in the pathway of a material particle, called the "quant" in physics. Relating to the first dream, the mother represents the core of the atom—the sun—around which the infant circles like a planet. I see the phenomenon of the quantum leap to be this, that our planet's circuit would be essentially altered—though not necessarily on the physical plane!

Through this alteration, there takes place a broadening of consciousness. This should best be experienced through an exercise. The following meditative exercise has been modeled on the images in both the dreams narrated above.

> ➤ *Put yourself in a peaceful place, sitting or standing, with an upright spine.*
> ➤ *Let your attention run along the spine a few times, and become conscious of the channels of force that run along it.*
> ➤ *Next, imagine that the spinal channel is getting slightly longer, both upward and downward.*
> ➤ *By this, I mean that the channel should be lengthened upward and downward from the heart center. The spinal channel can lengthen only in the region of the heart center, because the fractal of the divine presence in the heart makes this possible.*
> ➤ *This lengthening corresponds to the new position of the inner child in the first dream, which was above the usual level of consciousness. Feel yourself free to experiment with this to gain insights into the inner processes of change.*
> ➤ *In this way you can open yourself to the new quality of the consciousness field of earth or use the exercise for a deepened perception of the landscape.*
> ➤ *Finish by closing off your imagination, then ground yourself thoroughly.*